Strategy = Execution

I dedicate this book to my family, Colette, Nathan and Marah, for being my source of support, love and knowledge.

And to my parents, Wim and Irene, for imparting their love of books and the importance of curiosity and discipline to me.

I would like to express gratitude to Turner Consultancy's trusted clients, associates, colleagues, partners and alumni. My sincere thanks to the Turner management team and our extraordinary coach, Mieke Bello. This book would not have come to fruition without them.

STRATEGY =EXECUTION

JACQUES PIJL

Translated by Mischa Hoyinck and Robert Chesal

READ WHAT OPINION LEADERS HAD TO SAY ABOUT STRATEGY = EXECUTION

"*Strategy = Execution** **means driving change. This book brilliantly shows how leadership is fundamental to inspire people to want to change because they see the benefit and are engaged in the process. Rather than something being done to them, they participate in making the change happen. This is a hands-on book and a must-read for all leaders."

George Kohlrieser Ph.D., Professor of Leadership and Organizational Behavior, IMD, Switzerland, bestselling author of *Hostage at the Table* and *Care to Dare*

"Vision without action is a hallucination. Talking about strategy is easy, but as I have discovered far too often while working with CEOs, getting things done is a totally different matter. Taking care of its execution is what it is all about. People need to be mobilized to be aligned with the strategy. It is therefore refreshing to read a book where this important topic has pride of place."

Manfred F.R. Kets de Vries, INSEAD Distinguished Clinical Professor of Leadership Development and Organizational Change

"A wealth of well-founded insights and advice."

Ben Tiggelaar, behavioral scientist, author, public speaker and consultant

"Strategy is nothing more than a set of ideas until we move the molecules in the room. Strategy = Execution is about making ideas come alive and creates a much-needed bridge between insight and action. The methodology in this book is a success formula that's Monday morning ready. Read and thrive!"

Peter Meyers, founder and CEO, Stand & Deliver Group and visiting lecturer at Stanford University and IMD in Lausanne

"As we head into the fourth industrial revolution, the need for Innovation, Speed and Agility is bigger than ever before. This book provides excellent, reality-based insights into how we can achieve this."

Heiko Schipper, member of the Board of Management, Bayer AG; President Bayer Consumer Health

"It is important to take the time we need for strategy and reflection. But it will just remain paperwork if we do not turn this into practical steps with the same zeal. This book shows us how to do that and how to do it smoothly."

Ben Verwaayen, former CEO, Alcatal-Lucent and British Telecom and Commissioner, AkzoNobel and investor and partner, Keen Ventures

"Most management books are about strategy-setting, but precious few provide handles for strategy execution. Jacques Pijl's book is a notable exception. It's a must-read for every strategy professional."

Henk W. Volberda, Professor of Strategic Management & Business Policy, Rotterdam School of Management, Erasmus University

"In an increasingly VUCA world, good strategy-setting combined with organizational purpose is important, but effective strategy execution at the right speed is what determines success! After all, it's not your slide presentations that make the difference, but timely preparation for the new reality. In this book, Jacques Pijl shows that the next change is right around the corner. He inspires leaders and teams who face big changes and shares an abundance of good ideas for tightening our focus on successful enactment and execution of a change strategy."

Harry J.M. Brouwer, CEO, Unilever Food Solutions

"Strategy Execution is the No. 1 task facing executives. That's one of the most important arguments in this book."

Kees Hoving, Chief Country Officer, Deutsche Bank Netherlands

"Strategy = Execution *contains many clear, directly applicable ideas, taken from practical and proven cases."*

Karin Bergstein, member of the Executive Board, a.s.r.

"This book thoroughly demystifies the concept of innovation and the practicalities of how to organize it."

Jacques van den Broek, CEO, Randstad

"What a relief to be allowed to be passionate about strategy execution."

Lisette van Breugel, COO, Arbo Unie

"Jacques Pijl's practical book shows once again how an organization can remain relevant in our digitalized world. Slow down, read, and then accelerate again!"

Maarten Edixhoven, CEO, Aegon Nederland

"Jacques Pijl = strategy execution and much more, of course. In this book, he reveals his thorough and effective method. Which also makes it a great read for management consultants."

Meindert Flikkema, Academic Director, Amsterdam Centre for Management Consulting, Vrije Universiteit

"Jacques Pijl convincingly argues why it is not strategy, but the execution of it, that makes the difference. Highly recommended."

Ronald Goedmakers, owner and CEO, Vebego International

"This book connects thought with action in a unique way. It's a must read for anyone who wants to shape the future."

Henk Hagoort, Chairman of the Executive Board, Windesheim University of Applied Sciences and former Chairman of the Board of Directors, NPO

"This book goes to the core of change management: the hard is soft, the soft is hard. Balance is everything."

Cees 't Hart, CEO and President, Carlsberg and former CEO, FrieslandCampina

"Highly recommended reading for anyone who wants to understand the differences and similarities between established companies and new enterprises. How do they successfully carry out their strategies? How do they go about innovation?"

Symen Jansma, founder and CEO, TravelBird

"Strategy is static, but the new normal is continuous, daily adjustment and adaptation of execution strategy. This book is a crystal-clear guide on how to do that."

Patrick Kerssemakers, CEO, fonQ

"An inspiring and down-to-earth explanation of how new organizations and business models see to it that they can absorb growth while continuing to rejuvenate and innovate."

Agnes Keune, Director of Logistical Innovation, bol.com

"A stimulating book. Execution of your strategy is just as essential as the strategy itself. Pijl's writing makes for captivating reading."

Hein Knaapen, Chief HR Officer, ING Bank

"In this new world full of rapid change and digital innovation, the challenge is not only to have the best strategy, but also to execute it quickly and effectively. This book offers insight, inspiration and a wealth of actual cases, making it a must read for every executive."

Feike Sijbesma, CEO and Chairman of the Board of Directors, Royal DSM

"A strategy is nothing but a vision with a sell-by date, based on current information, on the best way an organization can achieve its objectives, its purpose. This book provides valuable and refreshing insights into how to turn that vision into action, how to get results and create social value through execution."

Tjark Tjin-A-Tsoi, General Director, Statistics Netherlands (CBS) and former General Director, Netherlands Forensics Institute

"In a fast-changing world, effective strategy execution is a critical success factor for businesses. Strategy = Execution provides many practical examples and tips on how to get it done."

Herna Verhagen, CEO, PostNL

"We live in a VUCA world (Volatility, Uncertainty, Complexity and Ambiguity). This is why strategy must continually be scrutinized and why its execution is even more important now. Strategy = Execution was written with passion, making it a particularly interesting and practical guide that belongs in every boardroom!"

Paul Verheul, COO, Van Oord

The greater the constraints I place upon myself, the greater my freedom and the more meaningful it will be. Whatever diminishes constraint diminishes strength. The more constraints one imposes, the more one frees one's self of the chains that shackle the spirit.

Igor Stravinsky

Translation: Mischa Hoyinck & Robert Chesal
Cover design: Dog & Pony, Amsterdam
Illustrations: Aad Goudappel
Layout design: Rienk Post
Layout realization: Justus Bottenheft, Rienk Post, Cor Barelds
Editing: Hans van der Klis
Copy editing: Dorseda de Block

Originally published in Dutch by Vakmedianet in 2017

ISBN paperback 978 94 627 6316 6
ISBN hardcover 978 94 627 6339 5
ISBN e-book 978 94 627 6353 1

TABLE OF CONTENTS

PREFACE

Ben Tiggelaar

As the brilliant management thinker Henry Mintzberg points out in his seminars, most of the strategies companies devise are never implemented. He has an inkling why.

During a discussion in the Netherlands a few years back, he asked who takes the blame when the implementation of a strategy fails. His answer was simple. Those who do the implementing always bear the brunt. Leaders tend to think: we think up excellent strategies from our head offices, but those bird brains in the rest of the organization just aren't smart enough to make them work. Well if you're one of those bird brains, Mintzberg continued, I've got the perfect comeback for you. Just tell management: if we're such idiots and you're so smart, why don't you come up with strategies that idiots like us can implement?

It's a strong argument. But is it fair? Not entirely, as Mintzberg himself was the first to admit. He said nearly every implementation misstep is the result of a disconnect between the formulation of strategy and its implementation. And this, he said, was caused by the mistaken belief that you can formulate a strategy in one place, corporate headquarters, and then implement it somewhere else, in the workplace. And it's precisely this crucial point that this book explores: the interface between strategy and execution. Or, as Jacques Pijl more radically expresses it, Strategy Equals Execution. There are four points in particular that I was struck by and that make it a must-read.

1 Strategy = Execution

A strategy that is not carried out is just as worthless as no strategy at all. Which is why you need to think about execution from the very moment you begin developing your plans. Strategy and execution are inextricably linked, and this book explains the implications of that in minute detail through the framework of four accelerators, each of which consists of four building blocks. That might sound very schematic, true. But the time for improvising and freewheeling in strategy execution is long gone. Strategy execution is a craft, and one which makes all the difference between winning and losing.

2 Honest about innovation

These days, renovations have to continue while the store stays open. Every entrepreneur and manager understands this problem. You need to devote attention to the going business because that's what makes your customers happy and earns you money in the here and now. And at the same time, you also need to put energy into what you want your business to be tomorrow and beyond. When we say innovation, we don't always mean the same thing. This book distinguishes three types of change: improvement, renewal and innovation. Each requires a unique approach. That's not easy, but it is the reality that experienced managers will recognize.

3 The work needs to be done by people

Why, what and how are important, Pijl argues. But *who* will carry out the strategy is the most important question of all. In the end, it's all about people, and about their qualities and engagement. That sounds great, but it has profound consequences. For instance, the people who will carry the execution have to 'check in' psychologically. In other words, they have to really commit to the strategy, the initiatives and the objectives that have been set. This book goes in depth on how to ensure that engagement.

4 Theory and practice

It's always good when a writer knows their literature. Some management book authors try to pass off the ideas they present as new, but that's only because they don't know their classics. No need to worry about that here. Jacques Pijl has done his homework. At the same time, he is keenly aware of the need for practicality. Which is why it's so helpful that Jacques and his colleagues are practitioners whose feet are firmly planted in the reality of consultancy. The result is a healthy dose of realism and lots of useful examples.

I love evidence-based work. Just one more thing about that. This book is a treasure trove of well-founded insights and advice. But its real value will only become apparent when you test these in your own organization. Then you'll see these great ideas come to life, and the words on the page will be transformed into good work and great results. Happy reading and happy learning!

Ben Tiggelaar

1

INTRODUCTION: **EFFECTIVENESS, AGILITY AND SPEED ARE KEY IN STRATEGY EXECUTION**

The rise of Netflix / Watson has earned a PhD / the whale curve is dead / Philips declined to buy Apple

1.1 Today's No. 1 Challenge is to Innovate Faster

We need to increase the speed with which we improve, renew and innovate our business models. This is the key management issue of our day. Organizations are caught between a rock and a hard place. They're notoriously bad at strategy execution, but this age of disruption leaves them no choice but to constantly improve, renew and innovate their existing business models. In other words, the skill that organizations are sorely lacking is the very one they need most in order to succeed. That's what leaders, professionals and entrepreneurs lose sleep over. And so they should. As one CEO recently told me, "All of us need to get better at this. Now. It's nothing short of our social responsibility. Our continued existence depends on it." This is exactly why I wrote this book. Obviously, there are worse problems in the world today. Just take a look at the news. Even so, I am convinced that increasing our effectiveness in strategy execution is a big deal. We spend the better part of our lives working, so it'd better be on something worthwhile. People want their work to be meaningful and have a purpose. Organizations are now deliberately choosing which social values they want to reflect. We are outgrowing our old obsession with shareholder value. What counts now is value in terms of social responsibility, diversity and regional and national development. This ambition has become one of our main strategic goals. Effective strategy execution creates value and the means by which we formulate meaningful objectives.

1.2 Organizations Suck at Strategy Execution

Research has repeatedly shown that organizations are not good at strategy execution. This is nothing new. We've known this for decades and the numbers are shocking. Estimates of the failure rate range from 60 to 90%. It depends how you define failure, of course, which is something I discuss in greater detail in Chapter 9. But even if we take a highly critical view of the percentages presented in most studies, the failure rate is never less than 50%.[1] We all know examples: massive government IT projects that get bogged down, private sector mergers that never deliver the projected synergies, big restructurings that go off the rails, and cultural change programs that evaporate into thin air. Organizations are full of good intentions, but these intentions often end up paving the proverbial road to hell. This is precisely where we can gain a competitive edge, but there is a more general imperative: every organization needs to become better at strategy execution.

1.3 The New Normal

The world will never be the same as before the financial crisis of 2008. There have been too many economic, social, cultural and technological changes. Globalization and changing consumer behavior are big factors, too. All these influences are ramping up the demands on our business models at mind-boggling speed. At the same time, the rate of change is accelerating. We no longer live in an era of change, but in a change of era, to quote Jan Rotmans, professor of Transition Studies and Sustainability.[2] Allow me to enumerate a few phenomena that I described in my previous book, *Het Nieuwe Normaal* [The New Normal].[3]

Business models are crumbling before our eyes. Business models are under great pressure in many industries—travel, real estate and financial services, to name just a few. These are known as *glacier industries* because they are simply melting away as a result of climate change in the business world. It's only a matter of time before other industries suffer the same fate. Studies show that digital disruption is affecting all sectors so we can expect a lot more melting business models in the years ahead.[4]

The traditional media are another glacier industry; in some segments, earnings are melting away by 10% a year. The director of Netflix brought up this problem at a recent keynote speech at the Cannes Advertising Festival. He asked how long media buyers would continue to attend that festival to decide on their viewers' behalf what they get to see and when. Just consider how bizarre it is that late night talk shows air when most people have already gone to bed. We spend a lot of time watching TV, yet it is one of the few products that does not allow us to choose what we consume and when. No wonder the rise of Netflix was so rapid. In the Netherlands, for instance, the channel attracted 600,000 subscribers in its first six months. This shows that linear television is fighting a losing battle. In the United States, 75% of late night shows are no longer viewed live but on demand. Yet even Netflix is now under threat from newer concepts.

Industries are converging. The triple helix model of innovation entwining government, education and business, probably offers as many opportunities as each of these sectors individually.[5] The parties involved in this helix understand the value of cooperation and are increasingly tackling challenges together to foster economic growth and regional development. One successful example of this is Brainport Eindhoven, a cooperative alliance between the Dutch government, knowledge institutes and companies like ASML (semiconductor equipment manufacturer) and Philips Medical. Another one, Yes!Delft, offers startup programs for young high-tech firms operating near the world-class research centers of Delft University of Technology.[6] In the USA, technology companies work side by side with institutions of higher learning in North Carolina's Research Triangle Park, in Silicon Valley, and at MIT, to name just a few examples.

State and semipublic institutions are not exempt. Senior managers know that state and semipublic institutions are just as vulnerable as private enterprise in the New Normal. Under intensifying social media pressure, politicians and citizens alike are demanding more transparency, lower costs, better service and greater effectiveness. Many public and semipublic organizations are not ready to step up their game. The demand for transparency is particularly tough to meet. Just consider the scandals that shook the Dutch government in recent years. The Ministry of Defense was forced to compensate employees who were exposed to highly toxic hexavalent chromium for years; housing corporation Vestia nearly collapsed when several senior-level managers committed fraud; and the Central Works Council of the National Dutch Police was found to have engaged in corrupt practices.

In healthcare, the meteoric rise of e-health reveals how the government, organizations and citizens are unable to keep pace with the introduction of new technology. Watson, IBM's supercomputer, has already earned a PhD and will soon be able to carry out the work done by a medical resident.

The New Normal is here to stay. By 2033, businesses will have an average lifespan of only five years, according to VINT, a Netherlands-based new technology institute run by IT firm Sogeti.[7] The life expectancy of Fortune 500 companies was 75 years in 1950, but in 2001 it was projected to plummet to less than 15 by 2012, as we can see in the Shift Index from Richard Foster and Sarah Kaplan's *Creative Destruction* (2001).[8] Other indicators tell a similar story. Standard & Poor's figures show the average lifespan of a business to be 61 years in 1958, 25 in 1980, and 18 in 2011.[9] We can extrapolate from these numbers that 75% of those listed on the S&P 500 in 2014 will have disappeared by 2027.[10] The topple rate, or the rapidity with which the market leaders in each industry are replaced, has more than doubled since 2010. Loyalty is a thing of the past, because customers now continuously reassess who best meets their needs. Competitiveness has increased by 100% and market positions can no longer be taken for granted. In short, the New Normal is here to stay. It is a reality, backed up with hard facts.

Figure 1 summarizes the facts that show why the New Normal is so different. The trend is obvious: continuity is no longer a given, and the most important reason for this is clearly digitalization.

Figure 1 — **The New Normal is here to stay. Its effects are there for all to see.** Innovation is a particularly tough game, but it's full of opportunities for those who know how to spot them.

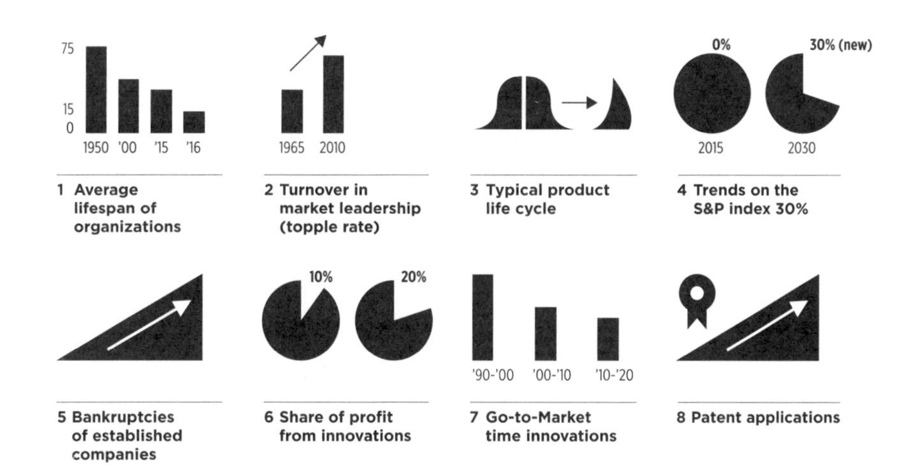

Sources:
1. In *Creative Destruction* (2001), McKinsey's Richard Foster calculated that the lifespan of Fortune 500 companies, which was 75 years in 1950, would sink to less than 15 by 2012.
2. Standard & Poor confirms this trend.
3. Verkenningsinstituut Nieuwe Technologie, Sogeti IT-services.
4. Deloitte Shift Index Series

Organizations underwent more change in the first decade of the 21st century than in the last five decades of the 20th century. In recent years, they have seen everything from process optimization to radical innovation; from outsourcing to rightsourcing; from joint ventures to complete mergers and acquisitions; and a constant stream of change programs. One leader who I spoke to while researching for this book even went so far as to say, "The last five years have brought more change than the fifty years that preceded them." And organizations see much more movement on the horizon. The digitalization of society and the pressure to keep up with disruptive innovations is bound to continue.

1.4 Digitalization Drives Innovation

In the 20th century, organizations rose to dominance by achieving economies of scale and gaining customer loyalty. At first, they succeeded at this through large-scale manufacturing (General Motors), and later by controlling supply chains (Walmart) and information (Amazon). But in the 21st century, it's the customers who call the shots. Customers read consumer reviews before every purchase and change their minds in seconds. The only way to win them over and to keep a competitive edge is to have a strategy that banks on knowing and engaging with the customer.

Companies that know how to play this new competitive game are what Forrester Research's James McQuivey calls "disruptors". The best disruptions do two things: they fulfill a basic need that end users understand, and they penetrate into the physical world of manufacturing plants and distribution networks, into the Internet of Things. The key issue is to focus on finding better ways to satisfying customers' fundamental and latent needs.[11]

Twenty years ago, disruption took years and required huge investments, as Harvard Business School Professor Clayton Christensen wrote in *The Innovator's Dilemma*.[12] But the digital revolution has changed that. Today's disruptors can radically transform every product and every service much faster and much more cheaply. They have a big influence on every aspect of business operations, from data management to pricing, to the management of labor and capital. It won't be long before all industries feel this influence, even those that have not yet been digitalized.[13] In James McQuivey's estimate, today's tools and platforms have multiplied tenfold the number of people who can bring innovative ideas to market. And that's a conservative estimate. The average cost of developing and testing these ideas is just 10% of yesterday's price tag. In short, our innovative power has multiplied by 100. But that also means every business now faces 100 times more competition.

Digital disruption speeds up competition and facilitates the advent of previously unimaginable numbers of ideas. The cumulative effect is devastating for any organization that operates 'old-school'.

Digital innovation changes everything. Airbnb's growth figures show that the classic whale curves of company life cycles are ancient history. They've been replaced by graphs that more closely resemble the Empire State Building. Let's face it: the whale curve is dead! Everything is accelerating. New business models are appearing at breakneck speed, while older ones disappear equally fast. No one can predict what will happen, but we can extrapolate from the trend that this acceleration has only just kicked into high gear. The longer you wait to join in, the tougher it will be to do so because competition is a key factor. Innovator, entrepreneur and investor Marc Andreessen summed it up nicely in a 2011 *Wall Street Journal* column, "Why software is eating the world."[14] If you were to draw up a list of organizations that didn't even exist 12 years ago but now either represent a big new market or have conquered a big share of an existing market, you would see some remarkably familiar names: Facebook, Twitter, YouTube, Uber, Airbnb, Snapchat, Instagram, Fitbit, Spotify, Dropbox, WhatsApp and Quora.[15]

Leaders, managers and professionals struggle with digitalization dilemmas. Should we digitalize or not? When? With whom? How? Menno Lanting, an expert on digital technology's effect on leadership, described what digital innovation and competition truly mean when he said, "All goods and services will either become digital themselves or will be surrounded by a digital shell of services." This also goes for services you would never expect to be digitalized. Lanting mentions the garbage collection services in the city of Philadelphia, where microchips in the garbage cans gather data that help the sanitation company devise smarter routes that require 40% less personnel. In short, we must learn to live with a new reality in which our lives and work are inextricably tied to technology.[16] Every organization needs to decide how to position digital innovation in their overall portfolio of strategy execution initiatives.

1.5 Uncertainty Galore

We all know our traditional way of setting up, managing and changing organizations no longer works. Thinking in blueprints, designs and cascades doesn't do the trick anymore. The ascendancy of unpredictability is best expressed by the concept of VUCA, which stands for Volatility, Uncertainty, Complexity and Ambiguity. This term originated in military jargon, but we now use it to explain how harsh the climate has become for businesses and public and semipublic institutions. *Volatility* refers to the nature, speed and dynamics of change. *Uncertainty* is about the lack of predictability combined with the fear and increased likelihood of unforeseeable big events and disruptions. Examples of this are big disruptive innovations like Uber and macro-economic events such as 9/11, or as Nassim Nicholas Taleb would call them, Black Swans. *Complexity* stands for the many-headed monsters of demands, markets, customers, managers and legislation that are making processes and systems ever more complicated. And finally, *Ambiguity* refers to the non-mathematical nature of business, that is, the fact that developments could lead to different outcomes and no one knows which one will become reality.

Facts can be explained in different ways. I have seen organizations that obstinately continued to operate on incorrect assumptions because they considered perseverance a key characteristic of successful execution. Yet, I have seen just as many organizations that pulled the plug too fast on some promising experiment. One particularly poignant example is Philips consumer electronics passing up on an opportunity to take over Apple in the 1990s. In his autobiography, former Philips CEO Cor Boonstra maintained he did not regret this decision. Apple, he wrote, would never have become what it is today under the umbrella of the Dutch electronics company.

The demands that come with the VUCA concept are just as interesting. Many long articles have been written about them, but in essence they come down to this: high volatility requires built-in buffers and flexibility; high uncertainty demands systematic data collection, analysis, interpretation and extrapolation; high complexity requires as much simplification as possible; and high ambiguity compels us to experiment with innovations, to learn through trial and error and to scale up what works.

The worst way to respond to VUCA would be to conclude that it makes strategic planning pointless. We do need to heed human fallibility, the workings of which we are slowly unraveling. Think of the human tendency to ignore that which we know nothing about and leave it out of our decision-making, "the known unknown" as Daniel Kahneman calls it. Rather than spurring us on to try ever harder to predict the future, knowing our limitations should spur us on to build in bigger margins and resilience. That's how we can deal with the unknown. In short, the demands put on us by the New Normal come down to the need to accelerate, to be agile and to increase our effectiveness in strategy execution.

1.6 The Last Competitive Edge

The New Normal leaves less room for trial and error. We are dealing with ever shorter product life cycles, high risks in innovation, and increasingly critical and fickle markets. This makes strategy execution even riskier and more challenging for leaders and professionals than it already used to be. This is why their focus is now shifting from "strategy for strategy's sake," to strategy execution. It is not the brilliance of a strategy or the analysis it is based upon that makes or breaks a company. It is the *execution* of that strategy. The difference between profit and loss depends on execution capacity. Organizations that excel in strategy execution and innovation see significantly bigger profits, productivity and achievement.

Actually, it has always been true that strategy is pointless without execution, but in the New Normal there is no escaping this fact. The newer books on strategy make this clear too. Take *Good Strategy/Bad Strategy* by Richard P. Rumelt, for instance. Or *Your Strategy Needs a Strategy* by Martin Reeves, Knut Haanæs and Janmejaya Sinha, and

Strategy That Works by Paul Leinwand and Cesare Mainardi.[17] All three books stress the need for a strategy that goes hand in hand with execution.

For leaders the world over, strategy execution is the No. 1 priority. As it is for you, apparently, or you would not be reading this book. Researcher Donald Sull from the MIT Sloan School of Management cited a recent study in which 400 CEOs from Asia, the Americas and Europe rated execution their top priority out of 80 issues they face, varying from political instability and innovation to growth.[18] Strategy was also the main issue identified in other recent research into leaders' main concerns.[19]

1.7 Methodology

Strategy execution is essential, but what makes or breaks strategy execution and innovation? At Turner, we dedicated three years to researching this question. We interviewed some 60 leaders, senior managers and senior program managers responsible for transformations of various sizes in the organizations they work for. We selected a cross-section of all levels, in the private, semipublic and public sectors, at both long-established and new digital organizations. In addition, we consulted over 300 of the most relevant books and articles in the field. Our criteria for inclusion were strict to avoid rehashing old answers to old questions. We also reviewed some 70 case studies. We did all this with just one question in mind: What makes or breaks strategy execution and innovation in our time? As you can see, the ideas in this book are deeply rooted in actual practice, and so are my Turner colleagues and I, with all the years of experience we've accumulated as organizational consultants in strategy execution.

This book is organized as follows: In Chapter 2, I make the case for a modern view of effective strategy execution. I base this on the top six success factors that direct our thinking.[20] In Chapter 3, I outline the concept and framework of the Strategy = Execution Model. The book contains a foldout of this model on the cover jacket for easy reference while reading the subsequent chapters. In Chapters 4 through 7, I explain the Four Accelerators in this model: CHOOSE, INITIATE, HARVEST and SECURE. Each accelerator consists of four practical building blocks, two dealing with hard capabilities and two dealing with soft capabilities. As a whole, these constitute the best method to successfully complete strategy execution and to drastically reduce the chance of failure. Chapter 8 talks about project and program management, both of which are indispensable to strategy execution during the four accelerators. Chapter 9 discusses why strategy execution so often fails and explores the price of failure.

The main objective of this book is to convince you to make strategy execution a priority in your organization by radically reallocating people's time and aiming for a real balance between hard and soft capabilities. This book is chock-full (80%) of how-to's that can help you achieve this. In keeping with this focus on execution, I have put my analysis of frequently occurring failure factors at the end of this book rather than the beginning—unlike most everyone else who writes about strategy, innovation and change management.

I conclude with an epilogue, an overview of everyone who contributed to this study, a research methodology and a treasure trove of additional how-to's. Some of these, such as the fact sheets and planning templates, are downloadable by using the QR codes in the appendices. We've made them downloadable so we can regularly update them and offer you added and lasting value.

Why is this such a hefty book? I wanted to write a comprehensive overview of modern strategy execution. There are several books out there that deal with aspects of this subject, but none that focus solely on strategy execution and how to organize innovation, let alone on the interaction between the two. Go ahead and Google it.

A win for both established and new organizations. From the initial reactions to our findings, I can confidently say that our research has struck gold. Another aspect that makes this book unique is its combination of thorough analysis with case studies and scores of interviews with people steeped in business practice. It's a candy store for every senior manager, professional and entrepreneur facing big responsibilities in strategy execution and innovation.

We know one thing for sure: organizations are less and less able to make accurate predictions. The next decade will probably bring even more change than the previous one. And yet I am confident that the principles in this book will remain valid. I believe this because they are new principles for a new age of exponential growth that's far from over. My main goal is to offer you lots of practical handles that you can put to use right away: 80% how-to. I show you

- how to **get an overview**: six success factors and the Strategy = Execution Model, which consists of four accelerators and 16 building blocks;
- how to **find inspiration and apply it**: 16 case studies and over 50 innovations and new business models for your inspiration; and
- how to **get to work**: five elaborated approaches + a free digital assessment that will help you assess your organization's execution capacity.

I know that managers like fundamental, practical pointers and are always pressed for time. For this reason, every chapter of this book can be read and used separately. In that sense, it is a workbook and a textbook rolled into one.

This is a book for leaders, professionals and entrepreneurs who have learned the tricks of the trade through experience. And because you are my audience, I use a particular type of vocabulary and jargon. Business has lots of jargon, and sometimes too much of it. Doctors, pilots and lawyers all have their own vocabulary and we consider that entirely normal. The same should apply to MBAs and consultants. I am no fan of excessive lingo, but I do like business-specific language. We need less generic professional jargon, but more specific terminology. As Eric Ries, startup expert and Silicon Valley businessman once tweeted, "I know that management jargon gets criticized, and often rightly so. But like every professional domain, we need specialized terminology with precise meanings." If you come across a term you are not familiar with, please check the glossary (Appendix 2).

And finally, the most important thing I want to say: Thank you to Turner Consultancy's many sponsors, business associates, colleagues, partners and alumni who helped to make this book such a rich reading experience. During my research, I realized once again that a team is so much more than its constituent parts.

Jacques Pijl, Owner of Turner Consultancy
December 2019

Want to respond? jpijl@turner.nl / @JPijlTurner
/ https://nl.linkedin.com/in/jacquespijl / #strategyisexecution

2

A MODERN VIEW OF STRATEGY EXECUTION: SIX SUCCESS FACTORS

Don't make a mess / dirty dishes on the Titanic / stop setting lazy goals / with friends like these, who needs enemies? / saying no pays off

What makes or breaks excellence in strategy execution? Turner's research identified six success factors that surfaced time and again as the essence of successful strategy execution. As a whole, these factors represent a fresh view of strategy execution, innovation and change management. These six success factors form the basis of our four strategy execution accelerators discussed in Chapters 4 through 7.

2.1 Success Factor 1: Identify and Execute 3 Types of Change

Insight comes from overview. So, let's first examine how I define strategy execution. What typologies help to make change manageable?

2.1.1 Excellence in strategy execution follows from excellence in Running and Changing the Business

Our research shows that leaders and managers regard strategy execution as their No. 1 priority, but have difficulty grasping the concept. They consider it too broad a term, too "holistic" even. To clarify matters, we need to make a distinction between the going concern and innovation efforts.

First of all, excellence in strategy execution is about how well the organization achieves its goals in its existing configuration; this is known as "managerial excellence." It is also called executive management or Running the Business. The way we look at this depends on our business model, as shown in Figure 2. This business model reflects our outside-in approach; the distinction between input, throughput and output; types of stakeholders; and business functions. In short, it is an elementary model we use to organize our thinking and actions.

Figure 2 — **The way we view organizations is determined by their business model.**

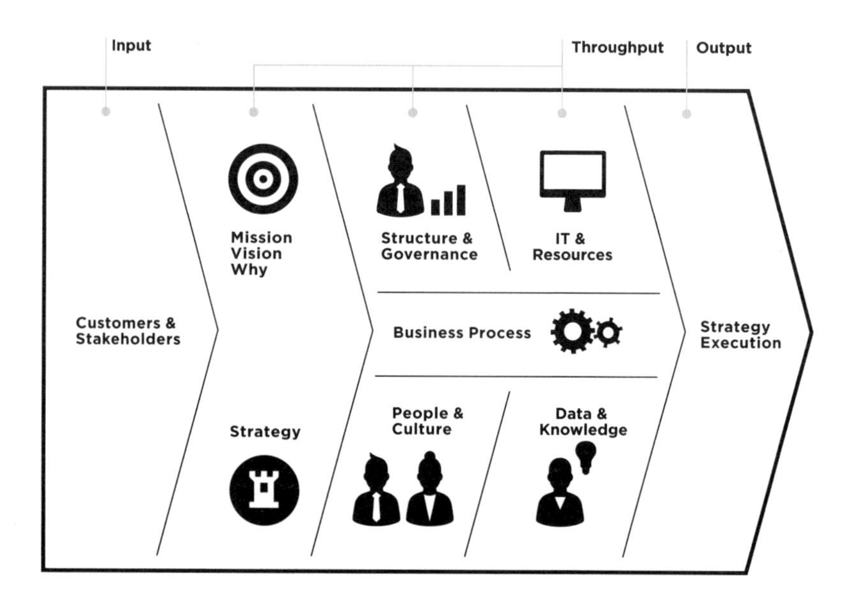

Source: Turner, 2016

Secondly, excellence in strategy execution is about how well the organization achieves its change objectives. Such objectives can take many shapes, such as projects, programs, acquisitions or interventions in your primary business processes. This is also known as change management, or in this book, Changing the Business.

Making a distinction between Running the Business and Changing the Business is crucial because it simplifies and expedites matters. Failure to make this distinction leads to suboptimal performance on both fronts. In my years as a consultant I have seen plenty of organizations that opted to have their line organization deal with every execution challenge, even though it's clear that most execution issues require a special focus and approach. The net result was an indistinguishable mess. By separating your change objectives from the going concern, you ensure you can properly manage and control both Running and Changing the Business, as Figure 3 shows. In my study, many leaders admitted to having realized too late how important this distinction is. As one professional put it, "You really have to be skilled at two very different things."

Figure 3 — **The distinction between Running and Changing the Business and the Three Types of Change: Improvement, Renewal and Innovation.**

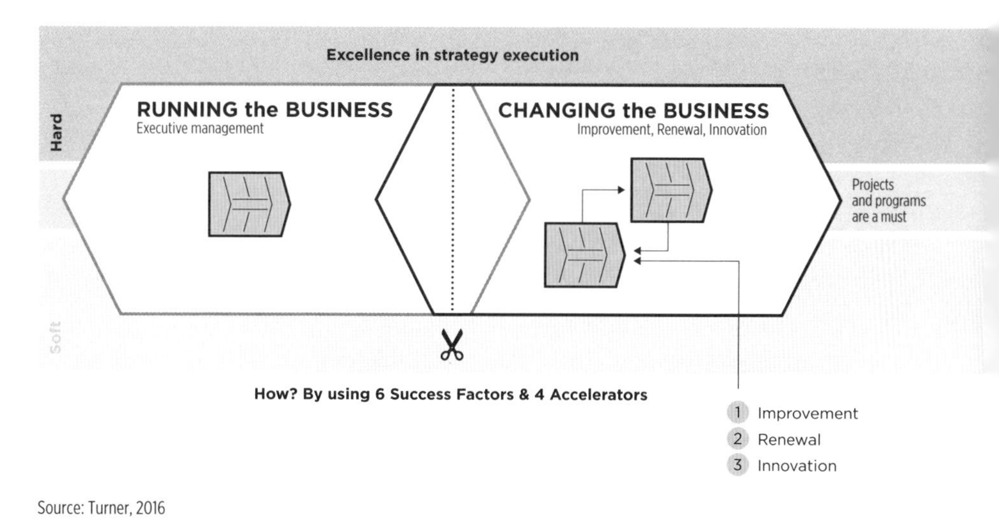

Source: Turner, 2016

This book uses the terms Running the Business and Changing the Business. The only way to structurally increase execution capacity is to select a particular focus and approach for each initiative and to execute it with full focus. No amount of training can beat that. For an illustration of the differences between the three types of change, see Figure 4.

By the way, it is a mistake to think your organization can coast and stay in business simply by focusing on running the business. Every organization must change. And yet I still hear organizations promise their employees that things will get back to normal once the dust from a tumultuous restructuring has settled. That's an illusion. Change is a constant. In fact, this phrase is so hackneyed it just elicits yawns. As one senior manager told me, his mind wanders every time a job applicant stresses they're not into 'just minding the store'. "Of course not," he said. "Who would hire anyone for that purpose in these times?!"

Figure 4 — **Three types of strategy execution: Improvement, Renewal and Innovation.**

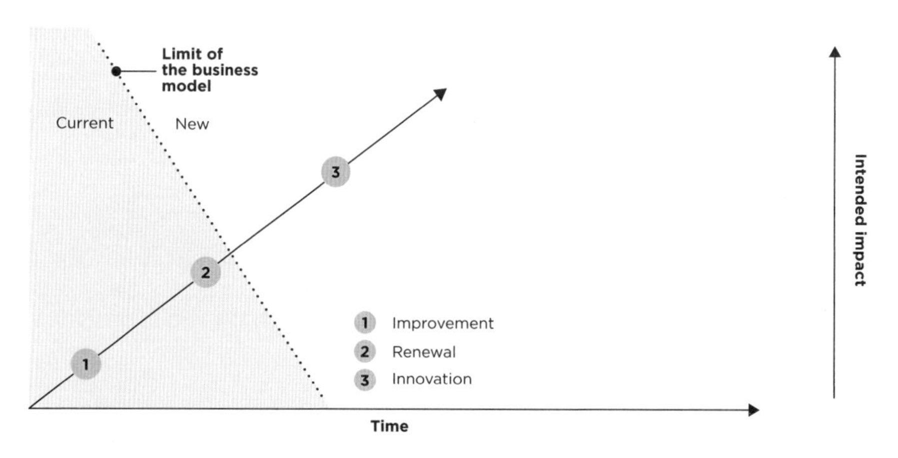

Source: Turner, 2016

Want to know more? Download more information about the necessity, complexity and art of distinguishing executive management from change management.

2.1.2 Demystify 'change' and differentiate three types

Not only should we disentangle Running and Changing the Business, we must also distinguish between different Types of Change: Improvement, Renewal and Innovation. Failing to make this distinction will once again create an indistinguishable mess. Obviously, every organization needs all three types of change, but also needs to find a way to offer a unique proposition. Every sexy startup that makes it big eventually becomes an established company. Even then, it needs to continue to innovate (Type 3 Change) in order to remain successful. At the same time, it must keep improving basic processes (Type 1 Change) and renewing its existing models (Type 2 Change). Amazon once started as a hungry young startup with an innovative business model (Type 3 Change). But now it rigorously improves and renews itself every day (Types 1 and 2 Change). Google and Apple do the same; they make headlines with their new ideas (Type 3 Change), but maintain the stability of their existing product lines and revenue and business models by continually improving and renewing their existing business models (Types 1 and 2 Change). Every organization needs all three types of change.

Type 1: Improvement. Continuous improvement and development of existing revenue and business models, aka "operational excellence"

Doing things better every day. That's how one senior manager described Type 1 Change to me. Although we enjoy a high standard of living in the Western world, it is practically impossible to schedule a repair or a delivery when it suits you best, for instance evenings or weekends. So, there is ample room for improvement. Excelling in Type 1 Change builds credibility with customers and fosters an execution culture within the organization: "change begets change"! That, in turn, fuels Types 2 and 3 Strategy Execution.

Type 2: Renewal. Overhaul of existing revenue and business models

Existing business models must be renewed too.
Type 2 Change is the kind of change needed when the existing revenue and business model needs to be transformed in order to keep running the business. This may entail drastic measures to cut costs or raise productivity, or leveraging the synergy attained through takeovers, or a rigorous revision of your customer value propositions and service concepts. This type of change nearly always requires a fundamental breakthrough in one of your company's key performance indicators, a real jump in performance.

Type 3: Innovation. Radical digital innovation, totally new revenue and business models, aka Game Changers

Define innovation. People often discuss innovation without knowing whether they are talking about the same thing. Definitions can also get blurred because product and process innovations are increasingly overlapping, as customers have come to perceive customer service as an integral part of whatever product or service they buy. And innovation can also mean a complete overhaul of the business and revenue model and the accompanying organizational structure. So, make clear what you are talking about when you discuss innovation, because your definition will influence your approach to innovation. It is vital to define what you mean, because the very survival of your company can hang in the balance. After all, how do you secure your earnings in a shrinking market when your existing business strongly depends on the commodity effect and profitability is shrinking year after year? No one can survive without innovation, but innovation can only be successful if it is manageable. Lee Iacocca once said, "The most successful leaders hold onto the old for as long as necessary and make the leap to the new as soon as this is the better move." They truly turn the page.

In a recent blog, Silicon Valley entrepreneur Steve Blank described the pitfall Microsoft and Apple face.[21] He argues that the successors of Microsoft's Bill Gates and Apple's Steve Jobs—Steve Ballmer and Tim Cook—are execution officers rather than visionaries. In his view, Ballmer and Cook must do more than just run, improve and renew their existing business models. They need to experiment with new business models too. If they fail to strike this balance, the downfall of their companies is merely a matter of time, Blank believes. Maintaining that balance is the challenge every organization faces.

The three types of change differ in terms of their impact; each requires a distinct approach. Figure 5 illustrates this. Types 1 and 2 Change pertain to a company's existing business and revenue models. Type 3 is about finding new business and revenue models by means of radical and digital innovation.

This distinction is not absolute. Business is not a science. I have seen Type 2 initiatives that were so radical that they could justifiably be categorized as Type 3. I have seen others brazenly presented as radical innovations (Type 3) that I would have hesitated to even classify as Type 2. Similarly, an initiative might start out as a Type 2 change project and gradually evolve into a Type 3, without anyone having intended for that to happen—serendipitously, in other words.

The essence of this categorization is to ensure that you are working with a single set of types and definitions, so the whole organization speaks the same language. This helps an organization choose a set of initiatives that as a whole, constitute an ambitious yet realistic portfolio.

Figure 5 — **The three types of strategy execution are fundamentally different in purpose and nature.**

	Type 1 — Improvement	Type 2 — Renewal	Type 3 — Innovation
Goal	Doing things better every day	Breakthroughs and increased profitability resulting from interventions in current operations	Ensuring continuity through timely earnings and profit from a completely new revenue and business model
Ambition level	Small, single digit differences in the KPIs of individual processes	Substantial	Substantial in the long run, with sufficient short-term traction to justify direction
Sample results	5% lower failure rate, 10% higher customer satisfaction about after sales service	10% more cross-selling, 15% cost reduction in secondary processes by leveraging post-merger synergy	5-10% growth in sales from new services resulting from new business model
Time Horizon	< 1 year, quarterly evaluation	1-2 years	2 - 5 years
Approach	Brief analyses, practical solutions executed immediately	Fundamental analyses and solutions, chopped into manageable pieces for execution. Agile	Manageable set of strategic experiments, trial and error, scaling up what works
Realistic # per division/ business unit	Max. 7 parallel	Max. 5	Define 5 to 15. Select no more than 5 for execution
Outside current revenue and business model	No	Possibly partly	Yes
Sample methods	Lean	BPR, PMI, BPM, BPO	Business Model Canvas

Source: Turner, 2016

Type 3 Change—Innovation—is crucial. Discover or create a new playing field. A third of your strategic initiatives should disrupt your own operation and the market you operate in. The distinction is motivated by a deeper business instinct. In *The Black Swan* and *Antifragile*, Nassim Nicholas Taleb describes what he calls black swans: big, unpredictable events that can bring organizations to their knees.[22] The solution to that problem does not lie in trying to predict black swans, but in trying to grow more resilient, because everything that wants to survive must grow stronger. That's the idea behind being antifragile. Taleb declares this principle applicable to practically all areas of life and certainly to organizations. The gist is that everything that doesn't kill you makes you stronger. Therefore, you would do well to shoot holes in yourself, too. The key is to be in the right position to deal with the black swan. Thanksgiving may be a black swan-type occurrence for turkeys, but it isn't for the butcher. In other words, you need to avoid ending up as a turkey. Discover or create a new playing field, and do it on time, so that it provides you with new opportunities without the risks a turkey runs. That's also what the Blue Ocean theory is about: the existing playing field is like an ocean turned red with blood. So, go ahead and find an uncontested market, a pristine blue ocean.

Type 3 Change, or innovation, is all about organizations disrupting themselves. Taleb would just as soon chuck Types 1 and 2 Change out the window; they merely contribute to making the existing organization more robust, which does nothing to address the company's vulnerability in the long run. He argues against academic experts with no skin in the game who describe how fragile organizations can make themselves robust at best, but will eventually go bust. As a pragmatic, I turn to John M. Keynes, who once said, "In the long run we're all dead." In the short and medium run, we need Type 1 and 2 Change. Without them we won't even make it to the long run, even in the New Normal where Type 3 disruptions are taking place in rapid succession. That takes nothing away from the undeniable fact that Type 3 Change is critical. Former Alcatel-Lucent and British Telecom CEO Ben Verwaayen said, "Part of every company must be in a constant state of disruption." Where I write about Accelerator 1, in Chapter 4, I explain that a sound portfolio of strategy execution initiatives must contain a third of Type 3 Change initiatives. That's a huge percentage, but it is necessary. Some people read Taleb's *Antifragile* and freeze up; they think it no longer makes sense to even try Type 1 and 2 Change. They reason that if the big innovations by other companies can blow you away (unicorns like Uber or Taleb's black swan), then there's no point. But that's just as senseless as not investing in Type 3 Change at all.

It is extremely important to keep the three types of change in balance. Some organizations scramble like mad to execute Type 1 Change as their industry shrinks by 10% every year. That's like worrying about the dirty dishes on the Titanic. And if a major financial crisis erupts, such as the one in 2008, those organizations are hopelessly unprepared. If you want to maintain dominance in a shrinking market, you are far better off working on Type 2 Change. Note that this is the most difficult type of change though, as the examples of Kodak and Nokia make clear. Once considered invincible, both businesses went under while trying to overhaul their existing business models.[23] Fortunately, there are also examples of businesses that made it through, like DSM[24], GE[25] and Toyota.[26] And yet, the most important type of innovation is still Type 3. Examples of this type of change can be found in both new and established organizations. In fact, established businesses like General Electric and Toyota might be more interesting in this respect than Uber or Airbnb. I will discuss the need for balance between the various types of change in more detail in Chapter 4.

We have sufficiently established the importance of Type 3 Change. But as a prudent Dutchman, I don't believe in throwing out your old shoes until you have a new pair. That's why you need Types 1 and 2 Change as well. They enable you to leverage your existing business model to the max and to fund the innovations that will result in a new model.

The four accelerators in Chapters 4 through 7 deal with the universal principles that apply to all three types of change (though of course, these should be applied with common sense and in differing degrees for each type).

Want to know more? Check out the world's best website about the world's best newspaper, and find out how difficult it is to innovate newspaper journalism.

2.2 Success Factor: 2 Resist One-Sidedness

What makes or breaks a modern vision of change management? What ensures that effectiveness and agility go hand-in-hand and serve both short- and long-term goals? Why are soft capabilities just as important as hard capabilities? And how important is a methodical approach?

2.2.1 Effectiveness and agility before perfectionism

Stop endlessly and pointlessly redrafting vision and strategy documents. Effectiveness and agility are far more important than perfection.

Modern strategy execution in the New Normal requires a fundamentally different way of working. Nowadays, the equation that works is Strategy = Execution. This doesn't mean strategy has become irrelevant. But every strategy requires another strategy: an execution strategy. In a column in the Dutch business paper *Het Financieele Dagblad*, INSEAD professor Annet Aris wrote, "A classic strategy analyzes market developments, looks at a company's strengths and weaknesses, pinpoints the competitive advantages that can be exploited and, based on these steps, devises plans as to where and how that company can grow. The result is a series of very precisely calculated projections for the next 3 to 5 years. More and more academics and even consultants and digital businesses are tossing this classic approach out. They are replacing strategy with a systematic quest for a higher goal, with lots of trial and error and unexpected outcomes, just like Columbus's sailing expedition to Asia."[27]

Organizations need a concise strategy that can be executed effectively and rapidly. The classic approach no longer works; taking months to chew on a strategy, analyze the context, set up the organization and prepare for implementation just takes too long. Choosing that route will only lead to a poor result. In the New Normal, organizations need a sound, concise strategy that is executed in short cycles.[28] Starting implementation of this strategy (that is, execution) right away teaches you how much agility you need to achieve your strategic goals. To make the most of your limited resources, your organization must make very deliberate choices and balance its strategic goals and execution capacity. And based on this, you need to pare down your portfolio of initiatives every year. Strategy as we once knew it no longer exists. Today, strategy equals execution.

You can't do without a clear vision, a sharply defined why, and ditto strategy. I regard the setting of vague long-term goals as sheer laziness. And while rigid blueprints may have lost their relevance, planning remains key. Leadership development expert Harry Starren calls this the planning paradox: you need to plan and look ahead, but also be prepared to change tack at the drop of a hat. It's all about balance. Lucid corporate visions and strategies are still rare, but more and more companies are working on developing a coherent mission and a concrete, inspirational long-term vision and strategy. Strategy expert Richard Rumelt hits the nail on the head in *Good Strategy/Bad Strategy* when he writes that many organizations have no strategy, even if they think they do.[29] What they call strategy is often no more than a (long) list of performance indicators, or worse yet, a vague wish list. Strategy means tackling challenges head-on. The essence of a good strategy is that it outlines the challenge and provides a roadmap, which form the basis for a concrete, coherent action plan. If this sounds rather obvious, be aware that few companies and institutions actually have such strategies.[30] Thinkers like Jim Collins and Hans van der Loo have shown repeatedly that profitability depends on a clear vision.[31] A well-defined vision is what enables a company to punch above its weight. Organizations with a robust and widely supported vision are over 25% more profitable than organizations that lack one.[32]

It is easy to see why strategy execution has fundamentally changed. Figure 6 shows why modern strategy execution and change management thrive on effectiveness and agility rather than perfectionism.

Figure 6 — **Modern strategy execution & change management:** effectiveness and agility, not perfectionism.

	Action	From		To
1	**Strategic scope**	Single product market combinations (PMC) at business unit level.	►►	Change at industry level, PMC portfolio, including consequences at all levels of business model.
2	**Nature of the goods & services**	Physical or stand-alone goods and services, one-off, single transactions.	►►	Hybrid of physical and digital services, services are priced (significant fragmentation and breakdown of value chain), multi-channel.
3	**Nature of innovation**	Planned, closed loop.	►►	Open source, open projects, assembly of subassemblies in the pipeline to propositions, continuous decision-making and adjustment.
4	**Nature of business models (processes, mechanisms, people, ICT, etc.)**	Unambiguous, maximum complexity is the hybrid matrix.	►►	Agile, open, flexible, demands beyond the matrix (while this must also keep functioning as normal).
5	**Industry structures**	Linear change (mostly erosion, glacier).	►►	Small and large evolutions and revolutions, shock waves, two steps forward, one step back.
6	**Nature of sales & marketing processes**	Sales effectiveness, mainly generic sales improvement techniques (gold, silver, bronze, light differentiation, coaching)	►►	Smart customer segmentation and sharp differentiation between sales and service concepts, from push to pull, distribution is just a fraction of sales management, marketing strictly supports sales.
7	**Nature and time horizon of execution**	Single strategy every 3 -5 years, using annual business plans as building blocks, sequential.	►►	Recalibration of mission, vision and strategy every 2 - 3 years if necessary; annual portfolio of individually structured initiatives. Note: living the paradox.
8	**Room for learning in execution**	Sufficient.	►►	Must occur in parallel, no time for classic learning curves.
9	**Nature of execution management**	Annual budget & target-setting in an etched-in-stone planning & control cycle	►►	Ever shorter lead times and life cycles, flexible budgeting and rolling planning & forecast models. Note: a highly structured approach remains necessary
10	**Method**	Analysis – overall design (blueprint) – detailed design – execution preparation – execution	►►	Concise yet solid blueprint (no vague goals!), executed in short cycles / work packages, each consisting of analysis/ design/execution/business case.

Source: Turner and Hans Strikwerda, 2016

Agility should be increased and managed from a helicopter view. Agility is a popular and important concept in modern strategy execution.[33] Cornell University professors Lee Dyer and Richard A. Shafer offer a clear definition of agility: "Organizational agility is the capacity to be infinitely adaptable without having to change."[34] Agile organizations have a built-in capacity to shift, flex, and adjust to changing conditions. There is a correlation between agility and profitable growth. Research at the Massachusetts Institute of Technology (MIT) shows that agile companies grow revenue 37% faster and generate 30% higher profits than non-agile companies. The Economist Intelligence Unit (EIU) has reported that 90% of leaders interviewed regard strategic agility as critical to their organization's success.[35] You should realize, however, that there is a difference between a capacity to be agile and actually being agile. It is essential to take a helicopter view at the monthly boardroom meeting, so you can rise above the fray and see where agility is needed.

We need to start conceptualizing change management in a new way. In Chapter 6, which deals with the question of how to scale strategy execution, I will talk about the idea of playing first and second fiddle. What it boils down to is this: sometimes you lead a strategy execution project—in other words, you play first fiddle—so it's your job to roll out the change for others; other times you take a back seat—that is, you play second fiddle—and you let others roll out the change. Sometimes you lead, sometimes you follow. In the New Normal, you tap everyone's renewal and execution capacity, you benefit from each other's work and you set the bar high. You don't have to be the driving force behind every initiative. That's perfectly normal in the *New Normal.* When effectiveness, agility and speed are crucial, you can't always play first fiddle.

Want to know more? Strategy professor Richard Rumelt talks about the difference between good and bad strategy.

2.2.2 Soft is hard and hard is soft: Balance is everything

It's the soft capabilities that ultimately determine whether change is successful. Big multinationals like Shell prepare all their new ventures and takeovers extremely well and evaluate them thoroughly afterwards. As it turns out, too few of their transactions are successes. And every time the reasons why are the same: not enough time and attention were devoted to the so-called soft capabilities. We're talking about things like cultural incompatibilities, an inability to agree on and strive for a common goal, an incapacity to bring potential synergy to fruition, and clashes in leadership and management styles.

In *Beyond Performance*, Colin Price and Scott Keller demonstrate that healthy companies outperform the market.[36] The health factors they identify largely coincide with what I call the soft capabilities. These elements make or break your ability to achieve goals. Luckily, we now have a quantitative underpinning for this argument. Price and Keller not only show that healthy companies outperform the market, but also that they are 2.2 times more likely to outperform the median.

Work just as hard on systematically analyzing and influencing your organization's soft capabilities as the hard ones. Explicitly discuss both types of capabilities. Soft capabilities include culture, behavior, leadership style and cooperation. Hard capabilities comprise processes, structure and ICT. Turner Consultancy's online research tool SECA.NU, developed to help determine an organization's execution capacity, is an excellent tool for systematically measuring its hard and soft capabilities.[37]

Many people think of this soft side of business as intangibles. Culture, climate, values, behavior and leadership seem to be the domain of a few experts who think they can tell others how to develop and perfect an organization's "soft side." No wonder the soft side remains a kind of black box to most employees.

The soft side is therefore often conflated with the concept of organizational culture. It is true that culture is considered the backbone of the soft capabilities, but attempts to change the culture for the sake of changing the culture are pointless. A far better approach is to identify five crucial behavioral issues, define what behavior is expected with regard to these, and make sure there is no room for excuses not to adopt this behavior. I will return to this when I describe Accelerator 2, Building Block 6.

The Strategy Execution & Change Accelerator—SECA.NU

Turner Consultancy has developed an online Strategy Execution & Change Accelerator called SECA.NU. This is a research tool that provides participants with online, real-time information about their organization's execution capacity compared to benchmarks. This feedback can enhance and accelerate strategy execution.

SECA.NU consists of 25 questions that generate a very accurate analysis of an organization's maturity in strategy execution. This can be broken down into four main metrics: maturity of executive management (Running the Business), maturity of change management (Changing the Business), the quality of hard conditions (processes and systems), and the quality of the soft conditions (leadership, cooperation). These are the four main dimensions of effective strategy execution.

I can't say it often enough: never invest in a culture change program. Culture is an outcome, not an independent issue. You can't independently change the corporate climate. Organizations are complex structures where every change has ripple effects. When employees are given new responsibilities, they will see their contribution in a new light and adjust their behavior and values accordingly. Just focus on real goals, tasks and initiatives in a way that keeps hard and soft elements in equilibrium and the culture will change in its wake.

Any program aimed exclusively at altering organizational culture is a waste of money.[38]

All eyes on the soft capabilities, in other words? No! Balance is everything. The balance between hard and soft is what really makes the difference. It is often said that a project's success is determined by how it starts out. Everyone agrees that there needs to be a robust, substantial roadmap and a clear goal. The soft element that is crucial at the start is the engagement of the executive who draws up the plan and gets others to commit to the project. This is what I call the psychological check-in, a crucial but generally forgotten or ignored aspect of every project. All too often, senior managers do nothing more than make a quick phone call the day before kickoff. The truth is, every minute invested in thorough discussion of roles and responsibilities pays off exponentially in the end results. But it has to be real engagement, not fake commitment.

In the New Normal, the choice between top-down and bottom-up change management is a false dilemma. As we all know, it's not either-or, it's both. The idea that top-down change doesn't work is an old, discredited idea that some people try to pass off as new. Similarly, we must quickly dispense with the dogma that bottom-up change is the only way. When large organizations start complex, multidisciplinary projects to execute real innovation, it's risky to assume that every individual involved is able to analyze and decide how things should be improved (bottom-up change). You can't do without a clear top-down framework. And it's unacceptable for departments or individuals to reject best practices just because someone else thought them up. The "not invented here" syndrome is an unproductive and undesirable characteristic for tomorrow's employee.[39] Leaders must take a modern attitude towards change management. New generations of professionals have come to expect that attitude and feel uncomfortable having to seek consensus on every decision. They want to deliver high-quality work when they're playing first fiddle on an initiative. And when they're playing second fiddle, they expect whoever is taking the lead to have the same attitude. The taboo on top-down frameworks and rollouts is unjustified. Many organizations make the mistake of not delineating clear frameworks because they believe "employees should come up with the ideas themselves." The solution is to strike the right balance between bottom-up and top-down.[40] There are other false dichotomies, like short-term versus long-term, results-oriented versus people-oriented management, and the tortoise-and-the-hare dilemma. Here's a hint: it's never either-or. Call it straddling-the-divide management, if you like.

2.2.3 Strategy execution is a process like any other

Nothing beats a good business process model. Modern strategy execution methods also need a business process model. Everyone is trained to think in business processes: sales, logistics, delivery, service, administration, management and human resource processes. But when it comes to strategy execution, this thinking suddenly seems not to apply, as if strategy execution can be taken for granted. Yet strategy execution is just another business process, which needs to be described and implemented like all others.

At the end of the day, everyone benefits from a practical model. It helps everyone speak the same language. And a process model or framework also provides a peg from which to hang best practices, so we can convert generic steps into concrete actions.

We execute strategy in an ever more complex and volatile world. Using a single method and a single language for strategy execution creates the time and flexibility to deal with our rapidly changing world. Taking a systematic approach and making sure you know which phase an initiative is in helps to successfully complete that phase and the whole initiative. This is true not only during analysis, but also during execution.

At one point, I helped a senior manager at a large insurance company to create a single method and language for strategy execution. Speaking about the use of a phased or step-by-step model, he said: "At any given moment, each initiative will be in a different phase from all the others. But every one of them has to go through every phase. In the heat of the moment, we often don't know what phase a particular initiative is in. And when it gets stuck or fails to deliver, we're surprised. But that's because we keep stepping into the classic pitfall of only approaching our initiatives systematically while we're defining them. When we most need to be systematic, during execution, our minds tend to be elsewhere." Thinking in accelerators, stages, phases or steps—whatever you prefer to call them—helps you realize what still needs to be done.

2.3 Success Factor 3: Disrupt or Be Disrupted

There are many big trends in the corporate world, but the biggest is digital innovation.[41] Customers' fundamental needs require radical, digital innovation from every organization. The kind of innovation we need now is digital transformation. We can no longer see innovation and digitalization as separate phenomena. Ninety-nine percent of all organizations worldwide are neither startups nor well-established successful digital innovators like Apple, Google, or Amazon. Yet, if you want to survive, you're going to have to come up with a digital innovation strategy.

In 2015, organizations expected to see 5 to 10% growth and efficiency gains in the next five years through digital experimentation.[42] So far, however, the results have fallen far short of expectations. Digital objectives are by no means easier to achieve than traditional strategy objectives. That's why we need to thoroughly analyze and redefine our strategy, value propositions, customer processes and organizational structure. Nine times out of ten, these issues are interconnected and multidisciplinary.

In essence, digital innovation is small experiments, quick fails, rapid scaling.
"First fire bullets, then cannonballs," said Jim Collins, and don't be afraid to fail. Anyone who has built a big company has been ridiculed somewhere along the way. Making room for failure also leaves room for what is known as "tactical serendipity."[43] Great ideas spring from the unplanned.

Digital innovation requires iterative and agile development and execution methods. It is also essential to work in projects to coordinate the business processes, technology and people. An organization's ability to shift into high gear is called its Innovation and Digital Quotient, or IDQ.[44] This is the digital DNA of startups and software companies that many other types of companies lack and need to acquire. IDQ is no mystery, but because it applies to every aspect of an organization, it can be hard to pin down.

Let me lay out the five areas in which you must excel in order to survive and be competitive in the digital age:
1. Digital Strategy and Value Propositions
2. Customer Need Identification
3. Digital Structures and Agile Management
4. New Capabilities and High Energy
5. Two-Track Technology

2.3.1 Defining your digital strategy and value propositions
Be sure to develop a clear and widely supported digital strategy. This boils down to a transformative digital vision that provides a new conceptualization of customers and their fundamental needs, as well as how digital innovation can meet these needs. Your digital innovation strategy must be a fresh chapter in your overall strategy. It will pull the other

chapters along in its wake! Define what digital innovation will be about in the next few years, on the premise that innovative goods and services will contribute more to your profits every year. Make clear that this is your goal, and that everyone is responsible for working towards this.

Your digital vision and strategy must shake things up. Your digital vision provides an unbiased analysis of your ideal customer experience, business processes and business model. This digital transformation must be inspired by a disruptive mindset: you are out to disrupt the market and hence your own organization, too. The strategy must jar things loose, inspire people and spur them into action. In the end, there is no such thing as a digital strategy. There is only strategy in the digital age.

2.3.2 Stop looking at your customers in cliché ways

The key is to look at your customers with fresh eyes. If you don't understand your customers' fundamental needs, you can't understand how to use digital innovation in order to meet those needs better, smarter and quicker. Customers have been king for so long, that our ideas about how to meet their needs have become old and stale. Digitalization challenges these fossilized ideas. It offers so many possibilities that it reprioritizes customer needs in a very refreshing way. Take the SNKRS app that Nike launched in 2015. The people at Nike saw that sneaker fans followed niche sites and online communities to find out when new products would be launched. So Nike launched SNKRS, a platform that offered these fans pre-release exclusive access to the latest models, as well as a channel for buying them directly from the manufacturer. The app provides personalized content based on buyers' preferences, whether that be Air Max or soccer shoes.

Co-creation is a value proposition in its own right. Don't hesitate to collaborate with other companies. There is simply no time to develop everything yourself. Why not enter into a smart partnership with a competitor who is way ahead of you in some area, whether content, distribution or marketing? This is a counter-intuitive idea that companies are afraid to initiate. But like I said before, customers care less and less which company is behind the products and services they use. If you want to offer your customers value, why let yourself get distracted by fights over territory with competitors? When you do, you lose customers. American companies have already embraced this idea. In *Digital Disruption*, James McQuivey cites the example of Amazon, whose Kindle runs on Android.[45] But if you want to read Amazon e-books on an iPad, you can simply download the free Kindle app. Similarly, movies on Xbox One are not limited to Microsoft's Zune platform. You can also use Hulu or Netflix. This is a new business model.

The profit margins may be lower, but in the end everybody wins—both companies and customers.[46]

Digitalization equals business process automation. Digitalization is about the need for and usefulness of automating business processes. Yet it also works the other way around: when implemented well, automation leverages rapid scaling and efficiency. Just consider how much efficiency is improved through deduplication, gathering information at the beginning of every key process, eliminating errors and shortening throughput times by means of "straight-through processing."

2.3.3 Navigating by means of digital structure and agile management

As Menno Lanting wrote, turning an oil tanker into a speedboat—or a fleet of speedboats—is not easy.[47] Going agile is a sea change: you shift from planning, development and rollout to experimenting, failing and starting over. That calls for a different culture too. But like I said, cultural change is an outcome of business process change.

Digital innovation requires strong top-down leadership. Ensure that digitalization is managed explicitly. Create a digital governance philosophy that serves as a substantial, recognizable and widely supported framework. For digital innovation to be effective, the necessary roles and responsibilities must be defined, assigned, and up and running before execution begins. Organizations should appoint a C-level executive who is responsible for digitalization, a chief digital officer (CDO) so to speak. That is the main digital leadership role, but responsibility for digitalization does not rest solely with that person. Each portfolio leader should know what their digital responsibilities are. This is why it is important to make sure leaders and key digital actors are on the same wavelength. They need to share the same digital vision, know it like the back of their hands, and promote it both within and outside of their own discipline.

Successful digital leaders seldom work from the bottom up. Letting a thousand flowers bloom doesn't guarantee success. Digital leaders need to manage transformations by providing direction and by persevering. This requires a great deal of coordination and strong top-down leadership, even if that runs counter to popular change management dogma.

Digital innovation must be a priority for the entire C-suite. It is not something that one radical innovator or a single dedicated team can do, no matter how hard they work at it. Senior managers have to lead. That's the bottom line.

The biggest obstacles to digital disruption are silos. The bigger the organization, the more difficult it is to break these silos down. Identify the silos in your organization and think of ways around them or straight through them. In other words, look at the organizational chart, identify the obstacles and remove them. That is change leadership. Typically, this boils down to things like speeding up legal and financial approvals, cutting through regional sales structures, and closing gaps between engineering and marketing.

2.3.4 Developing new capabilities and a high-energy culture

Every employee needs to have basic digital capabilities. You also need a few digital key actors who are way ahead of the pack and have excellent competencies. In short, you need a platoon of capable soldiers, but a vanguard too.

Digital capabilities are Human Resource Management's core business. Therefore, every HR process—whether recruitment and selection, training and education, coaching, evaluation or remuneration—should include a focus on digital innovation capabilities.

The CTO and the CFO are crucial leadership roles. In new, data-driven organizations, the Chief Technical Officer basically operates at the same level as the CEO. Chief Financial Officers are just as essential, because their job encompasses so much more than just financial control. But at the heart of every digital business model are the product owners and engineers, the tech people. They are the backbone of your business. Salespeople are easy to replace, but product and technical engineers aren't.

Startups look at HR in a fresh light. "When I think about what my employees might want, I put myself in the shoes of someone who quits to become self-employed," said one of the internet entrepreneurs I interviewed. "What is the first thing a self-employed person does? They buy an Apple computer. So, I bought all my employees an Apple computer." And that is just one small example of how to keep the entrepreneurial spirit alive in an organization, he stressed. This same entrepreneur assured me that he gives top priority to soft capabilities—education, purpose, job satisfaction and appreciation—for anyone who works for his travel organization.

Analytical skill is by far the most important capability for new data-driven business models. Understanding metrics and an ability to think and act in a well-structured way are crucial. A second competency no entrepreneur should underestimate is project management skills. Someone who excels at project management makes life easier for everyone else. "As an entrepreneur you love it when your people have a talent for project management and want to develop that skill," another successful internet entrepreneur told me. These capabilities are even more important than creative capabilities, although saying so seems to be taboo. Digital organizations spend so much money on marketing every month that you really need to know where it goes, and why, and how to manage that budget.

Specialists are where it's at for digital companies. Not managers. As one internet entrepreneur put it: "When a specialist wants to become a manager I sometimes say to them: 'Your added value here is your specialization. So why would you want to become a manager?'"

Obviously, your specialists and high-brow nerds have to be able to cooperate. Every organization has its high-performing oddballs and mavericks. That's not going to change, even in high-tech organizations. The old rule of thumb still applies: if you have fewer oddballs than one in ten, you've got a problem. If you have more, you've got another problem.

Digital innovation is part of your corporate culture. Work on building a strong, high-energy, digital innovation culture where employees are committed and motivated to help make digital transformation a reality. Too often, a company's digital strategy is just another policy document. Research has shown that usually two-thirds of employees don't even know it exists.[48]

2.3.5 Dual-track technology

IT works at two different speeds. Whether your organization is small or large, whether you're dealing with legacy systems or not, digital innovation always requires a two-track approach to IT. Track 1 deals with basic digitalization, while Track 2 is dedicated to digital transformation. You can only take real strides when these tracks have been separated and properly facilitated. Track 2 is characterized by small, autonomous IT teams that use modern methods such as DevOps and Scrum. They cooperate with marketing, sales and the customer base to design, build, test, change and scale prototypes.

Digital platforms are used for economies of scale. Digital platforms enable you to quickly introduce new products and to create and maintain customer relations. Today, this infrastructure is just as indispensable to your business as railroads, highways and aviation were in the previous century. A digital platform allows you to analyze how you can grow your profits exponentially without increasing your costs—and without the burden of having to pitch your ideas to investors or set up an HRM department. A digital platform enables you to reach out to your customers. A great example is HBO, which James McQuivey cites in *Digital Disruption*. In the USA, 28 million viewers watch HBO on satellite or cable, which makes them indirect customers. Just imagine having 28 million prospects. The company used the HBO Go app to connect with these potential customers and establish direct customer relations. This gained them access to a treasure trove of user information. Digital platforms prioritize customer relations and decrease friction: an ideal combination for innovation.

There are plenty of examples of companies that used a digital platform to become the greatest disruptor in their industry: Uber—a transportation platform without its own fleet; Facebook—a social media platform without its own content; and Airbnb—a lodging platform without its own real estate. Similarly, none of the big online retailers—Amazon, Alibaba/Aliexpress, Cdiscount—have their own inventory anymore.

Defining a platform strategy is the biggest challenge in business today and the main strategy puzzle for organizations with new revenue models. The puzzle is often multidimensional: which strategy do you choose for your B2B, B2C and B2B2C activities? Your platform strategy defines everything. You will want to maximize standardization and digitalization in order to make and keep your activities scalable. Scalability is key.

Data management is key in execution. Data management is the brain of digital operations. Metrics make strategic, tactical and operational analyses possible. Data management is key in digital innovation and the iteration of prototypes. The term "big data" can have a paralyzing effect. So, let's demystify big data analysis. Every organization has a huge cache of data that is just begging to be put to use for improving, renewing and innovating its business processes. The challenge lies in deciding which question you want to answer. Take Cattle Care, for instance. This company's technology provides dairy farmers with tons of data about their cows. But it's only when these farmers ask a well-defined question (e.g. 'Which numbers predict that a cow is going to get sick?') that they can actually mine the data.

2.3.6 Lastly: Startups are not as far ahead as you think

Established organizations tend to overestimate the convenience of new business models. They assume everything has already been standardized and digitalized. As we learned from the CEO and founder of a digital business model in the travel industry, there are some common misconceptions about his company. One is that his business is a success because its business model is highly standardized and digitalized. In reality, all he had was a great business idea: offering new, original travel packages every day. In fact, many of the processes needed to offer such packages are far from standardized and digitalized, because they're so dependent on suppliers. The travel industry might be one of the most promising industries in which to introduce new business models, but it's also one of the toughest because it depends so heavily on the availability, speed and reliability of immature suppliers. For example, *agriturismi*, high-end B&Bs on Italian farms, are very popular with Europeans, but getting reliable data on availability is a nightmare. Integrating this neatly into processes is a many-headed monster.

New business models face many challenges, just like ordinary, old-fashioned organizations. But new organizations with largely digital business models also face new challenges. They often double in size and sales every 2 to 3 years. This means their processes and their organization need to keep pace; otherwise they run a huge risk, because it's people who make or break their digital success. As our study showed, new organizations also have to deal with other challenges besides growth. First, there is personalization: using data analysis to tailor products or services to customers' existing or even latent needs. Content, message, messenger and timing have to come together in an airtight combination at a large scale. Second, there is the need for distinctiveness. Delivering a higher service level is getting ever harder. Since FedEx and DHL allow every online retailer to deliver overnight, overnight delivery is no longer a unique selling point. Digital entrepreneurs now try to deliver inspirational content with their product or service, or to find other ways that make them stand out from the crowd. Third, there's the principle of fresh inventory. Every new business model tries to mimic the "Zara effect." This successful Spanish retail chain's highly sophisticated logistics enable it to constantly refresh its collection and rapidly deliver new, surprising items that are very well attuned to its customers' needs, while keeping its inventory very small. This principle can be transferred to many other markets: finding ways to excite your customers with new releases in order to ensure their loyalty. The fourth challenge is attracting and keeping the right digital specialists. The fifth is getting your data management and reporting in order. The sixth frequently mentioned challenge is quality assurance. Last, but not least, standardization and digitalization of the supply chain are the seventh challenge.

Always aiming for straight A's, but never quite getting there. The CEO and founder of a new digital business model in retail told us it's self-evident that customer intimacy, operational excellence and product leadership all have to score an A+ in today's new economy. But you never reach that straight A status. You continually strive to meet ever higher demands. You continually look for the initiative that will have the most impact. Striving for straight A's, for excellence, must become second nature. Always. Every day you have to do better than the previous one.

Building a successful new business and revenue model is no picnic. The bar is set incredibly high. In the internet economy, the law of No. 1, 2 and 3 applies. Lower market positions simply don't survive. Most digital business models continuously improve their customer processes by A/B or split testing, but now find themselves having to continuously improve their internal processes as well. Welcome to the establishment.

Digital disruption? A critical note. Radical digital transformation speeds up innovation. Without digital innovation, there is no survival. Some people claim the age of great, world-changing inventions is over. They say we've gone from revolution to evolution that the past fifty years have just been about improving existing technologies. Yes, it's impressive what today's planes, phones and computers can do, but those are just improvements, not innovations. Economist Robert Gordon is one of the leading proponents of this view. In *The Rise and Fall of American Growth*, Gordon argues that the internet was responsible for a great increase in prosperity from 1994 to 2004, but that the effect of technological progress on the economy has since worn off. He points out that the growth of productivity from 1920 to 1970 has never been matched. [49]

The problem with Gordon's argument is that he links technological progress so inexorably to economic growth. There are two reasons to dispute this point of view. First, robotization, the free availability of information and the digitalization of business reduces rather than increases employment. Second, not everything can be quantified. The speed and ease with which we can now communicate with our customers, co-workers and employers has fundamentally changed the way we do business. But try quantifying that.

2.4 Success Factor 4: Emphasize Who over Why, How and What

This success factor focuses on the importance of people and on how to secure their engagement in strategy execution.

2.4.1 The right person for the right job

The most important success factor by far is the right person for the right job. Jim Collins points to this success factor as one of the main parameters that make organizations great rather than just good: "First, [get] the right people on the bus."[50] *Who* is more important than *what*. After all, your employees are your most important customers. Good people devise good strategies and create happy customers.[51] They're specialists in their line of work, they're smart and skilled. They're hard workers. We all know that willpower and stamina are much better predictors of someone's success than talent. I am a firm believer in the 10,000-hour theory proposed by psychologist Anders Ericsson and popularized by Malcolm Gladwell. According to them, you need to put in at least 10,000 hours to get really good at something, regardless of your talent or inspiration. Success is ultimately the result of hard work, particularly in strategy execution. However, many organizations have a lot of talented and hardworking people at senior level. That's where emotional intelligence separates the wheat from the chaff. Emotional intelligence is the capacity for self-reflection and the ability to empathize and connect with people, regardless of whether you like them or not.

Strategy execution is a craft and should be considered a core competency. Let me give you an example: one of the reasons Nestlé does better than many of its competitors is that it doesn't have a penchant for endless analysis. There is a bias toward action. Excellence in strategy execution is a more important topic than strategic analysis in Nestlé's boardroom.[52] That's the only way to foster agility and effectiveness where it counts most: in people.

Be tough and smart when recruiting, because finding the right people for the right job is key in strategy execution. Some senior managers have no qualms delaying a strategic program for 3 months while they search for the best people to fill the key roles. After all, your people are your most important lever. As business models change, you also need to change your recruitment practices. For example, the CEO of AFAS, a fast-growing software company, personally developed what he calls recruitment auditioning: shifting the focus from how someone talks about the job to how someone acts on the job.[53] Similarly, you need to redefine co-workership and take independent contractors just as seriously as permanent employees. Soon, the number of temps and freelancers will far exceed the number of permanent employees.[54]

Spend time on onboarding. Integrate the entire brand and customer experience in the on-boarding process and put new people on rotation through the entire organization. Encourage professionals to grow their careers by becoming super specialists rather than managers. Many professionals are more interested in growing and developing their skills in their field than in taking the classic route and being promoted to a management position. Another important tip: fire the same way you hire, decisively and honestly. In today's world, employees are responsible for their continuous development and every organization is responsible for enabling them to do so. This ensures employability. If an organization and an employee feel they no longer have enough to offer each other, this needs to be addressed immediately. If necessary, managers or board members need to fire people, resolutely and conscientiously. Every ex-employee is a potential ambassador for your organization, so everyone is better off if they leave on good terms. Fire the same way you hire, decisively and honestly.

Want to know more? Jim Collins coined the 'First Who Concept': people first, direction second.

2.4.2 Strong business case for engagement

Engagement is fuel. Engaged employees contribute significantly to all of an organization's strategic goals: profitability, customer and employee satisfaction, productivity, retention of talent and lower absenteeism. Engagement affects your customers and your results. In a 2015 poll, Gallup found that 68% of employees are not engaged.[55] Just over 50% were passively unengaged: neither hostile nor disruptive. Such employees get to work on time but do the absolute minimum expected of them. They are not committed to the organization's goals and ambitions. Another 17.2% were actively *dis*engaged: these employees were hostile and disruptive.

The behavior of disengaged employees not only leads to waste and demotivation, it lowers productivity too. Fortunately, the tide is relatively easy to turn. What you pay to retain an employee is a fraction of the cost of recruiting, training and onboarding a new one.

Engagement increases profitability. Organizations with an excellent ratio of actively engaged to actively disengaged employees show growth in profitability. Their Earnings Per Share (EPS) is almost 4 times higher than that of organizations with lower employee engagement.[56] Engagement also leads to significantly higher customer satisfaction. In these organizations, more than 60% of employees are actively engaged. This goes to show that employee engagement benefits everyone.[57] But how do these organizations motivate their employees? The study showcases some great examples:

- First of all, be like an Australian pasture: not fenced in, but with an alluring source of water. If your products, day-to-day work, leadership, co-workers and customers are attractive, your organization will be too.

Make sure your vision for the future is inspirational, explain to your people why their work is meaningful and why the various initiatives are necessary. In short, explain the real, basic *why*.[58]

- Good leadership is service-minded rather than charismatic. It is predictable, generous, caring and challenging. Be as compassionate as you are tough. Recruit rigorously, manage with a light touch! And most importantly, dare to get personal.
- Make staffing one of the main issues in setting up projects and programs. Find the right people to help set up new initiatives and give them personal responsibilities. This motivates and engages them.
- Be a "Rhine-Saxon": social and positive. Many Rhineland capitalists are hesitant to embrace Anglo-Saxon, American positivism, but you should learn to emphasize the positive. Never underestimate the power of real attention and a sincere compliment.
- Put time and effort into maintaining relationships. Few things harm your credibility more than seeking engagement, putting in the effort once and then neglecting the person you have given a key role in execution.
- Develop HR's role in recruitment, remuneration, organizational development, and most of all, in talent management. Ask your HR department today for a single sheet of paper listing the most important people to retain, and have them include a cafeteria menu of personal development options.
- When you assess and reward your employees, do not limit yourself to the quantitative and financial. Money is the most expensive way to motivate people. Obviously, remuneration should match performance, but personal development opportunities, personal attention, coaching, feedback, respect, equality, inspiration and compliments make much more of a difference. Make sure that your employees' goals and passions serve your organization's collective ambition, because engagement without alignment is meaningless.

Did I mention empowering people? I think it's self-evident that you should give your employees and teams maximum freedom within the right framework. The number of books published in the last decade on the topic of self-organizing and self-directed teams and the importance of autonomy to individuals in organizations could fill half a library. I consider the need for autonomy simply good hygiene, or pointing out the obvious. That is not to say that every organization always get it right. *Buurtzorg* got it right when it successfully introduced a new business model in which autonomous care professionals organize themselves at the community level without any management layers on top. But this is not a model that can be copy-pasted onto any situation regardless. If too hastily adopted, teams of employees will be expected to start operating autonomously, without having been adequately trained to make that change.

Don't underestimate the importance of behavior in relation to engagement; not all high engagement is functional. This is a delicate matter. First, you should always encourage bottom-up input, but you do not have to accept and implement every bottom-up suggestion for strategic change. As a leader, you must set, explain and adhere to a clear strategic framework. Yet within this framework, you need to leave maximum room for bottom-up interpretation and freedom. It's almost as if it's taboo to set clear boundaries.

There's also a dogma that dictates that any type of employee engagement is good. That's nonsense. A lot of money is spent on increasing motivation and engagement. I say, spend more time on fewer but better quality initiatives in this area. For example, let employees write a personal commitment statement. This popular and very effective HR tool is a great way to avoid formalistic HR processes while stimulating a more down-to-earth dialogue about what drives and motivates professionals.

To prevent the wrong type of engagement we need to stop using employee satisfaction as the only engagement metric. Let's look at people's behavior too. Someone may claim to be very satisfied, but does the walk match the talk? Sean Graber, CEO of training firm Virtuali, identifies negative, indifferent and positive employee perceptions and plots these against destructive, neutral and constructive behaviors.[59] The resulting matrix shows the all-star employee diametrically opposed to the saboteur, the brat to the martyr and the drifter, the underachiever, the cynic, the delinquent and the workhorse in between. They can all be equally engaged, but that engagement does not necessarily translate into a positive contribution to the organization. Clearly, you want to avoid destructive engagement. Each type of employee requires a different kind of leadership and coaching, both to encourage employee development and to let go of people.

Want to see what high engagement looks like? Watch a studio director in the last minutes of a live broadcast.

2.5 Success Factor 5: Make Strategy Execution Your No. 1 Priority

Just how important is strategy execution, and why? This section explains that every manager has only one core duty: Execution. That's why the E in CEO stands for Executive.

2.5.1 Strategy execution is a discipline in its own right

Strategy execution requires more than spouting ideas about leadership. You need to walk the talk, because actions speak louder than words. Writing down your strategic goals does not equal achieving them. The proof of the pudding is in the eating and the proof of your strategy is in its execution. There is a great anecdote about Conrad Hilton, founder of the eponymous hotel chain, who in his mid-80s finally retired and was honored by a dozen captains of industry. At the end of the evening, Hilton shuffled onto the stage to answer the MC's predictable question "Mr. Hilton, what is the secret of your business success?" His answer was as succinct as it was brilliant: "Remember to tuck the shower curtain into the bath tub." And with that he turned and walked off the stage.[60]

Obviously, this is an oversimplification. Leadership in strategy execution requires more. It requires all sorts of competencies and good timing: doing the right things at the right time. One change leader who proved himself effective time and again was Eberhard van der Laan, the late mayor of Amsterdam. He was not afraid of making hard choices or of putting his political future on the line. Many senior managers for public companies stress the importance of this. If you fail to take personal responsibility, you won't achieve a breakthrough. Mayor Van der Laan didn't shy away from speaking his mind either. While public debate dragged on in the city council and the media about how preventive frisking was a privacy violation, he dared voice the unpopular opinion that "a gun against your head is a much worse violation of privacy than preventive frisking."[61]

Operational intensity should be a required competency for every leader. A friend of mine is on the Board of Directors at Unilever. He's proud of the company's social responsibility policies and the growing bias for action he sees among his colleagues. This change goes hand-in-hand with well-chosen concepts and language. The notion of operational intensity represents a bias toward execution at every level, from the boardroom to the mailroom. As an example, my friend told me about a problem in Asia that required production to be shifted to a different plant. The company needed to make a series of important decisions with far-reaching logistical, managerial and even cultural implications. All its Halal products, which had been produced in a

Halal-certified factory in a Muslim country, would have to be manufactured in a factory that was capable of making the same products, but had no Halal certification. Using a WhatsApp group, the company was able to make all the decisions in less than 48 hours. It didn't matter where on the globe the decision-makers were.

Pope Francis is another good example. The pontiff does not involve the Curia, the Vatican's top administrative body, in all his decisions. As a result, guests regularly show up at the Vatican gate for an audience with the Pope, catching the Curia unawares and off guard.

As has been proven time and again, service-minded, constructive leadership is the best leadership. The most effective leaders do not have big egos. Executive coach, psychoanalyst and INSEAD professor Manfred Kets de Vries has explored the more perverse aspects of charismatic leaders' personalities.[62] We all have enough first-hand experience to know that organizations are full of egos and politics, from the boardroom to the mailroom. So, let's be real and put things on the table as much as possible. Let's respect each other's sensitivities and beliefs. Remember the saying attributed to Israeli general and politician Yitzak Rabin: "Always leave your enemies room to make an about-face without losing face."[63]

Want to know more? Larry Hrebiniak, professor at the Wharton School of Business and author of *Making Strategy Work*, talks about the alarming percentage of failing strategies and about what you can do to ensure that your strategy succeeds.

2.5.2 Magic and demystification in change leadership

Necessity, simplicity and focus have a certain magic. In *Must-Win Battles*, Peter Killing, Thomas Malnight and Tracey Keys describe how important it is to not fight every battle, but to pick a limited set of must-win battles.[64] However, beware of paring this set down too far. Don't wager everything on two big battles, but spread the risk a little thinner. Don't rack your brain about whether you should pick your battles based on urgency or excitement. These days, it's usually a mix. Your must-win battles are the arena in which you have to force the real breakthrough.[65] That's not easy, but it can be done. Leaders of large corporations always stress necessity, focus and simplicity. They word their strategic goals clearly and succinctly, often in three to five main points. Such simplicity is powerful.

Successful leaders in strategy execution excel at systematically creating focus. This means they also know when to say no. After the collapse of European electronic engineering firm Imtech in 2015, one of the senior managers of a large international trading company admitted he had earned his shareholders most by saying no to requests for new initiatives.[66]

Successful leaders in strategy execution know how to deal with the fears and temptations they face along the way. For example, a fear of having the wrong focus and falling even further behind the competition; or the fear of missing new opportunities, FOMO. One thing is clear: leaders without focus drive themselves, and everyone around them, crazy. If they don't even know where they're headed and why, why would anyone want to follow them? Would-be agility and flexibility projects a sense of vigor and freshness at first. But pretty soon, the underlying reality of a wavering organization without a true north will begin to shine through.[67]

Real strategy execution requires perseverance. It is about deferred gratification, by definition. Leaders who practice this meet a lot of resistance. The hardest moments are those when someone offers excellent arguments that reinforce your own doubts. After all, there are pros and cons to every option.

Modern leaders need new competencies to ensure success in strategy execution. Leadership is the most popular topic of management books, so finding resources is simple. What isn't simple, though, is identifying which leadership qualities determine success in strategy execution. But that is exactly what we have focused on in our research and case studies. The result is a list of competencies that distinguish an excellent 21st century leader from a mediocre one.[68] Any corporate HR department or headhunter is welcome to use it. Modern leaders:

- are strategically and analytically competent;
- can communicate the why, what and how in an appealing way;
- have a founder's mentality;[69]
- can simplify and remove obstacles;
- work systematically on expanding execution;
- create and force decisions and breakthroughs;
- believe in collective intelligence and so objectivize decision-making;
- build trust;[70]
- have authority and just enough paranoia;
- are always working on themselves;
- are curious and have more questions than answers;
- resist the tyranny of old-school change management.

A comprehensive version of this list can be found in Appendix 5, download #2.

If leaders don't develop themselves, chances are the organization won't develop either. More than half of the competencies in this list are known as "soft skills." This puts high demands on leaders' personal development. And that's a world unto itself, with training sessions, books, courses, gurus and coaches. All of these are geared towards helping you become a better person, parent, friend, co-worker and boss. But what a mixed bag it is, offering as many low-quality as high-quality methods to develop yourself. For high-quality courses, I can recommend IMD Professor George Kohlrieser, author of *Hostage at the Table* (2006) and London Business School Professor Brent Smith. They teach excellent programs for developing your leadership and team competencies in an academically sound, yet practical and personal way. Besides teaching you skills and offering tools, they also force you to dig deep and take a hard look at yourself. But as good as these programs are, you will learn far more about yourself in the harsh everyday reality of business. And that's what this book is about.

This new role description may strike you as a demand for the proverbial unicorn. But a closer analysis reveals a few striking shifts in perception of what good leaders are all about. Previously, leadership tended to be defined in terms of charisma and strong leadership. Think of Jan Timmer, who steered Philips through Operation Centurion in the 1990s. These days, the buzzword is authenticity. That's a quality you can never lay claim to, but that is used as a yardstick anyway.

Modern leaders are focused on open collaboration. That's how the new generation of CEOs lead their organizations, for example Ralph Hamers at ING Bank and Ton Büchner at AkzoNobel. They have to, because their organizations and their own performance are much more in the public eye these days. So, they find people that share their organization's vision and mission and then give leaders and teams room to grow.[71] A 2015 PwC study among 6,000 leaders showed that just 8% of them had the right competencies to achieve big transformations.[72] Most of these were women. The same study had been conducted in 2005, with similar results. The wheels of change turn slowly.

Mirror neurons work like magic. New research at the interface of neurobiology and organizational psychology—including work done by Daniel Goleman and Richard Boyatzis—is having a big impact on our thinking about leadership.[73] It's been proven that constructive, service-minded and positive leadership causes employees to follow suit, because of the influence of mirror neurons. This is pure biology. Mirror neurons are activated when you watch what someone else does. Interestingly, this action stimulates the same spot in the brain in both the observer and the person carrying out the task. [74] Knowing this, leaders need to take a closer look at their own behavior and the impact it has on others, and put this self-knowledge to positive use. This new knowledge even has an ethical dimension: it can help redress one of the most destructive behaviors leaders can display, namely manipulative tendencies that arise from a combination of high emotional intelligence and a big ego.[75]

Want to know more? Rosabeth Moss Kanter gave an excellent TEDx talk about six ways to lead positive change.

2.5.3 Continual alignment

Striving for alignment within the chain of command of the line organization is easy. Alignment is more than making sure the chain of command is well-oiled and that people who work at the same level in the vertical chain meet their KPI targets. Thanks to Peter Drucker and Kaplan and Norton's digital Balanced Business Scorecards (BBSC), many organizations use simple and transparent performance management systems these days.

The challenge is to align horizontally, outside of the chain of command. At least 80% of the work spent on strategy execution must be carried out in the main structure people work in. It does not matter whether the initiative is delegated to the line organization, the department or the team people are working in, or whether it has been organized in a project. If 80% is not carried out in the main structure it was assigned to, it was probably a bad decision to choose that main structure. In addition, the people who execute the strategy also need time to coordinate and manage across other initiatives and disciplines (which takes 10 to 20% of the time spent on strategy execution). Plus they need time to report on progress, to manage escalations and maintain collaborations, either in projects or programs or in their day-to-day work. This type of alignment, or old-fashioned coordination, is precisely what helps bring about success.

Alignment is a treacherous process, because a lot can go wrong. The higher up in the organization, the higher the risk of executive isolation.[76] Another problem is a "loss of levels" between senior management and middle management. Also, beware of disalignment under the guise of autonomy and self-organization. This can happen at any level. There can also be disalignment or even disdain between primary and secondary processes. The line organization may show contempt for back office jobs—"we're doing the real work while the rest just costs money and does nothing to alleviate our problems." But there may also be rivalry between different support departments, e.g. IT versus Finance versus HRM.

And then there can be disalignment between different line departments. Classic rivalries include "we created an excellent top line, but the delivery has failed us" (Sales) versus "they're not selling our stuff and they promise too much" (Operations). The mutual accusations between product management, category management and purchasing are legendary too. And finally, there is the most toxic disalignment, between the line organization and projects and programs. These issues always revolve around communication: how the steering group coordinates with the working committee, how the line organization coordinates with the program and vice versa, and how senior management communicates with the lower ranks.

To measure how well your organization does in terms of alignment you can make use of Turner Consultancy's SECA.NU tool. This online execution capacity tool helps you not only assess your company's maturity in strategy execution, but also your alignment capacity.

Obviously, leaders encourage the various disciplines to cooperate. They would do well to reference the need for alignment in each and every leadership message. Every business planning cycle should include an infinite exchange loop between the various disciplines and levels, both horizontally and vertically. It is important to think and work primarily in business process chains. Cross-functional collaboration should be the norm, and cross-disciplinary collaboration should be encouraged. This is the best way to break down silos.

Include collaboration KPIs in executive management, and communicate the results and the feedback on the quality of the organization to a wide audience. Don't facilitate silos. Define management information needs based on cooperation rather than organizational unit and check whether everyone interprets alignment as they should, that is, as a duty to exchange information. Lead by example in terms of alignment.

How do you go about this? It's fairly simple. Go back to the floor at least twice a week.[77] Yo-yo up and down a few times per month to determine which channels have to be unclogged. Real alignment requires real contact in a fixed rhythm. 'Listening posts' is what Jack Welch called such regular, fixed talking points and meetings. This is what allows you to stay connected to operations.[78]

Middle management is a crucial level in this traffic. This level has three parts to play: implementer, networker and signifier.[79] But middle managers can only be effective in their role if senior management invests time and energy in them. Middle managers need the right information and the right conditions to be successful, including enough time to be trained in strategy execution.

Want to know more? The famous 'Disconnect to connect' video shows how useful it is to turn off your phone for a while in order to really connect with people.

2.6 Success Factor 6: Go for 20% Strategy and 80% Execution

Time spent is going to be our new KPI. What does every leader's new use of time require? How can standardization and discipline help to put people and results on center stage?

2.6.1 Reversing how time and money is spent

Ultimately, time allocation is the biggest deciding factor in strategy execution. Strategy starts with words; successful execution starts with action. That's why you should spend 80% of your resources and time just on execution (and budget your time) rather than on strategy design and analysis. That truly is time and money best spent (see Figure 7). But apparently, this is very hard for managers and professionals. Conceptual analysis is a knee jerk reaction. Execution management requires more effort. Turning execution into a habit is a huge challenge. But it can be done. Here are some practical pointers:

- Halve your annual business plans, both in time spent and in size of the plans;
- Allow only single-page presentations for every initiative selected;
- Manage for iterative development and implementation;
- Make this a guiding principle in planning & control and in every action plan.

Track this for three projects for a year and compare the results with the preceding year. I am certainly not in favor of adding more KPIs, but this one KPI won't hurt.

Figure 7 — **Spend 80% of your resources (time, money, energy, motivation) on execution.**

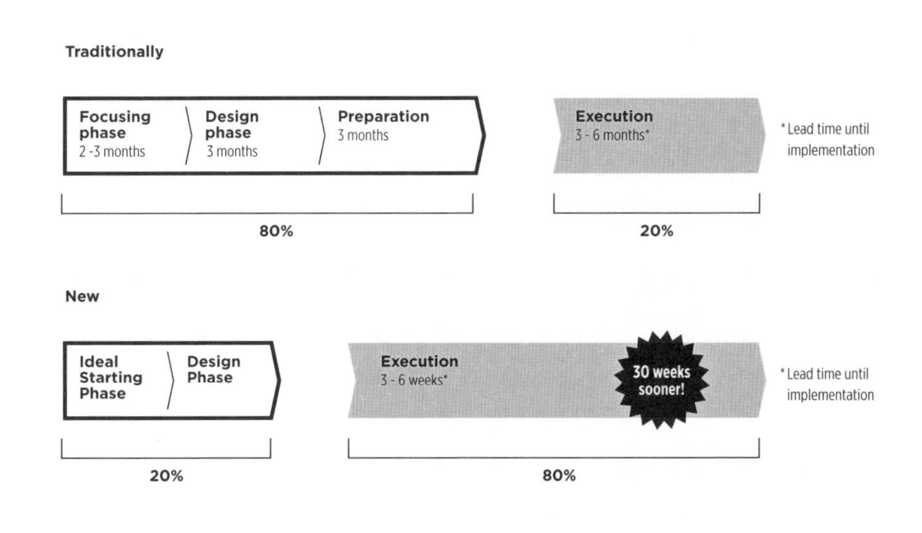

Source: Turner, 2015

Know and cultivate the value of time. "Time is the biggest luxury," as Privium, Amsterdam Schiphol Airport's premium concept, claims. An apt slogan for a priority program that allows travelers to skip the lines. In strategy execution, we're used to exclusively focusing on budget, never on time. That's a mistake. In Peter Drucker's classic, *The Effective Executive*, published in 1966, he writes that time is a non-renewable resource. Time flies and time past can never be recovered. Drucker therefore sees time as the leader's raw material. Productive use of this resource determines their effectiveness.[80] Economics traditionally distinguishes three major inputs: natural resources, labor and capital. Time should really be figured into this too. It may well be the scarcest and most important resource on the planet. It's also the only one that's equally distributed, which makes it a resource that could give you a competitive edge.

Strategy Execution is like running a marathon. You only know what you're up against at mile 20. That's when it really gets tough. Sponsors and co-sponsors only prove themselves to be real change leaders if they blaze a trail, remove obstacles and motivate people. They need to keep at it and not start freewheeling once they see the finish line. You'd better not squander energy or resources, because not only will you need a second wind, these days you'll need a third and a fourth. The biggest risk is that the cheering section in the boardroom you were counting on suddenly decides that it's time to pass the initiative back to the line organization. That's when you need to be on high alert. Even in the most successful strategy implementations we studied, the leaders on the leadership team felt the urge to let go of the reins at least three times. Dutch media tycoon and TV producer John de Mol is an excellent example of modern leadership. Everyone knows that he'll be there, even during the taping of the very last episode of *The Voice*, and that he won't mind doing a menial job like adjusting the lights. He works hard at keeping everyone's spirits up rather than putting up his feet now the format has been sold all over the world.[81]

2.6.2 Standardization, discipline, rhythm and excellence

Standardization creates freedom, time and flexibility. I realize that many employees will balk at the idea of more standardization, or at least regard it with skepticism. But it is one of the most brilliant ways to save time, which we can then devote to topics that really add value. IKEA is a great example.[82] Management insists on standardization of absolutely every repetitive process. It's non-negotiable. This has bought senior management a lot of time to spend on innovation, personal development and professional dialogue.[83]

Apart from standardization, we need structure. Clear goals and roadmaps ensure that people don't have to check back and coordinate all the time, but can devote themselves to what really matters. The trick is to start slow and gradually speed up—go slow to go fast.[84] People working in projects and programs often complain that there is not enough downtime, reflection and quality time to coordinate the most important issues with people in working groups or work streams. They are constantly putting out fires. Teams often lack the minimum required structure and clarity in the shape of a robust roadmap, forcing them to come up with something on the fly. Professionals tend to be quite dogmatic in their insistence on individual freedom, but that is absolutely unworkable in the New Normal. Collaboration is a must, people must be on the same page and speak the same language, so that there is time to spare in which to discuss the truly interesting stuff.

Discipline creates freedom, time and flexibility, as columnist Verne Harnish argues. Research has shown that discipline is an important success factor. The discipline we practice —prioritization, metrics, regular meetings—leads to more freedom, output and time.[85]

Choose the right speed and the right rhythm. Speed is just as important as agility. What's more, you can't be agile if you're going too slow. Speed also leads to better and more sustainable results, as research has shown (see Figure 8).[86]

You should aim for speed, but not without knowing the basic rate of change in your organization. Every organization has its own rate of change, whether for large-scale change programs, product launches, IT upgrades, or mergers and integration programs. This rate of change is not some vague random number, but can be objectively determined by analyzing the last three change programs, for instance. When did we start a three-month program and ended up spending nine? When was this the other way around, and how come? This knowledge enables you to reduce the uncertainty and subjectivity in strategic planning, which is incredibly valuable in these uncertain times.

Figure 8 — **Strategy execution is all about value creation.** Value creation works best at sufficient speed.

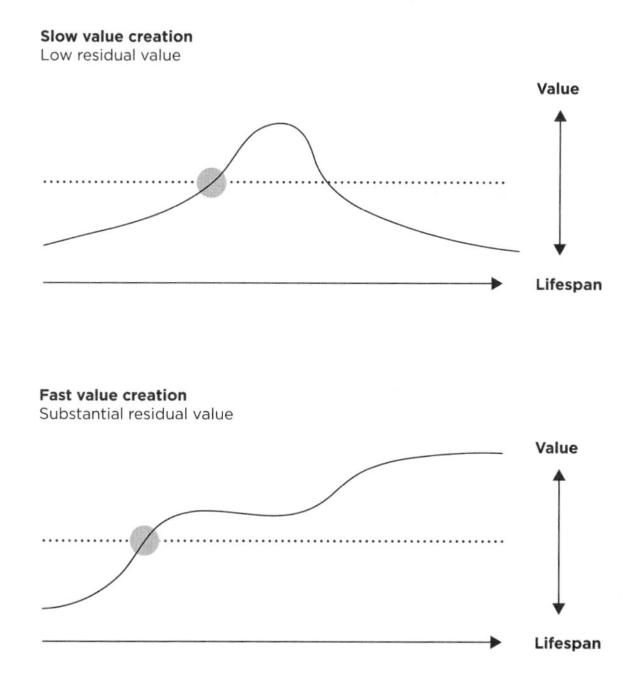

Source: Ed Boswell, Strategic *Speed: Mobilize People, Accelerate Execution.*

Focus on key moments. Focusing on natural key moments is important and kind of obvious. Onboarding a new co-worker, finishing a first draft, winning a contract, organizing a kickoff meeting, finishing a first minimum viable product, or completing the first leg of an implementation plan; each and every one of these are key moments you can put to use. Ask about progress and discuss shortcomings, failures and successes, and possible improvements for the next leg.[87] Use effective forms of consultation with a standardized agenda to mark these key moments.

Excellence is key. It is indispensable to survive. You should cultivate and encourage a mindset in which everyone is motivated to go the extra mile, to make sure that everything is done thoroughly and responsibly. At least there's never a traffic jam on that extra mile. My former colleague Patrick Davidson had a great way of motivating his people. At the end of each meeting, he would ask the same question: "Okay, people, about that extra mile ... Tomorrow, at that workshop at the client's headquarters, what's going to be our extra mile, our plus 1?" That attitude is worth pure gold, especially when it becomes second nature. You shouldn't just do what's expected, but put in some extra effort and realize that you're doing so mostly for your own benefit.

Setting the bar high is inherently satisfying. Obviously, many organizations have to comply with regulatory requirements or industry standards, but it's much more convincing when it complies with its own positive and self-instated product and service level norms. As Dutch soccer coach Louis Van Gaal said immediately after the Netherlands beat Spain 5 to 1 at the 2014 World Cup: "We ain't got nothing yet."[88]

Excellence can only be cultivated at the heart of your organization's primary process, on the job, by modeling excellence in the daily execution of products and services, in face-to-face meetings. You can't promote excellence by writing a memo.

Want to know more? 'Executing with Strategic Speed': Ed Boswell, CEO at Forum Corporation, explains why you have to slow down to gain speed.

In short

Success Factor 1:
Identify and Execute 3 Types of Change

Success Factor 2:
Resist One-Sidedness

Success Factor 3:
Disrupt or Be Disrupted

Success Factor 4:
Emphasize Who over Why, How and What

Success Factor 5:
Make Strategy Execution Your No. 1 Priority

Success Factor 6:
Go for 20% Strategy and 80% Execution

These are the six success factors that kept surfacing in our research. As a whole, and in conjunction, they are quite a big deal. Although I have phrased them as imperatives or strong recommendations, I am not trying to be arrogant or presumptuous. I am well aware of the amount and complexity of the work managers are facing. I know your plates are full. So, all you managers, professionals and entrepreneurs, please read these success factors as pointers, intended to help you deal more effectively with the complexity of strategy execution.

3

THE STRATEGY = EXECUTION MODEL: THE HOW-TO

Enjoy your meal from this placemat / a good chef relies on principles rather than recipes

3.1 The Four-Accelerator Framework: CHOOSE, INITIATE, HARVEST, SECURE

The six success factors discussed in the previous chapter are the foundation of excellence in strategy execution. But you also need a framework to achieve excellence: The Strategy = Execution model.

From my research results, I was able to distill four accelerators of strategy execution. Figure 9 shows these key elements and gives you a quick overview of the Strategy = Execution model.

The first accelerator applies to the organization-wide process of setting the overall strategy while the other three are intended for executing strategic initiatives such as programs and projects. Each accelerator consists of four how-to building blocks, two of which deal with hard capabilities, and two with soft capabilities.

The top row of hard building blocks deals with goals and benefits, or the *why*. The next row of hard building blocks refers to the contents of the strategy and the portfolio of initiatives, or the *what*.

The top row of soft building blocks is about the execution and change strategies, or the *how*. The second row of soft building blocks is about ownership of the initiative and the desired benefits, or the *who*. Altogether, the accelerators and building blocks are the how-to for the future. In that sense, they are "future practices" rather than best practices.

A necessary precondition to using these building blocks properly is an ability to work in projects and programs. This enables you to integrate all the hard, content-based capabilities with the soft, change-oriented aspects of strategy execution. You'll see that this integrated method forms the backbone of the entire Strategy = Execution model.

This is the framework that I will explain in the chapters ahead. I will go through the process, accelerator by accelerator, to build a complete strategy execution method and process. Each of the 16 how-to building blocks is followed by a concise case study in which it was successfully applied. Let's begin with a short summary of the accelerators and the 16 building blocks.

3.2 Four Accelerators and 16 How-To Building Blocks

Organization-wide:

Accelerator 1: CHOOSE

Accelerator 1 describes the process of developing a broadly supported strategy.

Building block 1: AMBITION. Your objective is to formulate an undiluted, purely content-focused strategy. Make sure you do it right, but spend a lot less time than you'd be inclined to. No matter how much time you spend on deciding your strategic direction, spend just as much on deciding whether your strategy is effective, agile and fast.

Building Block 2: SELECTION. This is where you translate strategy into a portfolio of initiatives. Be highly selective, so that you can set clear assignments and unambiguous requirements in terms of their execution.

Building Block 3: APPEAL. First ask for feedback on your strategy and then enrich it to ensure that it becomes a living, breathing plan. That takes more than one-way communication. The strategy's justification, or the *why*, must be perfectly clear. And the best way to convey purpose is to tell an appealing story.

Building Block 4: ACTIVATION. Your goal is to foster true ownership of the initiative. Leaders play a key role in this. Senior management must all read from the same script. Ensure that all assignees and key actors willingly assume ownership. Without engagement you may as well pull the plug.

For each initiative, project or program:

Accelerator 2: INITIATE

Accelerator 2 describes the process of analyzing, designing and starting execution of an initiative.

Building Block 5: MUST-HAVES. What are the basics every initiative requires? A clear mandate, a sense of excitement and a sense of urgency to carry out the initiative, an answer to the "small why", a business case and a hypothesis-oriented analysis.

Building Block 6: BREAKTHROUGH. Why content matters: it's the backbone of any initiative. The Minimum Viable Product (MVP) you develop must be based on at least one innovative breakthrough.

Building Block 7: EXCELLENT START. Using the execution cycle, which consists of a series of steps in a fixed order, the MVP is executed by an initial group of employees. In this first execution wave, your priorities are fast failure and success.

Building Block 8: PSYCHOLOGICAL CHECK-IN. The Execution Lead (the project or program manager) and the other key actors in the Execution Coalition psychologically check in to the initiative and its objectives.

Accelerator 3: HARVEST

Accelerator 3 describes the process of reaping benefits, continuous development and scaling.

Building Block 9: BENEFITS. Now that your MVP is in its first execution cycle, you can start monitoring and reaping benefits. Develop some metrics and introduce a benefit tracking system. Let yourself be led by the numbers.

Building Block 10: CONTINUOUS DEVELOPMENT. Develop your resources down to implementation level and set up a business case monitoring system. It should become second nature to constantly align with other initiatives and disciplines. Continue to develop the MVP based on customer needs and responses.

Building block 11: SCALING. This is where you select, concretize and operationalize scaling and rollout methods. You may need to scale up from 15 to 1500 employees at this stage. Just be grateful not all 1500 were involved in the initial analysis and design.

Building block 12: BRIDGE-BUILDING. Senior management and the execution coalition clear away any obstacles and make sure successes are celebrated. The point is to add value and be a positive influence. Any professional with skin in the game now becomes an avid ambassador, helping to make the change irreversible.

Accelerator 4: SECURE

Accelerator 4 describes the process of securing the benefits and learning from the execution process.

Building Block 13: ADJUSTMENT. Professionals need room to set their own priorities. Self-monitoring is more effective than supervision. The business case monitoring method you have chosen will help them do just that. Make use of visual management wherever possible.

Building block 14: OPEN ARCHITECTURE. Continuous development is facilitated by a simple, open architecture for the description of processes, technology, knowledge, competencies and conduct. That's how self-evident and easy maintenance and development of the MVP should be. The new method, the design, is secured, monitored and adjusted where necessary.

Building block 15: LEARNING. Organizations seldom take the time to learn from completed initiatives. This needs to change, because learning increases your execution capacity. Organizations that do bother to learn from each initiative get better at strategy execution by applying the lessons learned.

Building block 16: THE EXTRA MILE. Ultimately, every initiative is handed off to the benefit realization managers in the line organization. They become the owners of the goals and the new business model. Successful securement depends on their integration into your organization's primary processes. The best way to ensure this is by going the extra mile.

Working in projects and programs is a must. It is an indispensable skill and a core competency for most strategy execution initiatives. See Figure 9 for the Strategy Execution Model.

Figure 9 — **The STRATEGY = EXECUTION MODEL.** Strategy execution is a process like any other. Four accelerators for a modern process.

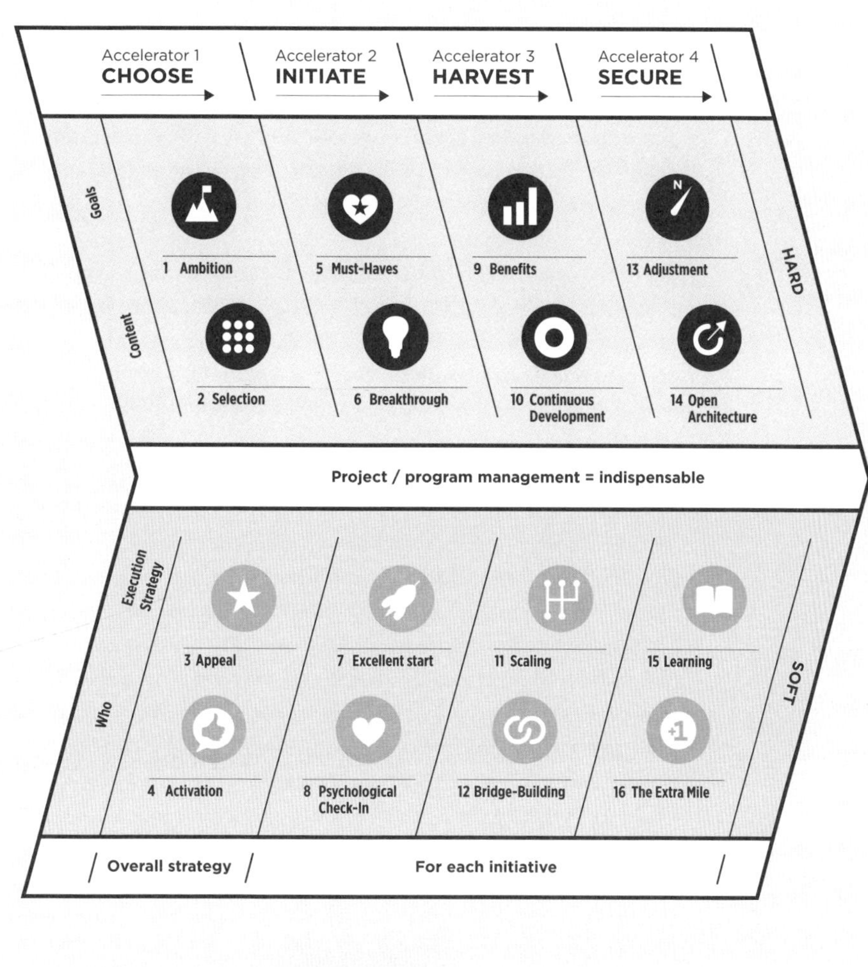

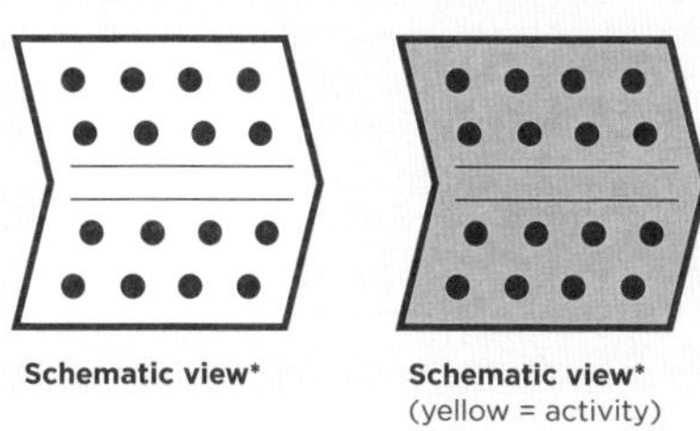

Source: Turner, 2016

3.3 Every Building Block Can Be Used Independently

In this book, I argue that strategy execution is a process. For any process to be effective, it needs to be comprised of logical steps with an overall coherence. The idea is to eliminate any redundant steps. Our research has shown that successfully executed strategies feature the four phases (accelerators) and 16 building blocks summarized above. These accelerators, building blocks and the balance between hard and soft capabilities were constants, which led us to conclude that they're universal. If they hadn't been constants, they wouldn't have made it into this model.

Their indispensability means that you can't just pick and choose any at will. Within the context of each building block, there is obviously room to tailor it to the specific needs of your project. And in some cases, you can skip a building block or two. For example, a small project aimed at introducing a regulatory change does not require appealing storytelling.

In real life, however, things are often tricky and you seldom start a project with a blank slate. There is no building from scratch. Therefore, I would advise you not to use the framework in a step-by-step, waterfall manner, but to work from right to left and from the bottom up. Every building block can be used independently. To use it sensibly, you will by definition need to take into account what industry you're in, what type of organization you work in, what issue you're addressing, and your organization's ambitions, capacities and maturity. A good chef relies on culinary principles, not standard recipes.

3.4 Using the Strategy = Execution Model Dynamically

Figure 10 shows the dynamics of the Strategy = Execution Model and summarizes the most important instructions for use. The left column shows the two most crucial checks, that tell you whether hard and soft are in balance and whether you're putting 20% of your resources into strategy and 80% into execution. The second column shows frequently occurring patterns in strategy execution that you want to avoid. And the third column shows how to use the model properly, in other words dynamically.

The Foldout

If you open the model on the cover jacket, you can keep track of where you are in the Strategy = Execution Model as you make your way through the following chapters.

Figure 10 — **Use the Strategy = Execution Model dynamically.** It is not meant to be used as a waterfall model. In fact, waterfall thinking is very risk.

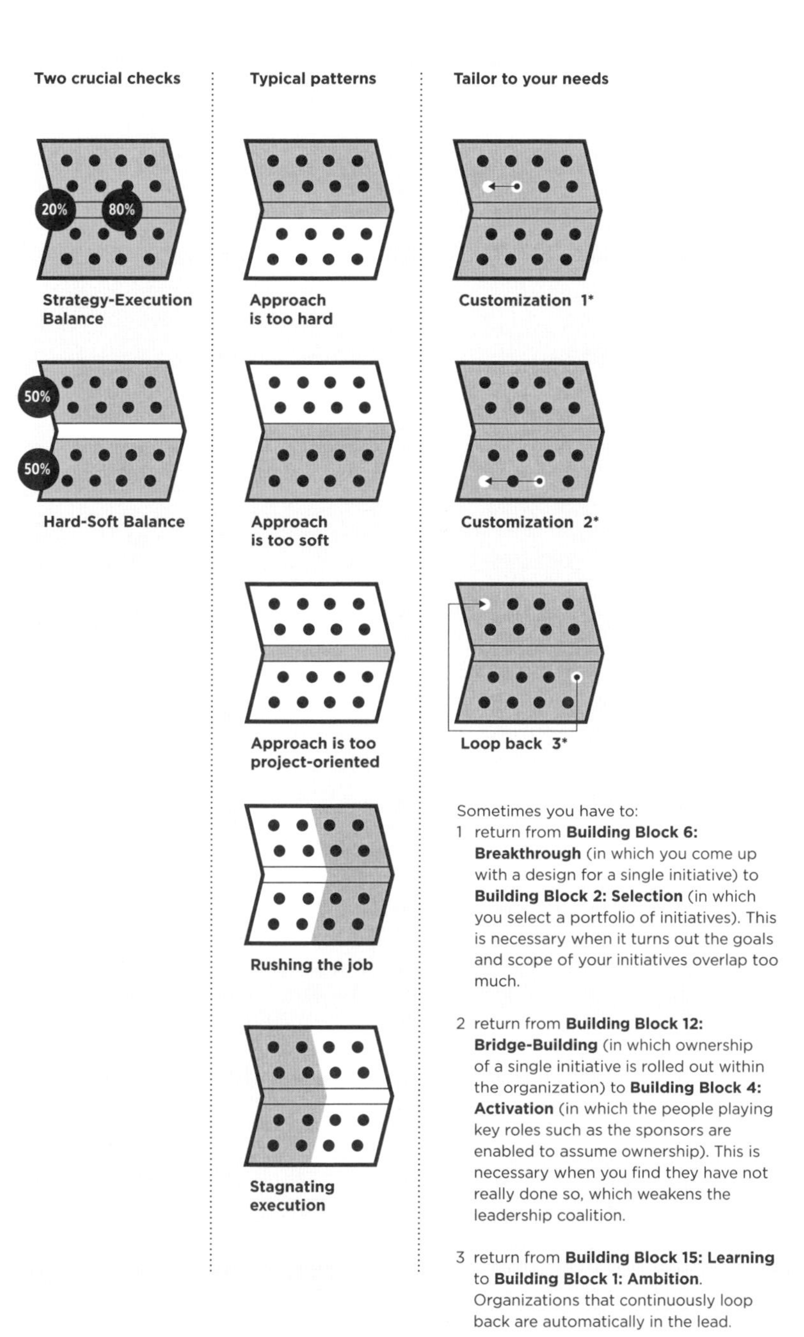

Sometimes you have to:

1 return from **Building Block 6: Breakthrough** (in which you come up with a design for a single initiative) to **Building Block 2: Selection** (in which you select a portfolio of initiatives). This is necessary when it turns out the goals and scope of your initiatives overlap too much.

2 return from **Building Block 12: Bridge-Building** (in which ownership of a single initiative is rolled out within the organization) to **Building Block 4: Activation** (in which the people playing key roles such as the sponsors are enabled to assume ownership). This is necessary when you find they have not really done so, which weakens the leadership coalition.

3 return from **Building Block 15: Learning** to **Building Block 1: Ambition**. Organizations that continuously loop back are automatically in the lead.

Source: Turner, 2016

3.5 Distinction Between Strategy and Execution

You can't have strategy without execution, but you should be able to tell them apart. In the course of our research, the more philosophically inclined leaders we interviewed raised the question whether there was any difference between strategy and execution; weren't they the same thing? In the 1990s, Professor of Management Studies Henry Mintzberg pointed out the importance of the strategy-execution interaction.[89] That's a key dichotomy to keep in mind, especially in the New Normal. Strategy and execution have an impact on each other and iterations between the two must be possible. Yet it is necessary to distinguish between them. Otherwise, you get the same problem as with responsibility: if everyone is responsible, no one takes responsibility. There are essential steps in strategic planning and strategy execution that can't be lumped together. Each requires a special focus and approach. Just like there's a difference between making a grocery list and going grocery shopping. If you don't pay heed to this difference, you will get neither your strategy nor your execution right. That is why there are four distinct accelerators in our model: Accelerator 1 is about strategy setting, while Accelerators 2, 3 and 4 are about execution. (Although you could argue that Accelerator 2 is mainly a matter of analysis and is therefore not really about execution either.)

The main tenet to keep in mind is that strategy equals execution. I did not make that the title of this book on a whim. If strategy is defined as deciding why you want to achieve a particular goal, how you go about it, and with whom, then the act of devising a strategy with co-designers already influences and initializes a process. And if execution is defined as carrying out that which has been devised, this does not mean execution has to be a passive, mindless job. In fact, you expect the professionals in your organization to keep adapting the strategic plans as often as necessary, depending on what does and doesn't work, especially in the New Normal.

Open or closed, fixed destination or unplanned backpacking: who cares?

No one should really give a toss whether this is an open or closed, planned or evolving, green or purple change vision. Who cares whether it's a fixed destination or an adventurous backpacking model? Change management experts are too keen to pigeonhole every approach. This generates a lot of unnecessary polarization. The Strategy = Execution Model describes universal elements, or building blocks. Each building block has proven its worth in strategy execution. At the same time, the model allows for tailor-made adaptation and situational use. That's why I emphasize the dynamic use of the model in this chapter.

Nonetheless, an open or "journey-based" approach to change management can be a great way to kick off the process and can even lead to a measurable and tangible strategy execution result. Such an open approach will gradually become more closed as the process evolves and moves towards an increasingly clear goal and set of solutions. This is true even in Type 3 Change (radical innovation), where the only possible approach is targeted experimentation, which you plan as well as you can in order to end up with as much information as possible. So, let's not waste time on pointless debates on planned versus emerging change.

Instead let's focus on taking the most direct approach possible—taking concrete initiatives and seeing them through from start to finish to achieve success. If someone wants to characterize a big part of my argument as an appeal for a blueprint or "structured view" of strategy execution, so be it. If that's what you want to call it, be my guest. I believe structured strategy execution is one of the best ways to free up time for customization, flexibility and much-needed human interaction during a change process.

4

ACCELERATOR 1: CHOOSE

The laziest of change agents / corporate Korsakoff syndrome / zombie projects / Amsterdam Taxi Dispatch / down-to-earth and off-the-wall afternoon sessions

When and where is this accelerator relevant?
According to our research, radically changing how you allocate the limited time and resources at your disposal is one of the main success factors in excellent strategy execution. In essence, 80% of your time and resources should be put into execution rather than analysis and strategy-setting. That doesn't mean strategic planning is less important than execution. Nothing is as pointless as perfectly executing a project that shouldn't have been carried out to begin with.

Recommended maximum time/resource allocation for this accelerator
Timebox: five weeks per year

Recalibrate your strategy once a year. Spend a maximum of five weeks from start to finish. Every third year, recalibrate more thoroughly, but take no more than 10 weeks to complete the process. And once every five years, make even more thorough adjustments, but don't spend more than 25% longer. I'm not trying to be presumptuous. I know no two organizations or situations are the same. But it's good to take the spirit of my recommendation to heart. And, as one senior manager confessed: "We should take it quite literally, because we tend to spend too much time on strategic planning anyway."

The hard building blocks in Accelerator 1: AMBITION and SELECTION

Every accelerator has two hard and two soft building blocks. The first two building blocks in Accelerator 1, AMBITION and SELECTION, are hard.

Building Block 1: AMBITION. Your objective is to formulate an undiluted, purely content-focused strategy.
Building Block 2: SELECTION. This is where you translate strategy into a portfolio of initiatives.

4.1 Building Block 1: AMBITION

In Building Block 1, your objective is to formulate an undiluted, purely content-focused strategy. Make sure you do it right, but spend a lot less time on it than you'd be inclined to. No matter how much time you devote to deciding your strategic direction, spend just as much on deciding whether the strategy is effective, agile and fast (EAF). In this building block, you decide on your mission, vision and values, and go looking for the Big Why. Your analysis must be thorough, coherent and consistent.

4.1.1 Determine your mission, vision, values, and the Big Why

Building Block 1 is made up of the following components: your mission, vision, values and the Big Why. Together, these create a good jumping off point for further development of your strategy, the *how* and the *what*. Key questions are: Why does your organization exist? What does it want to be and for whom? What does it believe in? It's always good to clarify your answers to these basic questions, because these concepts are especially prone to causing big misunderstandings. Your mission expresses your organization's goals, or its raison d'être. Your values describe your organization's motives, which are reflected in every employee's conduct. Taken together, they are the compass that sets everyone's daily course. Your vision, which is worded in ambitious, visionary and inspiring language, expresses your organization's future position in the market and in relation to its customers. The Big Why addresses purpose, the reason your organization does what it does in terms of its more deep-seated motives and drives. Let's take a closer look at that last point.

The why is hot. The example of President Kennedy's assertion in the early 1960s that America would put a man on the moon by the decade's end is something of a cliché as far as ambitious goals go, but it makes the point well.[90] A more down-to-earth example was expressed by Paul

Polman, CEO of Unilever, who said he wants his organization to have doubled its revenue and halved its carbon footprint by 2020.[91]

Another good example is Starbucks, which was once a small company with a seemingly impossible goal. The well-known coffee brand started in 1971 with a single coffee shop in Seattle. When Starbucks CEO and spiritual father Howard Schultz bought the company in 1987, its mission statement was to "[e]stablish Starbucks as the premier purveyor of the finest coffee in the world, while maintaining our uncompromising principles while we grow."[92] At the end of that fiscal year, the Starbucks Corporation had 17 coffee shops and Schultz's mission seemed pretty outlandish. But as everyone knows, he stuck to his guns and in 2015 the company had 22,519 shops and Starbucks coffee was sold in more than 65 countries.[93]

The point of these examples is that there must always be a Big Why underlying an organization's ambitions, whether those are to take one big step for mankind or to create a world-renowned brand of coffee.

There are various terms in use that are more or less synonymous with the Big Why, which can be confusing. One well-known example is the Big Hairy Audacious Goal (BHAG).[94] Specifically in the field of digital innovation, there is another one: the Massive Transformative Purpose, or MTP. According to Yuri van Geest of Singularity University, every exponential organization has an MTP, which is defined as a higher purpose for making radical changes while also making the world a better place.[95]

Exponential organizations are those that perform at least ten times better than average, both in time and quality. They make ten times as much profit per employee as the average company in their industry. In practice, these organizations meet at least four of the ten critical success factors identified by the authors of *Exponential Organizations*. Examples include Airbnb, Uber, Netflix, Tesla, Quirky, WhatsApp, Waze and Xiaomi. Van Geest names six secrets to success: formulate a higher purpose, create an 'on demand' workforce, make use of communities and the crowd, use algorithms, use other people's property and create engagement.

It makes no difference whether you're talking about socially responsible goals or commercial ambitions, or whether the company in question is big or small. In all contexts, you need a lofty goal to shoot for, to motivate your workforce, to hold on to talent, and to give meaning to what you do every day. But such an audacious aim has its own criteria too. It should appeal to a deep need in the market or in society, and it should be based on logical arguments.

And yes, before you start raising objections, I know those are subjective criteria—but that shouldn't stop you. It wasn't too long ago that a 16-year old Dutch kid said he'd design a way to rid the Great Pacific Garbage Patch of plastic. People claimed it was impossible, but today Boyan Slat's Ocean Cleanup system is actually in the Pacific. The dream was turned into a series of tangible experiments; iterations generate quick fails and successes and show what does and does not work. Innovation = Execution.

The Big Why is the most important anchor for all subsequent questions. Why do you, as a leader, do what you do? And why does your business do what it does? What are the underlying motives and drives that make it feel worthwhile to work on reaching your goals every single day? Another great example is the Salvation Army, whose purpose is to help people who are really in need. That is their deepest drive; they live by the creed: 'We believe, but not in indifference.'

Whenever you do a strategic analysis and plot your course, answering the Big Why is the only sensible way to start. Simon Sinek explains this in his popular book *Start With Why*.[96] He argues that companies can only maintain the justification for their existence if it is clear why they do what they do and if they are able to communicate their belief in this why to their customers and employees. If these two groups believe in your motives, they will continue to be ambassadors for your company.[97]

You need more than a why, however. Only the laziest of change agents would be content to merely answer the why. "Start with why," wrote Sinek, not "leave it at why." After *why*; what, when and how follow. And as our research showed, *with whom* is even more important than what, why, when and how.

Objectives. The main question is: what are we shooting for? What kind of goals are we going to set and how high are we setting the bar? Objectives must be formulated as end goals and output goals, continuity, profitability, customer and employee satisfaction and flexibility.

Our research supports two recommendations related to setting goals. First, you should ensure a healthy balance between objectives that affect customers, employees and shareholders. Those are the objectives that have to do with profitability, costs, productivity and flexibility. Second, don't forget to explore which areas need investments rather than cuts. Use the process models in Appendix 5, download #8. Processes are an objective means of pinpointing a quality or a capability that needs strengthening. By using them, your discussions about objectives become more level-headed and practical.

These two recommendations are based on the trends we discovered in the course of our research. For example, we came across the case of an insurance company that was feeling the heat from unmet benchmarks and had therefore been implementing one austerity program after another. But it was an across-the-board measure; the company didn't do a sensible analysis of where it should tighten its belt and where it would in fact be better to invest. Ultimately, the company's customer service deteriorated badly and customer satisfaction plummeted. It reminded me of a cartoon I'd once seen of a medieval galley with a busy management team holding a meeting on the top deck, discussing the umpteenth Lean program to cut costs. Meanwhile, down below deck, there remained only one crew member doing the actual rowing.

The book that lays the best foundation for setting objectives is Kaplan and Norton's *Balanced Scorecard*. Translating the big strategic goals into individual goals for each initiative takes great precision.[98] So we're not going to rehash that; we're going to apply it. Figure 11 includes examples of strategic goals and Appendix 5, download #9 provides a detailed list of KPIs. Most leaders know by now that it's a bad idea to set too many goals. They also realize that it can be just as harmful to set unclear or incorrect goals. In our interviews, many subjects mentioned the Objectives & Key Results (OKR) Model which originated at Intel and is now used by Google, Uber and the like to set clear goals and monitor these down to the level of the individual.

Setting goals has but one purpose: achieving them. That's why benefit realization management is a process which you will find neatly embedded in Accelerators 1 through 4. In other words, if you use the Strategy Execution Model, you will automatically include this in what you do.

Figure 11 — **There are clear, generic categories of goals.** The contents are always highly specific to each individual initiative!

	Objectives	Sub-objectives
1	**Continuity**	Buffers in relation to trends in working capital and financing
2	**Profitability**	Return on equity, EBIDTA
3	**Market & Customer Targets**	Market share, competitiveness, share of customer spending, brand recognition and brand value
4	**Customers**	Satisfaction, loyalty, turnover, growth, for each segment
5	**Employees**	Satisfaction, absenteeism, turnover, loyalty, flexibility
6	**Society**	Corporate Social Responsibility goals
7	**Efficiency & Effectiveness**	Productivity, capacity utilization, reliability, service levels
8	**The Outcomes**	Achievement, overall and for each initiative
9	**Execution & Change**	Contribution to goal from improvement (Type 1), renewal (Type 2), and innovation (Type 3)

Source: Turner, 2016

We just looked at the importance of your organization's mission, vision, values and the Big Why—an important step in the first building block. But you know as well as I that you can't just look at what you'd like to achieve in an ideal world; you also have to face the hard facts. What can, and can't, your company achieve? What capacities does your organization have? Let's have a look at these aspects.

4.1.2 Take a critical look at your point of departure

In management terminology it's known as analyzing your capabilities. But let's refer to them as qualities. Measure your organization's hard and soft qualities. Hard qualities include structure, performance management system, business processes and technology. Soft qualities include culture, conduct, and leadership and collaboration styles. Hard and soft qualities can apply to daily management, or Running the Business, but also to transforming your existing business model, or Changing the Business. Analyzing the qualities that determine the effectiveness of your company's strategy execution is a key step you need to take before finalizing your mission, vision and strategy. This analysis gives you an idea of the strength, maturity and coherence of your business's basic qualities.

When your basic qualities are good, your ambition or bar can be commensurately high. When you have lower basic qualities, this is not necessarily the case. Your strategic ambition must be in line with your organization's execution capacity or change capacity. A low score on hard qualities does not necessarily mean you have to lower your ambitions, but it does mean you'll need to put in extra effort to realize them. For example, if your analysis of hard qualities reveals that your main structure is not an effective platform for management and renewal, then it makes sense to adapt that structure before launching a new strategy. An old or faulty structure can never be a good jumping off point for strategy execution.

At this point you may find yourself in a chicken-or-egg situation. Imagine you determine during Building Block 2 that you want to have five strategic initiatives in your portfolio, but discover when measuring hard qualities that your senior management structure needs an overhaul, which is a project in itself. This, in turn, can become a preparatory project, a separate initiative in itself.

Go to SECA.NU to fill in your Strategy Execution & Change Accelerator (SECA) online and see your organization's score in the areas of Running the Business and Changing the Business, as well as your hard and soft capabilities. It takes less than 20 minutes to learn how you can bolster and accelerate your strategy execution. During Building Block 1, the point is to analyze your hard capabilities. See Figure 12 for how to assess your key competencies in strategy execution.

Figure 12 — **Assess your organization's strategic capabilities in strategy execution.**

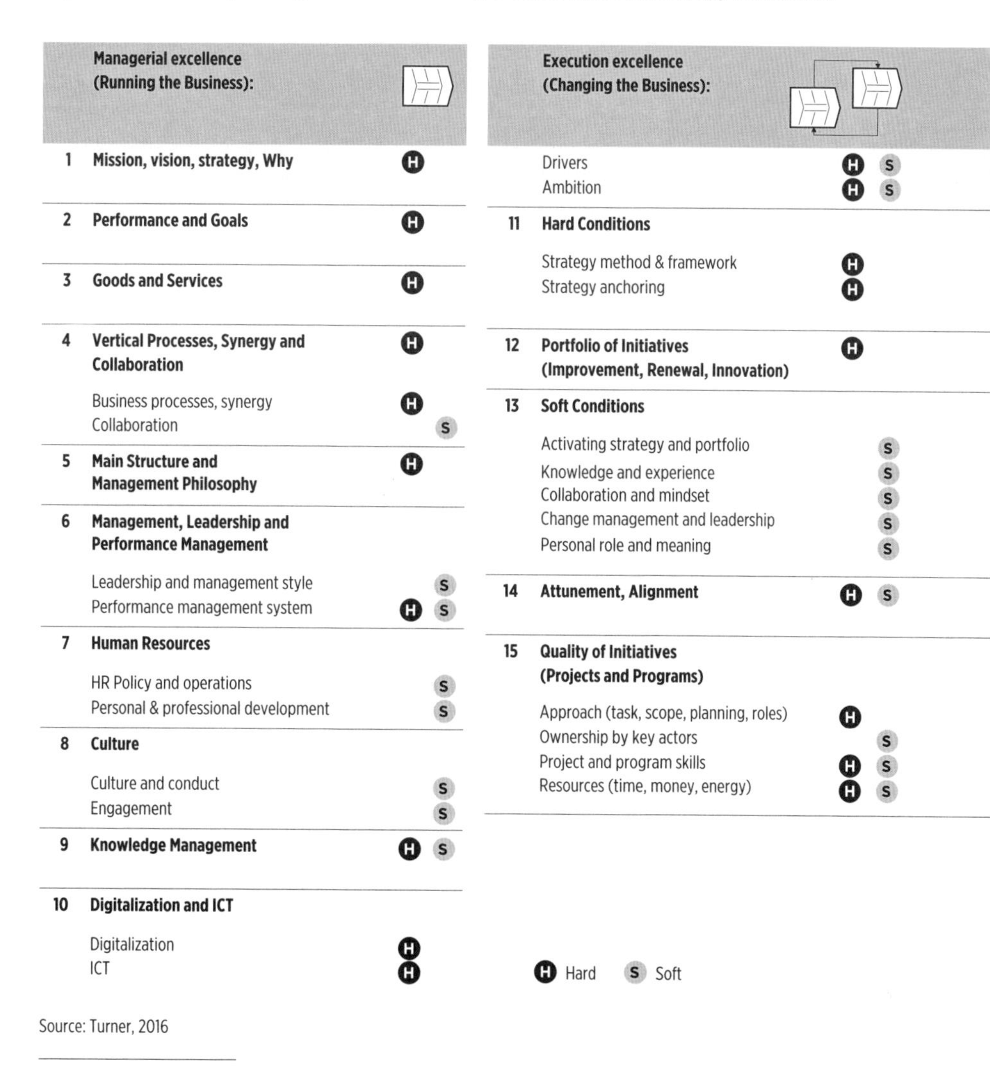

Source: Turner, 2016

It goes without saying that it pays to discuss the results of the SECA.NU analysis during strategic analysis because this enables you to align your strategic ambitions with your capacities. I would suggest three agenda items for this discussion:

1 Choose the specific hard competencies and capacities that need strengthening in order to achieve your strategic goals.
2 Where does the business model lack coherence and require restoration?

3 What decisions need to be made to achieve (2)? Which of these management decisions are on the Running the Business side, and which are initiatives on the Change side?

Use the same tool to measure the soft capabilities when the time is right.

So far so good. You now have a basic idea of your organization's capabilities for executing its strategy. But there are bound to be areas that require more in-depth exploration before we can draw conclusions about strategy.

4.1.3 Carry out in-depth analyses

External analysis. The key question is: how can we meet our customers' needs? Customer, market and competitor analyses are, and will always be, the basis of your strategy. Michael Porter's generic strategic models still serve their purpose. The main point of external analyses is to find out what your customers want and what is actually delivered to them. Far too often, we lose sight of the customer and fail to go beyond some crude market and customer analyses in our strategy documents. But the real heart of the matter is revealed in detailed analyses of your most important customer segments and customer perceived value. One example of a useful value analysis is plotting the supposed benefits of a product or service against the assumed price. That should be a pretty good indicator of the market share you stand to gain or lose. And remember that satisfied customers are all you need to achieve most strategic targets.

Internal analysis. The key question is: how should we be organized? Internal analysis, that is, an analysis of your own organization, is just as valuable as external analysis. This is the dirty work, especially if your organization does not yet have a periodic review system. But there are various aids to help you get it done. In Appendix 5, download #3, you will find a summary of the 16 most relevant methods and models for determining your growth strategy, such as Porter's 5 Forces Model, the BCG Growth Share Matrix , and Ansoff's 4 generic strategic options.[99]

Strategy-setting should be differentiated according to type of organization and context. We tend to take a generic approach to strategy-setting, but we need to account for the fact that there are big differences between organizations and the contexts in which they operate. Strategy-setting is a completely different animal in the petrochemical industry than it is in software development. The former is all about big capital investments that require thorough justification, while in the latter you can plan all you want, but rapid developments tend to completely change the ball game. When tech giants like Microsoft or

Oracle decide to accelerate innovation, they can blow their competitors out of the water. That puts very different demands on your strategy.

Martin Reeves, Claire Love and Philipp Tillmanns of the Boston Consulting Group did fundamental research into strategy-setting, which resulted in their book *Your Strategy Needs a Strategy.* [100] The model they describe distinguishes markets according to their high or low predictability and malleability. It details five archetypal strategic styles and imperatives.

1. **Adaptive.** Be fast!
   (in markets with low predictability and malleability)
2. **Shaping.** Be the director!
   (low predictability and high malleability)
3. **Classical.** Be big!
   (high predictability, low malleability)
4. **Visionary.** Be the first!
   (high predictability, high malleability)
5. **Renewal.** Remain viable!
   (in industries that are under such great pressure that the organization must first recover lost ground by growing its resilience and vitality).

4.1.4 Safeguard the preconditions

In the old days, there were several strategic preconditions you could pick and choose. In the New Normal, however, all of these are considered standard and indispensable.

Every organization must score straight A's on the classic triangle of customer intimacy, operational excellence and innovation. Most classic strategy-setting methods have been declared obsolete because of the New Normal. This is justified to an extent because some of the rules of the game have fundamentally changed. For instance, Airbnb and Uber were launched in several countries simultaneously.[101] According to classic strategies, a new product or service would first be launched in a single country and then rolled out geographically later.[102] Another example is Treacy and Wiersema's strategic triangle, which was used for decades to determine whether an organization was focused on excellence in customer intimacy, operational excellence or product innovation. [103] Organizations were meant to score an A on every process in one area of the triangle, which made it acceptable to score a B or a C in the other two. At the time, the triangle was useful for forcing organizations to select a clear focus, but it is now entirely obsolete. In the New Normal, every business must score at least a B+ in all three aspects of the triangle, and preferably an A+ in one of them. All well-known disruptive organizations beat established businesses in every respect: customer service levels, operational excellence and product innovation.[104] Every company needs to both leverage its existing business model and innovate to create new ones. Changes are happening so fast in the New Normal that continuity is no longer guaranteed. You've got to keep up with the times.

Every organization must grow. Growth generates the resources for you to attract new talent and invest in leveraging and innovating your business models. In the New Normal, this is becoming more and more important.

Every organization must build buffers, gather data, simplify and experiment with innovation. Basically, it's eat or be eaten, or in Nassim Nicholas Taleb's metaphor: the best way to avoid being the turkey that gets slaughtered for Christmas, is making sure you are the butcher for whom Christmas is peak season. And the best way to become a butcher is to structurally carry out the four steps from the VUCA model (see Glossary of terms, Appendix 2): (1) build buffers ('well-stocked grain silos for hard times') so you can roll with the punches, (2) make data gathering second nature, (3) continually simplify, and (4) experiment with innovation. I challenge you to name just one successful organization that can get away with not doing this.

4.1.5 Ensure agility

Agility in strategy execution is just as important as effectiveness and speed. There are many methods and schools of thought operating under the banner of agility whose intention it is to increase flexibility. And that's a key notion in this book, too. Innovation and strategy professor Michael Wade, from IMD in Lausanne, writes in his blog that world-class athletes can still afford to use classical strategy execution.[105] After all, athletes know which race to prepare for; they know the distance, location, their competition, the date and time. Organizations, by contrast, are facing increasing uncertainty about all of these criteria. Classical strategy-setting requires the same information that athletes have, so you can cascade your strategy, prepare and implement your strategy step by step. In the New Normal, this is a luxury few businesses can afford. Uncertainty is the name of the game. Wade illustrates this by asking why it took Volkswagen so long to react adequately to the emissions scandal. And how many taxi companies saw Uber coming and had any strategy at all to deal with it? Wade argues that a long-term strategy can act as a pair of handcuffs that rapidly leaves you handicapped. In the New Normal, it's all about effectiveness, agility and speed (EAS). We need iterative strategy-setting and execution. The burden of proof for a strategy lies with its execution.

Enacting this vision of strategy execution requires the highest degree of self-awareness, or what Wade calls hyperawareness. This is a capacity to make a timely assessment of changes in your context, of what will and won't work in that context, and to change course based on your assessment. Wade doesn't see many businesses that possess this quality. "Most organizations are mainly just hyperaware of themselves," he says.

This vision also requires informed decision-making. And that, in turn, is only possible if your organization routinely and systematically gathers, analyzes and interprets data to make informed decisions. That's how you know which interventions to make. But even then, this will only work if the intervention is executed rapidly enough. Execution must be targeted, and those who carry it out must learn quickly from what doesn't work and rapidly scale up what does. Our research revealed 12 factors that determine agility; these can be found in Figure 13. Next to

Figure 13 — **Agile strategy execution enables organizations to deal with continuous change.**

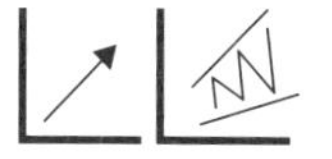

	Agility	Agile
1	**Strategy content**	Clear vision, flexibility along the way. Short-term and long-term strategy are equally important. Iterative development, emerging rather than a blueprint. Time and resources spent: max. 20%
2	**Business Model & Propositions**	Single focus: creating customer value. Scope: the entire value chain and network
3	**Structure**	Structured but not fixed. Flexibility created by multidisciplinary teams and collaboration.
4	**Innovation Vision**	Dualism: different speed for innovation. Enabled by separate structure & ICT.
5	**Processes**	Harmonized wherever possible, flexible where necessary. Vertical chain processes rather than departmental processes.
6	**Structure & Governance**	Small teams. Autonomy and freedom (carte blanche). Rapid response to opportunities and threats, effective risk management and rapid iteration and adjustment based on success/failure. Decisions based on systematic data collection and analysis.
7	**Leadership**	Letting go of the desire for the one and only right solution + leadership qualities.
8	**Culture & Workforce**	Intrinsically motivated ownership, "want to" rather than "have to". Self-management. Cross-disciplinarity is second nature.
9	**Execution Vision & Methods**	Strategy equals execution. Strategy based on evidence obtained from execution. Design a prototype / MVP, rapidly start executing, learn from failure, adjust, scale what works.
10	**Alignment**	Across all configurations, all the time.
11	**Flexibility & Perseverance**	The wisdom to know when to persevere and when to adjust course.
12	**Focus & Simplicity**	The less ballast, the easier it is to pivot.

Source: Turner, 2016

each factor, we have listed some practical ways of checking the agility level in your organization.

What makes a strategy agile? Let's look at a few key points from Figure 13 in more detail. The key question is: What factors determine whether your strategy, your strategic analysis and planning are agile?

What makes your strategy execution agile, is spending a maximum of 20% of the available time and resources on the basics of strategy-setting. It's only when you carry out your strategic plans that you see proof of success or failure, so that's why you need to invest the other 80% of your time and resources in execution. Execution is where you get the feedback that leads to adjustments, which makes your strategy agile. That's why I make "maximum time" recommendations in the introduction to each accelerator.

Stop holding those arduous strategic planning sessions every three or five years. You're better off defining a long-term vision that spans a longer period of time. It should be neither too vague nor too detailed, because there's no point to either. Your vision, mission, strategy and the Big Why should be a tight, coherent whole that stays fresh for at least five years. This "shelf-life" enables managers to decide along the way how the organization can adapt to the changing circumstances. There's nothing wrong with thinking about the future, but keep strategic planning concise. The old habit of planning your strategy every three to five years takes up too much time. Do it every three years, but keep it short.

The same goes for business planning. Make your annual business plans very practical and brief. Make sure your plans make a distinction between the targets set for daily management (running the business) and those meant to renew your existing business model (changing the business). On the change side, define no more than five must-win battles.[106] This is all the strategy you need to start executing. Scale what works and remain agile so you can make the necessary adjustments.

Your strategy also becomes more agile if you make strategic analysis and planning an iterative process. Think of it as a developing, emerging strategy rather than a finished strategy set in stone. If the three-year interval I mentioned has not yet elapsed, but strategic recalibration is necessary, then do it. In fact, you may find that there are two or three strategic issues per year that require recalibration or adjustment of your long-term strategic direction. I call these strategic priority questions.

Don't be afraid to work on various elements of strategy-setting simultaneously. One manager told me that, to his surprise, some of the employees involved in a mission and vision discussion got angry when they discovered that underlying projects had already been defined and some projects had even started. They had expected the mission and vision process to be rounded off first, and all subsequent activity to take place later, step-by-step, in a logical order. However, we can't afford to work that way anymore. Parallel and iterative processes are sound ways of working. The definitive strategy depends on its execution. Strategy equals execution, remember?

Agility must not lead to fickleness. Agility depends on the wisdom to know where you need to persevere and where you need to adapt your strategy. Agility is the capacity to look at all developments and patterns and pinpoint areas that need to be addressed with an eye to staying the course of your long-term vision. I once heard a sponsor in the financial services industry sigh about how often he and his team had to make a 180-degree turn. Six months earlier, he had helped design a new marketing strategy that had to be implemented in a rush because an important niche market had collapsed. However, soon after the strategy was ready to go, the company's newly hired CEO said the priority should be on target group segmentation, so the marketing team had to go back to square one. Perhaps this is an example of agility. But it might also be a serious case of corporate Korsakoff syndrome, in which every manager feels the need to reinvent the wheel, not as a means to an end but as an end in itself.[107]

Our research revealed that one of the main failure factors is a lack of smart agility, in other words neglecting to seize opportunities and control threats. One leader I spoke to called that responsible agility. To execute your strategy with agility, you need a clear framework. Vacillating too much is like having a compass that keeps giving you wildly different readings for true north.

Myths about new digital organizations abound. Many people think their business is organized for agility because they have a modern, hip internet company. This misconception is based on the fact that their business is growing rapidly. In the past, fast-growing (non-digital) organizations also had to adjust their processes, structure, management, culture and systems every few months. Any company that didn't do so would implode. That's simply inherent to growth, and it makes little difference whether your organization is new or old. People overgeneralize: startups are flexible and established companies are unwieldy. But flexibility is not necessarily innate to modern internet companies. As one entrepreneur said: "We're growing so fast it can feel like we're an oil tanker already, while we're really still just a speedboat." Really? You can't afford to assume that you're agile. If you do, you might realize you've already become an oil tanker—but by then it'll be too late.

4.1.6 Check for coherence

Your hard strategy must ultimately pass what I call the Rumelt Check, named after American professor Richard Rumelt whom I mentioned in the section on Success Factor 2. The Rumelt Check is this: Does the strategy contain an accurate enough description of your business's core challenges and the actions required to meet them? The key question is: What are you out to achieve and how? This lays the foundation for execution, and for many companies they constitute a major challenge in and of themselves, Rumelt explained in *Good strategy/Bad strategy*.[108] The gist of a good strategy is a sharply defined challenge, a plan of attack, your strategic options and scenarios, a sensitivity analysis and a list of practical, coherent actions that arise from the strategy and address the company's Big Why and fit the company's core capacities. That may sound obvious, but few organizations actually have all these ducks in a row. A good analysis is indispensable. People tend to be on the lookout for competitors and disruptors, but threats may come from a completely different angle than you expect.

Key topics and questions that need to be answered:

1. Which markets and customers do we want to serve? Why there, and why them?
2. With which products, services and value? Using which business model? What is our unique value proposition?
3. What demands does that make on our business model, and hence on our business processes, structure, management, competencies and culture, technology and data management and knowledge?
4. What portfolio of initiatives do we need? (This is what Building Block 2 is about.)

When elaborating your key topics, you must make clear what choices you are making and why you believe you will succeed in these.[109] In other words, which competences put your organization in a position to deliver the value proposition better than anyone else? Determining and defining these key topics is the heart of your strategy. If you put in the hard work here, the rest—the plan of attack and the portfolio of initiatives—will follow with relative ease.

The key topics listed above can be used as all-purpose standard parts of your strategy. More detailed work formats, arranged by accelerator, can be found In download #10 from Appendix 5 that you can use to access the fact sheets and planning templates for every accelerator.

Successful Application of Building Block 1, AMBITION

Case study: Ditzo online insurance makes an impact on the market
Breakthrough: In 2007, Ditzo's parent company, ASR insurance, spearheaded online insurance sales in the Netherlands. In the US, Progressive, Esurance and GEICO had been active in online insurance sales since the late 1990s. The breakthrough was dealing with customers directly (direct written premium), without having to go through brokers. ASR's success was due to effectiveness, agility and speed. Effectiveness, or rather decisiveness, was necessary to make clear decisions when faced with a difficult choice. Agility allowed the company to respond and adjust as it developed. But the biggest reason for the breakthrough was speed, which enabled the company to be the first in the Dutch market and a pioneer in online insurance.
Impact: The advent of online insurance sales channels radically transformed the property and casualty insurance market, making it more transparent, lowering premiums and narrowing margins. The fact that ASR was ahead of the game is one reason the company is still an important player in the Dutch market to this very day. In the meantime, Ditzo has successfully entered the health insurance market, too. In the first year, ASR sold over 50% more new policies.

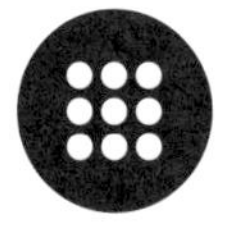

4.2 Building Block 2: SELECTION

In this building block, you translate strategy into a portfolio of initiatives. You need to be very selective so that you can set clear assignments and unambiguous requirements in terms of their execution. Before you decide which initiatives to include, you must purge your existing portfolio, restructure your organization so you can execute the initiative, and understand why you need to shoot for a two-track approach.

A carefully balanced portfolio of experiments feeds the strategy.
Strategy equals execution. This phrase will likely rub old-school leaders and strategists the wrong way, but their more modern counterparts will understand exactly what you mean.

4.2.1 Purge your portfolio

Cull your portfolio of strategic initiatives to attune your aspirations to their feasibility. Some discrepancy and overreach is good, but only in moderation. Usually the portfolio of initiatives is overflowing and some of those initiatives need to be weeded out. You can make quick headway by disentangling managerial excellence (daily operations) from execution excellence (real projects). Many successful managers told us that purging the project portfolio always yields quick results. The essence of an activity that deserves to be organized as a project is a change that is too complex to be achieved in daily execution. Initiatives that are multidisciplinary in nature always need to be organized in projects. Projects that do not meet these criteria basically consist of routine line operations. In every portfolio, 33% of project work turns out to be routine work.

The taboo on adding projects can make people reluctant to tackle an initiative as a project, even when this is the only right approach. When reluctance wins out, work that should be organized as a project ends up on the line organization's plate, which is just as detrimental as when projects get saddled with routine work. The remaining projects and programs need to be condensed, because another 33% of the project work in a portfolio likely has an outdated, overlapping or poorly-defined mandate, scope or approach. This leaves your organization's change capacity badly hampered. After purging, what's left must be assessed by strategic priority criteria year by year.

Then there are zombie projects, projects that sprawl because something is forever being added or subtracted. Such projects can almost grow into separate little businesses, with their own corporate culture. They are easy to spot. Just look at how long they've been around (for ages), their scope (constantly shifting), their structure (practically non-existent, under the guise of freedom), their management (ditto) and their communication (ad hoc, largely fact-free, full of opinions and emotions). The strange thing is that no one seems to question why these projects are allowed to drag on.[110] Fortunately though, they are becoming less common.

Translate strategic targets into initiatives. In Building Block 1, you defined strategic objectives. Now it's time to translate them into initiatives. To do this, use the portfolio fact sheet that you can download using download #10 from Appendix 5. Aside from pruning your initiatives, you'll also want to know whether you're selecting the right initiatives and whether your portfolio is balanced. Usually, ambition levels exceed execution capacity. Prioritize, integrate or consolidate wherever you can. Make smart and well-defined choices. That may again lead you to consolidate, slow down or even halt many existing and new initiatives. Check again whether your execution capacity is great enough to match your ambition. In Building Block 1, you established your organization's execution capacity with the help of SECA.NU. Now is the time to use those insights to establish the appropriate tension between your strategic ambition and your execution capacity.

Recalibrate your portfolio every six months. A 500-employee organization could execute a mission, vision and strategy with four programs and ten projects, or with two programs and four projects. The former is likely to fail while the latter stands a real chance of success. Organizations often overestimate their execution or change capacity and launch far too many new initiatives while others are still ongoing. They let initiatives and expectations pile up without any real link to their actual ability to change, and in so doing set themselves up for failure.

You should update and recalibrate your portfolio of strategic initiatives every six months. This doesn't have to be a difficult or time-consuming exercise as long as you set aside a strictly limited time to do this and prepare by assessing the true status of all existing initiatives beforehand. Once you've done that, you can get pretty far in a single afternoon.

Make a "to-don't" list. "Organizations earn just as much by not doing things as by doing things," one manager said. Explicitly describing what your organization does NOT do prevents opportunism. You want to make sure that pet projects that were eliminated during the portfolio recalibration are not sneaked back in by being included in the scope of another initiative.

4.2.2 Balance your portfolio

A good portfolio consists of well-aimed shots at a strategic target. How good your aim is, is determined by the four dimensions represented in Figure 14.[111] This is a practical, widely-used matrix meant for reviewing strategic initiatives and matching them to a company's change capacity. Figure 14 is highly valuable from a content and communication standpoint; if it's not in the matrix, it doesn't exist!

Figure 14 — **A sound portfolio balances the three types of execution, types of targets, and the long vs. short run.**

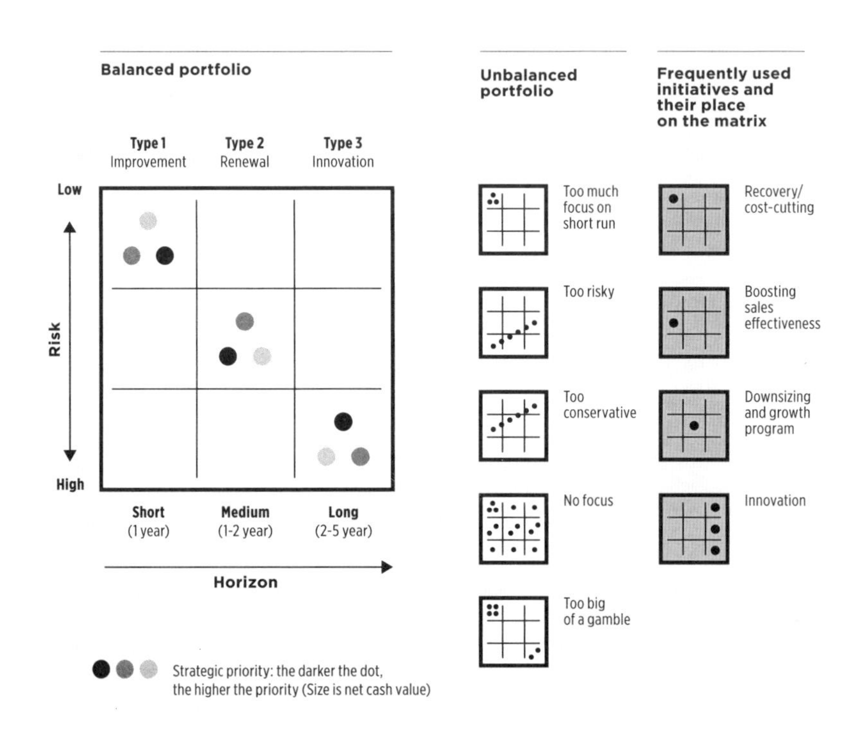

Source: Bettina Buechel, Xavier Gilbert and Rhoda Davidson, *Smarter Execution*; Scott Keller and Colin Price, *Beyond Performance*.

First you want to assess whether you have struck a good balance between initiatives that are Type 1 (improvement), Type 2 (renewal) and Type 3 (innovation). Each type has its own appropriate execution horizon. A lean optimization project (Type 1) should be completed within a year. A business process redesign project (Type 2) should be completed within two years, and a greenfield innovation project should have a five-year horizon at most.

The second dimension for assessing your portfolio is risk and hence your chance of success. Risk is the vertical axis. It's fairly obvious that Type 1 is low risk, Type 2 is moderate risk, and Type 3 is high risk. Don't use this insight to make predictions. As we know from Taleb, our ability to make accurate predictions is sharply diminishing. See it, instead, as an exhortation to keep things in balance. Taleb himself was a Wall Street broker before he became a revolutionary thinker in the field of statistics. His success as a broker was due to the so-called Barbell strategy: put 85-90% of your resources into low-risk investments (Type 1 and Type 2, even though Type 2 are higher risk than Type 1), and 10-15% into extremely speculative funds (Type 3).

The third dimension is the total number of initiatives, and the number for each type. The right number of initiatives is the number at which you can attain the best balance between ambition and realism. As a rule, executing three to five initiatives of each type works best. The following chapters provide a fact sheet for each initiative. This enables you to hammer out the details of each initiative's ambition, scope, goals and approach and to make an honest appraisal of the best balance between ambition and feasibility at an early stage in the process. You don't want someone shooting for greater customer satisfaction—a real umbrella term—without establishing clear choices in terms of customer target groups and scope.

For Type 3—radical innovation of new revenue and business models—things are a bit different. In this area, you're dealing with great uncertainty and low odds of success. Achieving your aims depends on conducting a bigger set of experiments. Fortunately, there are more and more effective rules of thumb to deal with the world of disruptive digital innovation. Personally, I use the following: Generate ideas continually and limitlessly. Select 20 ideas every year and analyze them. Elaborate 10 of them in detail and select three to five of these for execution in the shape of experiments. Selecting fewer than three is playing Russian roulette, while choosing more than five signals failure to make a choice. Leaders who are good at digital innovation share an ability to make clear choices that are neither too narrow nor too broad. They choose experiments that can lead to a significant increase in customer value and expectation, that deliver quick results, and that are fundamentally innovative. Such leaders understand that fast failure and fast learning from failure are also valuable results.

Use explicit criteria for selecting experiments. First, every experiment must contribute to the customer's most fundamental unmet needs. Second, the experiment must be feasible, and fit in with your organization's existing competencies and capacity, or with those you can mobilize. Finally, each experiment must be conducted in the same market where your company aims to achieve growth.

The last two dimensions of a professional portfolio. The fourth dimension is the initiative's strategic value. That value can be expressed by the tint of the dot you use on your chart. The fifth dimension consists of assigning a code for the type of target an initiative is aimed at. Is it meant to address (A) share (of customers, revenue or market),

(B) costs and productivity, (C) employee satisfaction, (D) flexibility, (E) effectiveness, (F) corporate social responsibility or (G) compliance? In answering this question, you can also weigh whether you are meeting the needs of your various stakeholders: customers, employees, shareholders, management and society.

Check the matrix to see whether it shows a neat incline. A well-balanced portfolio shows a nice diagonal line from top left to bottom right on the chart, and not the cliché hockey stick. You need all three types of initiatives. The unbalanced portfolios on the right side of Figure 14 are a quick reference guide to determine if something is wrong. Some managers are flabbergasted when they see their company's situation mapped out that way. A pattern of dots scattered all over the place sends a blunt message that you're lacking focus. A combination of one or two lighter dots and a few very dark ones reflects a risky portfolio. If you see lots of dots near the bottom, you know you're being too careful. And in case you didn't know it, playing it safe is the riskiest thing you can do in volatile and disruptive times. Finally, the letter codes of the targets tell their own story. In some sales-driven organizations, you see nothing but Code A, or sales projects. Industries with small margins, in which all services are a commodity, often have a large percentage of Code B, or cost-cutting projects. There, people are so dispirited by trying to survive in a shrinking market, they don't even think of trying to meet a sales target.

Decision time: full speed ahead or back to the drawing board? If you decide to stop at this point, it usually means that there are still too many differences of opinion among the key actors regarding your goals, the why, the mandate, the approach, the organizational structure (sponsor, assignee, key actors, benefit owners), the capabilities and the success factors for each chosen initiative. If this is the case, you need to dig a little deeper and find out whether people's expectations are compatible. This is an exercise in change management in its own right, which is bound to reveal clashing interests that must be addressed.

And now it's time to roll up your sleeves and start writing. Write out the entire strategy and portfolio fact sheet. Use the fact sheet for Accelerator 1 (accessible through download #10 from Appendix 5). You wouldn't be wrong to call this a strategy and portfolio fact sheet.

4.2.3 Plan and organize each initiative

A recalibrated portfolio of initiatives won't help if the initiatives aren't organized well. Successful leaders have a refreshingly down-to-earth attitude. They hold detailed quarterly discussions about the portfolio and discuss the critical initiatives once a month. In Accelerator 3, I describe how management and monitoring can play a vital role in accelerating the initiative. But let me first explain how to organize your initiatives.

How to organize Type 1. There are countless tried and true methods of continuous improvement. Lean and Lean Six Sigma are the best known of these. Lean, for example, is a framework organizations use to structurally enhance customer satisfaction and generate (financial) results (see Appendix 5, download #5, where you'll find a reference to the 10 main principles of Lean). By focusing on customer value and reducing execution errors, you reduce the number of process steps (Lean) and make the result of the processes predictable (Six Sigma).[112] Examples of successful Lean Six Sigma implementations can be found at Motorola, General Electric, Ford and Dell. GE Medical Systems used Six Sigma to develop a diagnostic scanner that sped up the scanning process from 180 seconds to 17 seconds. And a Six Sigma team at the GE Plastics division boosted plastic production by 10 million pounds.[113]

Crucial parts of the Lean philosophy are badly needed for Types 2 and 3 Change (renewal and innovation, respectively). A typical characteristic of Lean is the small, bite-size waves of performance improvement. It is precisely this iteration that is key to Types 2 and 3 Change. It's better to go into execution with a Minimum Viable Product (MVP) than to wait a year to finish your strategic blueprint. As one manager told us in an interview: "I want plain old business projects to start using what has been the standard in IT projects for quite a while: agile and Scrum-type methods."

Types 2 and 3 changes are usually a matter of incremental improvements in performance by implementing a series of small projects in a single division or discipline: in other words, a series of Type 1 changes. Such changes don't involve other divisions or disciplines, so there's really no excuse for not making them. All you need to do is settle on a method and find a division or person who wants to throw their weight behind it in order to make the whole organization work lean. Many would argue that this is all part of Running the Business, but it isn't, because it requires too many specific methods and competencies; it really is part of Changing the Business.[114]

How to organize Type 2. Business Process Redesign (BPR) is still the most relevant of the proven generic methods to achieve renewal. Fortunately, BPR in its current form is brief and iterative. Where it used to take months of analysis and design before you could start execution, now it takes just weeks. We call these methods "business agile and Scrum." Always settle on one specific method for Type 2 Change. And regardless of the method you select—whether business process management, redesign, Scrum or some other agile method—always make sure you excel at it.

You really can't do without a good, generic method for Type 2 Change. At the same time, a generic method is not a panacea, because relying purely on a generic method is risky. Modern times call for specialized expertise and methods. It's important to add specific methods for specific issues. Reducing overhead, for instance, requires overhead value analysis, while to achieve synergy you need a post-merger integration method. Increasing your revenue per user requires customer and sales process analyses, and so on. We'll discuss this in more detail in Accelerator 2, Building Block 5.

How to decide whether a Type 2 initiative belongs with line management or in a separate project or program. Let your line organization handle as much as it can, but don't be afraid to set up projects or programs. Sometimes I get the feeling there's a taboo on the P-words: project and program. Time to get over it. Any initiative that has (1) fundamental goals and is (2) multidisciplinary must always be organized in a project or a program, like it or not. This applies to any Type 2 Change (renewal), and also to Type 3 (innovation) for that matter. If you know this and still insist on foisting it on your line organization, you are guilty of oversimplification and setting everyone up for disappointment. The polarization between execution in your primary process and in programs is one of the most damaging false dilemmas plaguing organizations.

Paradoxically, it is a sound impulse to want your line organization to execute your projects and programs wherever possible. That's a healthy dualism that many managers rightfully try to foster because they want to avoid endlessly, aimlessly meandering programs. So how do you go about this? By applying this dualism at every level and in every meeting as if it were the norm, and by setting up cross-functional teams and vertical consultation.

There are a few reasons for this perceived dichotomy and the apparent taboo on the P-words. First of all, you know that any renewal goes fastest if you organize it separately. However, you also know that eventually it has to be integrated back into the regular business processes, the going concern. Secondly, organizing initiatives separately in projects or programs triggers the existing prejudice that projects and programs are time and money-wasting operations with a bad track record in terms of results, and that they tend to become silos within the company, sometimes even developing their own culture.

How to organize Type 3 initiatives. Type 3 Change, or innovation, is often delegated to a separate startup, but it can also be organized as a separate initiative within an established organization.[115] Both options share one important feature: a history of multiple failures in order to score the one success. It's a story of blood, sweat and tears, of endless patience and endurance. That's why established companies organize such initiatives in various ways. The question of how best to organize radical innovation—which is almost always digital in nature—is so elementary that it deserves a separate section (see below).

4.2.4 Take a two-track approach

Radical innovation (Type 3 Change) has preoccupied organizations for the past ten years. There are many different strategies for organizing and managing such change. Most recently, new digital business models have been the main drivers of innovation, putting successful innovation at the top of every boardroom agenda. Innovation gurus have seized this opportunity and, either deliberately or inadvertently, created a hype around innovation. They've suggested that the creativity and brilliance needed for successful radical innovation are smothered by structure and management. They've vilified metrics as the ultimate death knell. This misconception has created a tendency to indiscriminately try out all kinds of ideas, at enormous financial and intangible cost. Such innovation gurus had free rein until Eric Ries published his bestseller *The Lean Startup*.[116] The basic idea behind his excellent innovation method is validated learning: a way for startups operating in uncertain conditions to prove that they are making progress.[117] This is much more practical, accurate and rapid than market forecasts or classical business planning. It's all about learning. Anything extraneous—that is, not required for learning from customers—is eliminated. Validated learning is learning based on the actual development of the organization, substantiated by real customer data. All a startup does is carry out experiments to learn and successfully navigate the company through a period of uncertainty.

In practice, Type 3 Change, digital innovation, is organized and managed in many different ways. Figure 15 details the various organizational and managerial forms we came across in our research. To do well, you need to organize a healthy dualism. Running your existing business model and implementing changes to this model (Types 1 and 2 Change: improving and renewing), are aimed at fully leveraging your current business model. Your existing organization can handle this. But Type 3 Change is of a different order. This is about radical innovation, introducing new business models, radically changing the way you do business. This type of change can only be achieved through a differentiated, autonomous execution strategy, separate from your regular structure but with at least a minimal interface to facilitate linkage and cross-fertilization. This is not to say you shouldn't foster innovation in your regular organization, but don't put all your eggs in that basket.

How do you organize management of all three types of change in relation to day-to-day executive management? How do you organize Changing the Business in relation to Running the Business? The solution is to institutionalize dualism. Figure 15 lists the ways in which Type 3 Radical Innovation can be organized; this is crucial for established organizations to survive. But startups become scale-ups and there comes a day when they're established companies. As you can see, the organization formerly known as Google has opted to explicitly differentiate its established revenue and business models (like Google Search and YouTube) from its Type 3 innovations (like Google X and Google Capital) by introducing a new corporate structure called Alphabet. This is an excellent example of strategy execution that requires differentiation into the three types of change. Google can leverage its existing revenue and business models using Types 1 and 2, while simultaneously ensuring that it leverages Type 3 innovations, its moonshots, in ways best suited to that particular business model. Type 3 innovations may for this reason always remain separate organizations that are never integrated into a larger, existing business unit.

Shareholders also like this logic and transparency, because it makes clear which risks pertain to which division. By rigorously separating its activities, Google—or Alphabet, rather—can protect its brands and experiment with them.

Management thinker John Kotter advocated this dual operating system in his 2014 book *Accelerate (XLR8)*.[118] In his dual operating system, regular execution operates separately from, yet in conjunction with, innovation.

Another great example of this two-track approach comes from Alex Osterwalder, inventor of the Business Model Canvas, in his successful book *Business Model Generation*.[119] In his blog on the Strategyzer website, titled "6 Roles That Can Position Your Company for The Future," he presents a modern organizational chart. It shows how the two separate tracks work, and what improving and renewing existing revenue and

Figure 15 — **Six organizational strategies for managing radical innovation (Type 3).**

	1. Integrated	2. Quasi-independent (50%)	3. Independent (100%)	4. Joint venture	5. Acquisition	All of the previous options
Organization	Each division in the organization innovates individually.	Innovation takes place within the existing structure, but is organized separately.	Innovation takes place outside of the main structure, usually at a different location.	The parties start a new joint venture, specifically for the purpose of innovation.	Completely separate from the going concern.	All of the previous options.
Management	Business as usual. It is vital to distinguish between Running and Changing the business.	If the innovation is close to the going concern in nature, management needs to be done by the line. But separation of activities is crucial.	Often, a back-office support department monitors progress and reports directly to the CEO.	Each party contributes its own competencies and resources; the joint venture will attract outside expertise if necessary.	The market is systematically scanned for promising and necessary innovations.	Often, a back-office support department monitors consistency between activities.
When to use	When it is clear which innovation is necessary and the organization has proven itself capable of innovation.	When it is unclear which innovation is necessary and the organization has not yet proven itself capable of innovation.	When it is unclear which innovation is necessary and the organization has not yet proven itself capable of innovation.	When each party's motives complement the others' and there is a balance between giving and getting.	When there is an opportunity or necessity and acquisition is cheaper, faster or better than another strategy.	When the organization has the opportunity, or feels the necessity to differentiate.
Benefits	Sustainable.	Speed.	Speed.	Risk and cost sharing.	Speed.	Innovate when possible, buy when necessary.
Drawbacks	Slow and impossible if internal competencies are inadequate.	Complicated integration.	Complicated integration.	Slow decision-making.	High costs and complicated integration.	Risk of half-hearted approach.
Examples	PostNL	New York Times, Zwitserleven	NPO: NLZiet	School of One, a European public - private initiative	ING and Aegon bank	RELX,

Source: Turner, 2016

business models (Types 1, 2) and innovation (Type 3) look like organizationally.[120] On the Innovation side of the chart, Osterwalder distinguishes six modern roles: the Chief Entrepreneur, the Chief Portfolio Manager, the Chief Venture Capital, the Chief Risk Officer, the Chief Internal Ambassador and the Entrepreneurs. All these forms and models meet management's needs to purposefully separate operation of the existing business model from the timely innovation of new business models in order to survive. They prefer some form of slight interaction between the two "engines" to maintain a relationship and enable cross-fertilization.

Management. A very practical example of dualism is the A and B agendas used by one manager I spoke to. The A Agenda at a meeting deals with day-to-day executive management, while the B Agenda deals with progress of the 3 Types of Change, which together determine the Execution Agenda. This highly systematic approach kills several birds with one stone. It keeps Running the Business and Changing the Business separate, while distinguishing between the three types of change and between short-term and long-term goals. This is the most practical application of agile strategy execution I have ever seen. But whatever innovation structure you decide on, always make sure you create a second speed, a second track, for radical innovation (see Figure 16).

Figure 16 — **Whatever innovation structure you decide on, always make sure you create a second speed, a second track, for radical innovation.**

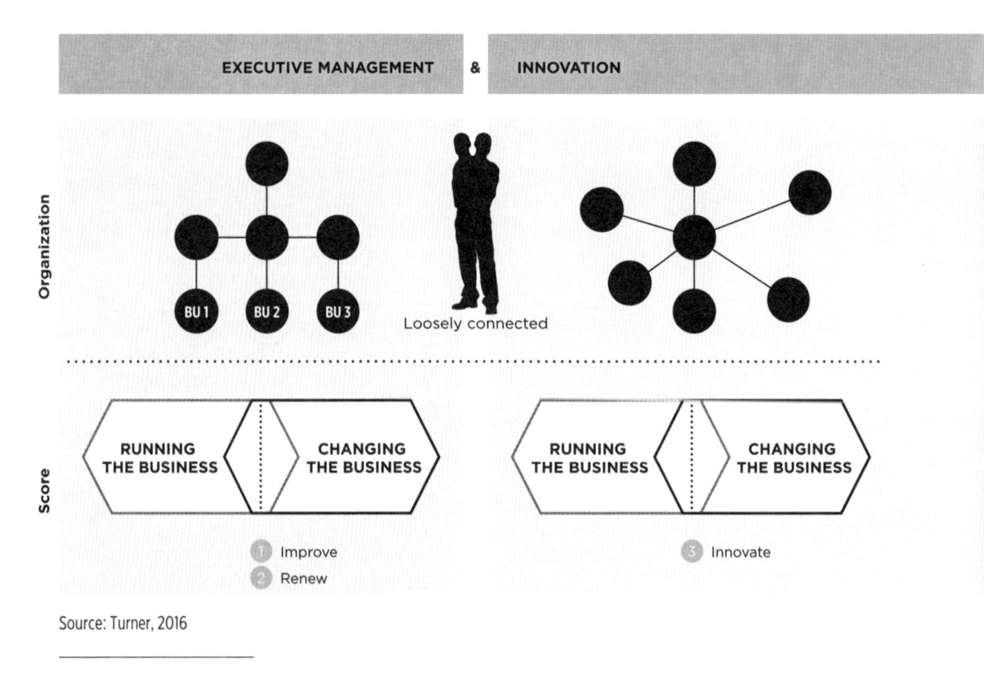

Source: Turner, 2016

As a result, the organization will end up with a robust two-track approach, each running at its own speed. It's quite a radical step to consistently implement this approach in your organizational structure. Some organizations will find it easier to live with this type of 'healthy schizophrenia' than others, but it really is the best way to use your existing workforce to generate radical innovations. If it sounds complicated, that's because it is. All workmanship gets complex now and then.

General Electric is a good example. In mid-2015, the company announced plans to sell most of its finance unit and focus exclusively on industrial manufacturing. At the time, the GE Capital business unit was good for half of the overall turnover, but the company decided to retain only part of its aircraft and equipment lease operations. In 2018, these activities are forecast to bring in 10% of its earnings: a real sea change. But GE's industrial segment is also undergoing a radical transformation. These days, many of the machines GE manufactures—deep-water oil-drilling equipment, military and commercial jet engines, and trains—are equipped with sensors that collect data. So, GE developed Predix: predictive maintenance software that uses this data to monitor performance and identify opportunities for improvement. GE now has a new Digital Business Unit, which is exploring the possibility of offering deep-sea drilling as a service rather than a product.

And let's be honest: if the establishment had approached modern strategy execution professionally, the media industry would have created and marketed Blendle and Netflix itself instead of wasting a decade daydreaming about new business models. And Hilton would have come up with the Airbnb model, and the Amsterdam Taxi Dispatch would have thought of Uber.

Successful Application of Building Block 2, SELECTION

Case study: Aegon Bank. A single team, a single vision, a single execution
Breakthrough: The years 2008-2010 were a tough time for the financial sector. Aegon Life & Mortgage was under great pressure to make strategic choices. The life insurance market had bottomed out and the mortgage market was on the verge of collapse. Yet Aegon's strategy was clear. To realize its vision, the bank had to make incremental changes in various areas. It was crucial to invest in the team charged with drawing up the change agenda. This team translated the strategy into clear one-page plans for each business unit. The portfolio of initia-

tives contained crystal clear assignments, and conditions and deadlines, based on an unambiguous strategy of coordinated change with a steep learning curve, while the team ensured everyone stuck to the change portfolio.

Impact: The result was a substantial improvement in execution capacity. This included not only structural, procedural and management interventions, but also behavioral and cultural changes. No less than 90% of the planned projects and line operations were completed. The results were real and substantial. The mortgage portfolio grew, bucking the market trend, and since 2008 the business has quadrupled its market share.

The Soft Building Blocks in Accelerator 1: APPEAL and ACTIVATION

Each accelerator has two hard and two soft building blocks. Accelerator 1's soft building blocks are APPEAL and ACTIVATION. **Building Block 3, APPEAL**, serves to review and enrich your strategy. In **Building Block 4, ACTIVATION**, you work on establishing real ownership for every initiative in which leaders play a key role.

4.3 Building Block 3: APPEAL

In **Building Block 3, APPEAL**, you ask for feedback on your strategy and then enrich it to ensure that it becomes a living, breathing plan. That takes more than one-way communication. The strategy's justification, or the *why*, must be perfectly clear. And the best way to convey purpose is to tell an appealing story. Leaders need to be systematic in their approach, embrace feedback and funnel creativity.

4.3.1 Tone from the top: Live the strategy

Leaders must review each other's ownership of the initiatives selected. To actually mobilize the leadership team everyone has to declare ownership. If *you* don't believe in it, no one else will follow. Three-year strategic planning sessions tend to be technical procedures that are finalized when the strategic documents have been drawn up; this limits their value. The enrichment procedure described below can help to increase their usefulness, but its goal of involving people in a strategy review is rather broad. What you really need is to ensure that the whole team of change leaders share the same views and expectations of the portfolio's ambition. You need to make sure that everyone is reading from the same script.

Figure 17 — **Get under the surface when assessing the soft capabilities for strategy execution. Dive into people's mindsets.**

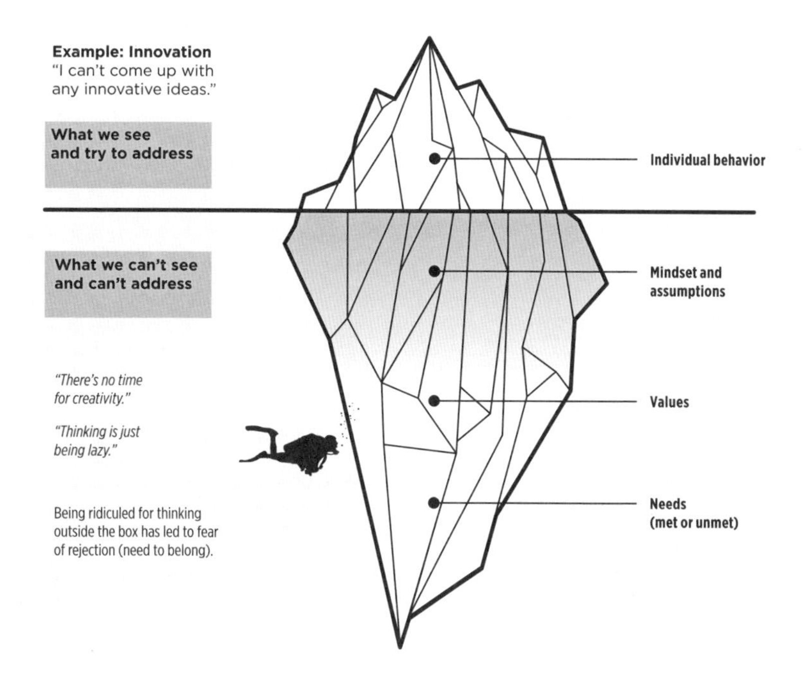

Source: *Beyond Performance*, Scott Keller, Colin Price, Figure 4.3

Take time to review each other's true commitment. Start by assigning each initiative in the portfolio to a change leader. Then make sure there is enough time to fully appreciate the nature of the choices made, to see eye to eye and share your intentions, principles, preferences and expectations. The trick is to get under the surface and ask: What really drives us? What assumptions determine how we look at each other and what we do?[121] (See also Figure 17). The demystification of the soft stuff is well underway. Use techniques and formats to get a grip on it.

Figure 18 shows that the deeper you go, the more personal it gets. Depth is also necessary to achieve authenticity. Boards of directors are usually happy to do a color test, because that is relatively safe. Digging deep and being able to make the right interventions in the leadership team requires personal courage and highly developed leadership skills (see the middle and right side of Figure 18, and the leadership qualities in Appendix 5, download #2).

Figure 18 — **The deeper you dive, the more personal the soft skills become.** Ranging from 'soft' methods to soft personal skills.

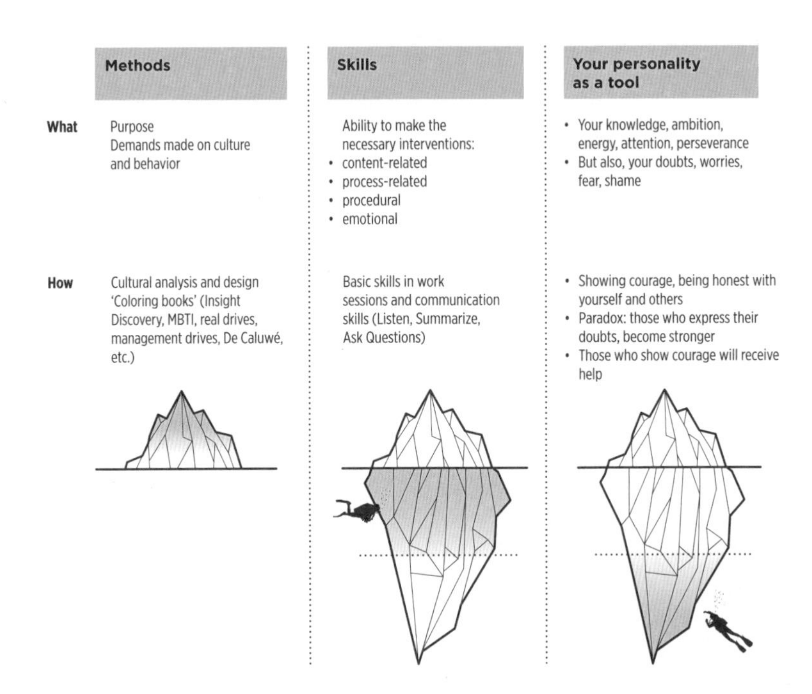

Source: Turner, 2016

A practical pointer is to conclude the strategic phase that this accelerator encompasses, by organizing a day off-site. A different context can help to mark the shift from strategic analysis and course plotting to mobilizing yourself as a leadership team, focused solely on the points made in this section. This makes for a truly memorable moment.

4.3.2 Review and enrich your strategy

Expand ownership beyond the inner circle through review, communication and interaction. The strategic framework is set by board and management only. The steps from Building Block 1 and 2 are carried out by the right people in an appropriate way. I am not going to waste my breath on that; I think it's safe to assume that no one is going to take an overly long-winded approach to strategic planning any longer.

A general rule of thumb is that just 5 to 10% of the organization is involved in strategy-setting. You don't want any more than that, because, as we know from experience, full bottom-up strategic planning leads to superficiality. That has been demonstrated time and again. The leaders and the lower-level employees who are involved in planning need to come up with a clear mission, vision and strategy. That is their mandate and it includes involving a representative cross-section of the organization in planning: a few individuals from every rank. The framework for the organization's long-term mission, vision and strategy has to be explicit and sharply defined, yet flexible enough to allow room for enrichment.

Enriching the strategic framework is an all-hands-on-deck operation. Once you have hammered out the strategic framework, it is time to enrich it. Enrichment involves more than just communication. The framework needs reviewing, improving, supplementing and specifying. The word 'communication' is an oft-used and far too narrow definition of what needs to happen. If communication is a one-way street—which it often is—it is a lost opportunity at the very start of strategy execution. Enrichment is not a formality whose results you stick in a drawer. On the contrary, it is vital that you open yourself up to all feedback, because that feedback is worth its weight in gold. You want to absorb all feedback and constructive criticism like a sponge. If you can't take criticism, you won't succeed.

Embrace feedback. When you have labored with a deliberately diverse group to formulate a new strategy or a new plan, it can be hard to put it "out there" for a larger group that hasn't made a commitment yet, but do it anyway.

If you can't explain the story of the strategy or plan in simple terms, there's something wrong. So, you want to get any feedback that can help you improve your story. Nothing stays with you quite like constructively worded feedback and criticism that rescues you from some disaster in the nick of time or dramatically improves the quality of an initiative. That's the best example of how human synergy works.

Dare to weed out unsupported criticism and questionable feedback. The conventional wisdom is that any and all feedback and criticism is good. But that dogma gets in the way of staying level-headed. Remember that any feedback and criticism you receive always includes some nonsense that stems from a lack of experience. I've met managers who insist on incorporating each and every piece of feedback in their strategy. This feedback tyranny robs them of their ability to think straight and they end up including bad feedback in their strategy too.

Feedback from those whose motives you question can paralyze you. Their arrogant, cynical or narcissist attitude and tone can be so nasty that you might find yourself thinking: "With friends like these who needs enemies?" This does not mean they never have a valid point, though. Even a stopped clock shows the right time twice a day.

Your strategic framework delineates and funnels creativity and ideas. But ideas sprout outside the box too. Don't hesitate to include those, because you can strike gold outside the box just as easily as inside. Management thinker Verne Harnish says the power of ideas is crucial for driving tomorrow's strategy execution and hence for survival and growth.[122] The more leeway you give yourself to think about ideas, away from the day-to-day, the bigger their potential. Organizations that tap into the most ideas by the most people win. To this end, surround yourself with people who are smarter than you. And don't be "the one genius with 1,000 helpers" as Jim Collins calls leaders who fail to surround themselves with others who are smarter.[123] You need to trust that the people who are in charge of the enrichment process, who prepare, facilitate and report back, have enough experience and the right skills.

By the way, the digital age is a great time to be enriching your mission, vision and strategy. You have so many wonderful and proven social and technological means at your disposal to creatively, effectively and efficiently involve the whole organization in enriching the strategic framework. As I said at the beginning of this section, you should not involve the whole organization in devising a strategy from scratch, because that will lead to superficiality. But once you have a framework, you want as many people as possible to review and enrich it.

It pays off to systematically implement the steps that lead to enrichment: communication, review, supplementation and specification. Select an appropriate format for every step and target group. It is smart to differentiate; you might want to communicate the strategy to everyone at the same time ('broadcast'), but follow this up with differentiated interactions per target group ('narrowcast'). For example, because middle management often plays a crucial part in many strategy execution initiatives, it pays to organize a number of tailor-made reviewing carrousels for middle managers and pull out all the stops to get and incorporate their input into your strategy. Another example of appropriate differentiation is this: in the upcoming strategic plan, some divisions are hit much harder than others and will need to 'stomach' more change than others. You will need to adjust the nature and intensity of your enrichment activities accordingly. See also Figure 19. This is how you give your organization a voice.

Figure 19 — **Enrich your strategy and build ownership.** Adapt your format and technology to your goal and target group.

	Format and resources Note: separate from regular resources in production and HR	Broadcast semi-targeted, roughly differentiated	Narrowcast targeted, finely differentiated	Two-way traffic?	Online options in addition to live interaction?	Accelerator			
						1	2	3	4
1	Storytelling	●		✗	✓	●			
2	Customer Experience Panel Discussion		●	✓	✓	●	●		
3	Challenge and dialogue sessions		●	✓	✓	●	●		
4	Letter of credence	●		✗	✗	●	●		
5	Personal manifesto		●	✗	✗		●	●	
6	Q&A's	●	●	✗	✓			●	
7	Ambassadors' stories	●	●	✓	✓			●	
8	Experience forum		●	✓	✓			●	
9	Master-apprentice		●	✓	✗			●	
10	Coaching menu		●	✓	✗				●
11	Execution and peer review carousels		●	✓	✓				●
12	Icons and symbols	●		✗	✓				●
13	Celebrations or incentives		●	✓	✗				●
14	One on one intervention		●	✓	✗			●	
15	Action-based learning	●	●	✓	✓				●

Source: Turner, 2016

Look for and create a sense of urgency and excitement. Don't wait for everyone to experience this in the exact same way. In the old days, people would debate which would be the best driver: a shared sense of urgency to change, or a sense of excitement at new opportunities. Let's not waste any more time on this. That sense of urgency is part and parcel of the New Normal. Goals without urgency are pipe dreams and a sense of excitement is a necessary precondition at all times. So, it's not either-or, it's both. Organizations that can operate on excitement alone are rare indeed.

It is good to discuss where you stand in terms of urgency and excitement when preparing your story in your leadership team. Symptoms of a low sense of urgency include people insisting on staying in their comfort zone; inflating past achievements; irritated customers and talent; settling for mediocrity; beating around the bush; hands-off, distant management; downplaying issues; and meetings without action.[124]

So again, you need both urgency and excitement. Beware of the myth that you should only appeal to people by creating excitement. It's a matter of simple psychology that people are more inclined to avoid loss than to realize a dream. That's why a healthy dose of urgency is a good thing.

4.3.3 Tell your story

In communicating your strategy, you need to both appeal and inform. More likely than not, your sharply delineated and fully enriched strategy is dull and boring. Despite all the hype about storytelling, most companies are still fairly clueless about how to sell their mission, vision and strategy to their own organization and beyond. That sad state of affairs is even worse in Rhineland than in Anglo-Saxon countries. You won't believe how ill-prepared some huge corporations and executive committees are to address large town hall meetings. They fumble their way through far too many PowerPoint slides, hopelessly ignorant of the three-minutes-per-sheet rule. Their projected 20 sheets per 30 minutes is guaranteed to make them go 30 minutes over time. It's that simple. And that doesn't even address the other rule of thumb—that a quarter of the available time should be reserved for questions and debate.

A good strategic story doesn't magically appear. The veil of mystique that surrounds storytelling needs to be pulled away. Turning a strategy into an appealing story requires a sequence of steps. Granted, some things can't be planned, like some leader's eureka moment about the best peg, metaphor or example that hits them during their Saturday morning jog. But you can't do without a systematic approach. Figure 20 lists the main storytelling imperatives and checkpoints. "This is hard work, too," one senior manager said. "Remember, it's all about perception, not about what you actually say."

Don't forget the facts! Who ever said that a story has to be a fairytale and can't contain any hard facts or figures? I notice a shortage rather than a surplus of numbers. Open a random PowerPoint presentation and you'll see mainly qualitative statements in endless bulleted lists (often without numbers, another deadly sin). Or you'll see just images, since everyone knows that a picture is worth a thousand words. But facts are conspicuously absent.

Figure 20 — **Storytelling imperatives and checkpoints.**

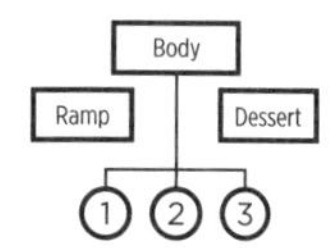

1	**Preparation**	• Consider your audience and your goal • Get into the right state • Give yourself enough time to prepare
2	**Ramp**	• The ramp is essential. Pick an acute angle, a hook
3	**Body**	• Deliver 3 messages at most • Speak passionately and professionally, qualitatively and quantitatively • Balance content and emotion • Use both verbal and visual aids • Incorporate a sense of urgency and excitement • Use pauses and silences, but don't overdo it • Use humor: indispensable, but tricky • Keep it simple, but not too simple • Consider interaction
4	**Dessert**	• Prepare an attractive final statement, possibly a cliffhanger

Source: Peter Meyers, Stand & Deliver Group / Turner, 2016

A good story will miss its goal if it's not delivered right. Peter Meyers, an authority in strategy communication, says that the body of a story should contain no more than three messages.[125] In *As We Speak* he also explains that content and delivery are just two of the three important factors that determine the success of your story. The third is the mental state of the person who delivers the story. In such a high-stakes situation, the speaker needs to perform his or her best to get the message across. Otherwise, it might get lost. And yet this crucial factor, the state of the communicator, is often neglected.

Ensure that employees can find enough inspiration in the goals your story sets. Social scientists like Danah Zohar have discovered that managers and employees strive for impact in five places: society, the organization, customers, co-workers and themselves.[126] Leaders tend to emphasize impact on the organization and customers, neglecting 60% of the motivational potential in a story. What a shame! This also implies that it makes a lot of sense to co-create the corporate story with colleagues.

Successful Application of Building Block 3, APPEAL

Case study: Unilever integrated its autonomously operating companies into one operating company per country.
Breakthrough: This integration took place ten years ago, but is still cited as a successful case study in business administration. Meticulous preparation ensured seamless integration and excellent results. In the Netherlands it yielded lower overhead (< 8.7% of earnings); more autonomy (50% reduction of higher management); larger span of control (10-12); a simplified structure (15% reduction in management levels); a platform for growth and sustainability; and no undesirable turnover of customers and talent (the No. 1 problem in mergers and integrations).
Impact: The real breakthrough was in the careful balance between hard and soft targets. The Day One Kickoff—featuring a compelling video based on U2's song *One*—consisted of a rock-solid story that "really made you excited about the future," as one employee put it. It really appealed to people. But a cool video is not enough. It was a cascade of team discussions about the opportunities and responsibilities in this new situation that brought the integration to life. Practically every employee saw the opportunities.

4.4 Building Block 4: ACTIVATION

In Building Block 4, ACTIVATION, your goal is to foster real ownership of the initiative. Leaders play a key role in this. Senior management must all read from the same script. Ensure that all assignees and key actors willingly assume ownership. Without engagement you may as well pull the plug. This building block is about the nature of true ownership, assembling your execution coalition and assessing your soft execution capacity.

4.4.1 Assemble a leadership team based on your goals

In strategy execution, your goal is to execute your strategic goals. Ownership—or responsibility, engagement, commitment—is a means to this end. Some change management theories argue that people's engagement with their organization is the ultimate goal and that performance and results follow from there. This idea is often worded so skillfully that you can't really disagree. High engagement indeed leads to significantly better results for all stakeholders, but engagement only has real impact in organizations that take their own vision, mission and resulting strategic goals seriously. In this chicken-and-egg debate, strategic goals come before engagement.

4.4.2 Distinguish between Execution and Benefit Ownership

There are two main types of ownership and various roles in which people need to take ownership. This is an elementary distinction, and the chain connecting the two needs to be strong enough for strategy execution to work. Let me first explain the types of ownership. The first is ownership of the execution of an initiative, and the second refers to ownership of the initiative's intended benefits. The actors playing the key roles in the analysis, design and execution stages are responsible for execution. The actors with key roles in reaping the benefits of achieved strategic goals "own" the benefits and bear responsibility for them. Any one actor may fulfill either key role, or both, in any stage of the execution process. That is why the distinction is relevant.

Let me give you an example. Someone may be responsible for the execution of new sales procedures and systems without winning as much as a single new customer. You also need explicit benefit owners whose gut feeling is: "All those new procedures and systems are wonderful, but how are they going to help me attract more customers?"

An actor fulfilling a key role in strategy execution may have to assume ownership of the benefits, simply because he or she is responsible for the services or processes the execution pertains to. The same person may or may not play a key role in the analysis, design and implementation stages of execution. Such an actor might, for example, be a sales manager who was not involved in the initial analysis of a project aimed at improving sales effectiveness, but who now has to use the new business processes to achieve results and meet targets.

4.4.3 Launch the Execution Coalition

The Execution Coalition is an important innovative concept in this book. As Figure 21 reveals, the execution coalition consists of five key roles that are consistent across all accelerators. Our research identified the need for each of these interdependent roles. They're necessary to clearly define and assign execution and benefit ownership. The execution coalition institutionalizes two important principles.

First of all, it establishes the necessary distinction between people who come up with solutions (roles 1 through 4) and those who realize the benefits (role 5). This distinction and its importance are seldom recognized. In fact, benefit ownership (role 5), which is by far the most important of them, is usually treated as a fifth wheel.

Second, these five roles are key to alignment, an important element in the list of success factors discussed in Chapter 2. The power of the execution coalition is that alignment ensures the best odds of success—and by this I mean alignment between Running the Business and Changing the Business as well as cross-disciplinary and vertical alignment. The execution coalition is a powerful tool because it frees you of your dependence on accidental actors and their alertness or willingness to align. The division of roles in the coalition makes alignment a daily routine, a fixed item on the agenda. And this routine increases your chances of success.

The coalition signals a fundamental change. It is so much more than strategy execution project management. It is the change engine that drives every initiative. It pays systematic attention to the change leadership provided by the sponsor(s) and the execution lead, and to the change management provided by the execution lead, those involved in the execution, and the benefit owners.

This might sound a bit dull, but nothing could be further from the truth. The execution coalition is a true "throughput engine," as one professional called it. Not because of its formal power, but because it's an a priori coalition that connects the boardroom with the mailroom and because its multidisciplinary composition institutionalizes alignment.

Figure 21 — **The Execution Coalition: Five roles for clearly defining and assigning Execution and Benefit Ownership.**

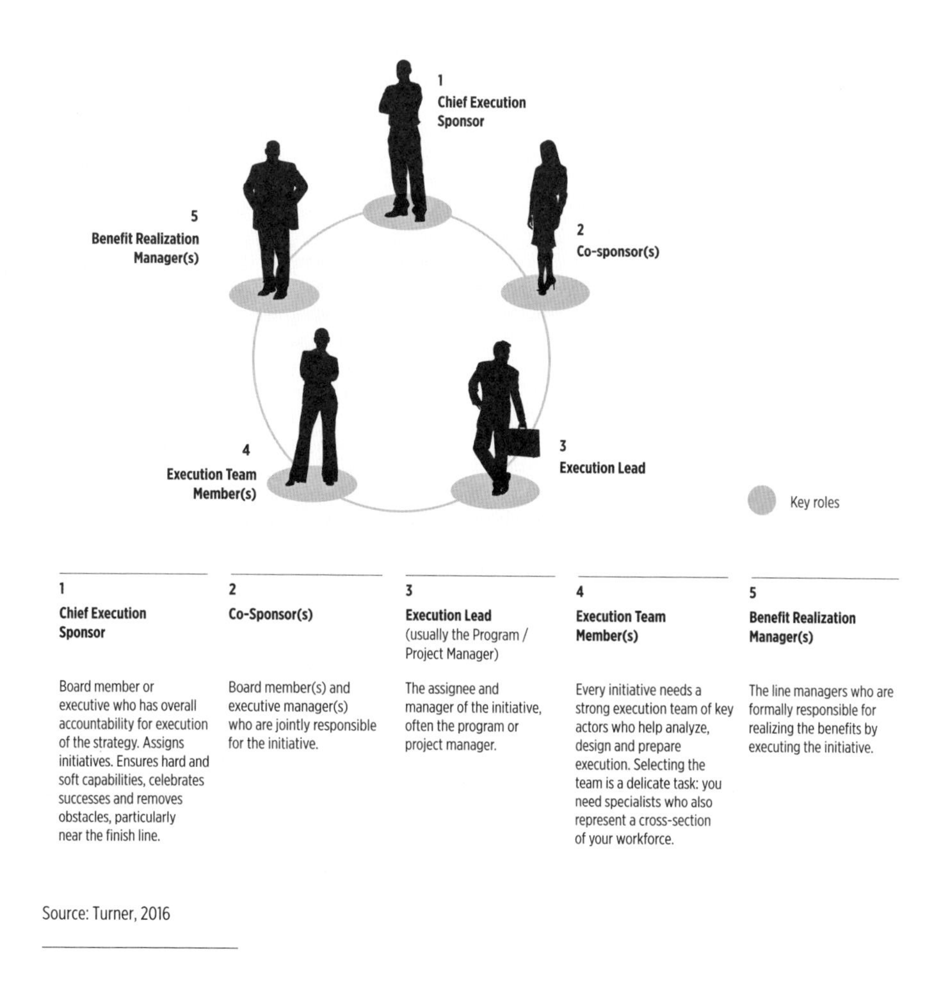

Source: Turner, 2016

1 **The Chief Execution Sponsor.** This is the Board member or executive manager with overall accountability: the chief sponsor. This person ensures hard and soft capabilities, celebrates successes and removes obstacles, particularly near the finish line. Every individual on the leadership team—usually the Board of Directors or the executive management team of a division or business unit—is Chief Execution Sponsor of one or more strategic initiatives.

Business leaders should not just embrace change, but actively lead change, and not just once, but all day, every day and at every level. They play a key role in ensuring that the portfolio of initiatives is in line with the strategy. They regularly align the portfolio with the overall strategic goals. They maintain a close connection to the key actors in the various program. As senior managers, they are important constants in the execution of the strategy.

The role of the Chief Execution Sponsor tends to be underestimated. It's no accident that there's a host of books and courses on how to be a good sponsor. As we shall see, the Chief Execution Sponsor's behavior can make a big difference in any of the four accelerators.[127]

2 **The Co-sponsor(s).** Board member(s) and executive manager(s) who are jointly responsible for the initiative. In fact, an initiative's wide scope often means it has an impact on various departments and responsibilities. Take a sales effectiveness project, for instance. While overall accountability and sponsorship typically lies with the sales director (CCO), the project will also depend heavily on operations and have implications there, too. Therefore, it makes sense for the COO to co-sponsor the initiative. This is the only way to create the type of "strong guiding coalitions" John Kotter advocates in *Leading Change*.[128] The co-sponsors' responsibilities are so entwined with the initiative that they might as well have been the chief sponsor. It goes without saying that the entire Board is squarely behind the business plan and the initiatives it describes. Board members who wait to voice their doubts about an initiative until halfway through the execution process, or undercut it completely by asserting the opposite of the initiative's goal, are not worth their paycheck.

3 **The Execution Lead** (usually the Program or Project Manager). This is the assignee and manager of the initiative, often in the role of the program or project manager. The execution lead is the first to lose sleep over, or celebrate, the initiative's progress. He or she is the initiative's linchpin and does whatever's necessary to make it a success.

4 **The Execution Team Member(s).** Every initiative needs a strong execution team of key players who help analyze, design and prepare execution. Selecting this team is a delicate task; you need specialists who also represent a cross-section of your workforce. Your criteria are both qualitative and quantitative. Quantitatively, there is a clearly definable amount of work, which requires a specified number of hours. Qualita-

tively speaking, you need people with the right, specialized capabilities and expertise. But it is also logical to include all the business units the initiative will have an impact on. Hence, soft criteria also are key considerations in the selection process. It might be prudent to include some of the most defiant people, and you'll also want to make sure that the right "blood types" are included. Innovation requires key actors with an outward-looking approach and an inward-looking ability to act.

5 **The Benefit Realization Manager(s).** These benefit owners are the line managers who are formally responsible for realizing the benefits that come from executing the initiative. This is what it's all about! Let's revisit my earlier example of the sales manager who was not involved in the initial analysis of a project aimed at improving sales effectiveness, but who now has to use the new business processes to achieve results and meet targets. Other benefit owners would be the people responsible for part of the execution's results under the sales manager's wing. For example, they might be responsible for a higher conversion in a particular subsegment. At this level, this could be a dozen team leaders, who in turn have their own team of a dozen people.

These five roles are universal in any type of strategy execution and any kind of change process. In the age of agile and Scrum, many different names and definitions are used, such as product owner, Scrum master, agile coach, tribe member and chapter member, but my list is different. My five roles are universal. They are indispensable in any kind of execution. Working with fewer than five creates the semblance of simplicity, but actually confuses matters. Working with more than five causes complexity and inflexibility. Appendix 5, download #11 gives an overview of the roles in popular innovation methods like agile and Scrum and the Execution Coalition's universal roles.

Hierarchical, you say? I am not going to waste my breath on polemics about the question of whether defining key roles is old-school hierarchical thinking. It's quite simple. In the New Normal, you make use of individual professionals' qualities and offer them maximum autonomy and freedom. Since most initiatives in strategy execution involve radical, innovative, multidisciplinary, complicated issues, you need to amalgamate the professionals' results to achieve the overall benefits. To ensure maximum individual freedom, it is helpful to work with standardized roles. It's conducive to creating flexibility and time for human interaction because there's no need to waste time on defining the necessary roles along the way.

Real, psychological ownership means so much more than formal ownership. Responsibility equals formal ownership and accountability based on role and task descriptions. This is often determined with the help of RRA or RACI tables.[129] Psychological ownership is its "soft" counterpart, but it needs to come from deep within. Does everyone realize what they are responsible for? Have they actively sought this and subscribed to it? Are they fully committed, psychologically? The key question is whether someone *wants* to assume ownership and responsibility, not whether they *have* to.

4.4.4 Execution Coalition: Lay the foundation for Execution and Benefit Ownership

In essence, you want to build ownership for every strategic initiative in your portfolio. That's why in every accelerator, you are prompted to reconsider how you've filled the key roles and what the priorities should be.

Building execution and benefit ownership requires a systematic approach. Ownership doesn't just appear out of nowhere. Figure 22 shows the types of ownership and roles in Accelerator 1.

The execution coalition leads and implements execution. Taking the lead, aka change leadership, requires that leaders personally analyze and reinforce the necessary capabilities, and convey and enrich the hard strategy and its soft counterpart (storytelling). True enrichment only happens through real interaction with people, by uncovering and discussing their personal motives, mindsets and patterns. This helps you to forge and structure the execution portfolio. Our research has shown that successful organizations systematically choose strategic initiatives, balance their portfolio and define each initiative from start to finish in terms of mandate, scope, method, planning, etc. This may sound like drudgery, and to a large extent, it is, but as our research has shown, a systematic approach is more effective than reinforcing risk management systems.

The strength of the Execution Coalition is that is has a built-in alignment structure between Running the Business and Changing the Business and across disciplines and chains. This gives you the greatest odds of success. In Accelerator 1, alignment is all about timeliness in involving supervisory and external target groups, such as the Supervisory Board.

Figure 22 — **The Execution Coalition: Execution and Benefit Ownership in Accelerator 1.**

1
Chief Execution Sponsor

- Analyzes and reinforces capabilities.
- Conveys the story and enriches strategy.
- Explicitly assumes ownership.
- Drafts an assignment.
- Informs the key actors relevant to this stage of the process.
- Identifies and talks to the execution coalition.
- Makes final choices and starts coproduction.

2
Co-sponsor(s)

- Stand(s) shoulder to shoulder with the sponsor at key moments.
- Show(s) co-sponsorship in word and example.

3
Execution Lead (usually the program or project manager)

- Commits to the initiative, if motivated.

4
Execution Team Member(s)

- Form(s) an idea of the initiative and takes on their role and ownership.
- Propagate(s) their role and ownership in the team, solicited and/or unsolicited.

5
Benefits Realization Manager(s)

- Form(s) an idea of the benefit ownership and the attending responsibilities.
- Figure(s) out what contribution they need to make to the initiative, which role they can play and prepare(s) accordingly.
- Do(es) the same with their team.

Source: Turner, 2016

4.4.5 Assess soft execution and change capacities

In the first half of this chapter I talked about why it is important to take stock of your organization's competencies and capacities; you need to know your core capabilities and assess which need reinforcing. The SECA.NU tool is a fast and convenient way of doing this. The same tool can also be used to analyze your organization's soft capabilities.

This analysis is crucial, because soft capabilities make or break your ability to reach your goals, as we learned from Success Factor 2. Organizations with strong soft capabilities are 2.2 times more likely to perform better than the median.[130]

Soft capabilities include organizational culture, conduct, and leadership and collaboration styles. These capabilities play a role in both running the business and transforming your existing business model. Contrary to popular belief, soft capabilities are eminently quantifiable. Analysis of the soft variables that determine the effectiveness of an organization's strategy execution is not only possible, it is necessary. It is a crucial step and a prerequisite to delineating the scope of the organization's mission, vision and strategy. It really pays off to discuss your SECA analysis results in one of the strategic analysis and course plotting sessions you devote to aligning your strategic ambitions and capabilities.

Successful Application of Building Block 4, ACTIVATION

Case study: FrieslandCampina: simultaneous team building and planning, with incredible depth
Breakthrough: This Building Block was used to activate the Top 70 people at Royal FrieslandCampina. Facing tough times together builds a strong team. Before starting execution of a multiyear strategic program, senior management at FrieslandCampina decided to first invest in its people. "Who is on the bus is just as important as the destination." There is a clear correlation between the execution team and the organization's strategic goals. Senior management started an intensive program to take the company's leadership to a higher level and formulate a common vision. The program didn't just address who was "on the bus," but also their collaboration style and personal development.
Impact: having a common starting point and finish line helps to plot the best course. Based on personal and professional development methods, the Top 70 people took off-site trips in the Netherlands and abroad, in order to connect, challenge, discover and shape themselves and each other, individually and collectively. These shared experiences played a pivotal role in how the company's strategy was formulated. The bond they forged removed all sorts of potential (role-based and status-based) resistance. It turned strategy-setting into more than just a cognitive exercise by a bunch of intelligent people and made it into a shared experience. The entire Top 70 felt personally engaged. This helped to cement the strategy, encouraged the Top 70 to authentically carry it, and hence promoted its execution.

Useful Tips From Successful Leaders

Every chapter concludes with several proven, practical ideas that have helped leaders and professionals make a difference in real world situations. You can also use these as mini case studies and learning points.

1. **Down-to-earth and wild afternoon sessions.** A senior manager in financial services looking to renew his existing revenue and business models and to radically innovate, found that every time he tried to do both at the same time he ended up with neither fish nor fowl. His solution was to separate the activities and organize down-to-earth afternoon sessions for renewal and off-the-wall afternoon sessions for fundamental innovation.
2. **Portfolio doctor.** A business development manager got so frustrated with the ever-increasing number of projects outgrowing his organization's realistic change capacity that he decided to put a stop to it. He put this priority so high on the executive committee's agenda that it has become one of the board's core duties to cull the portfolio every six months, much to everyone's delight.
3. **One-pager.** One senior manager who believes in the power of simplicity has elevated this to an art. He demands that every strategic measure and every project from the portfolio is described in razor-sharp, concise language on a single page. Want to do the same? Use the fact sheet from Accelerator 2, accessible through download #10 from Appendix 5.
4. **Business planning minimalism.** A senior manager told me he prioritizes conciseness in every way, both in terms of time and the thinness of plans on paper.
5. **Storytelling.** One leader I interviewed is known for his "little black book." He pulls this notebook out of his pocket to jot down the details any time a "story" presents itself, either from a customer, an employee, or a supervisor; it doesn't matter who. And he systematically uses these stories.
6. **Shoulder the burden.** One executive board president at a Dutch university admonished his fellow board members to take their sponsorship of projects and programs more seriously. He felt many sponsored them only in name.

All these ideas call for valuable, but time-consuming involvement. To a great extent, time expenditure is what effective strategy execution is all about. "How would our time be best spent?" is a question well worth asking.

5

ACCELERATOR 2: INITIATE

Don't stifle the imagination / sensitivity analysis 13c / water is wet / 1016 soldiers / straddle the divide / Radio Moscow

When does this accelerator come into play?
This accelerator describes how to determine the content of every strategic initiative you have chosen, how to choose your approach and how to execute each initiative. This focus on single initiatives is crucially different from Accelerator 1, which describes the overall, company-wide strategy. From this point on, every accelerator focuses on what's required to successfully execute each strategic initiative you have decided to go with. That means we have reached the point where execution itself begins.

Recommended maximum time/resource allocation for this accelerator
Time box: five weeks on average for each strategic initiative.

That's extremely fast, and yet there will always be managers and professionals who want to get started on execution even faster. Don't fall into that trap. Keep in mind that it is prudent to proceed with caution, to go slow to go fast. In any case, both your analysis and design will have to be thorough if you're to succeed in accelerating during execution.

The hard building blocks in Accelerator 2: MUST-HAVES and BREAKTHROUGH

Every accelerator consists of two hard and two soft building blocks. The first two building blocks in Accelerator 2, MUST-HAVES and BREAKTHROUGH, are hard. **Building Block 5, MUST-HAVES**, is about the basics each initiative requires, namely a clear mandate, a sense of excitement and urgency, an answer to the Small Why, a business case and a hypothesis-oriented analysis. In **Building Block 6, BREAK-THROUGH**, you see why content matters. It's the backbone of any initiative. The Minimum Viable Product (MVP) you develop must be based on at least one innovative breakthrough.

5.1 Building Block 5: MUST-HAVES

This building block is about the basics each initiative requires, namely a clear assignment, a sense of excitement and urgency, an answer to the Small Why, a business case and a hypothesis-based analysis. You're going to explore the Small Why, your outstanding strategy questions, your main issue and how to choose the right approach and tailored expertise.

5.1.1 Answer the small why and outstanding questions

From the Big Why to the Small Why; how do you get there? In my description of Accelerator 1, CHOOSE, I argued that a good strategy defines a clear, appealing Big Why. Why are your vision, mission and strategy expressed the way they are? Why should you, as a professional, feel motivated to go through hell to achieve this? The answer to this question lies in what you do in Accelerator 2, INITIATE. Break down the Big Why and, for every initiative, define the Small Why so simply that even a child would understand how it contributes to the Big Why. But don't confuse the Small Why with thinking small, because that's far from the truth.

Imagine that your company is preparing an initiative—in this case, a takeover. Then the Small Why should answer the question of how the acquisition will help the company achieve the Big Why. It might read something like this: "This takeover will enable us to accelerate the renewal we aspire to. The business we are acquiring has a significant and growing share of our target market and has intellectual property rights that will lay the foundations for continued innovation."

Every initiative has outstanding strategic questions. Once the Big Why has been translated into the Small Why, there is another important step, namely identifying and answering those outstanding questions. Even the very best strategies leave some underlying questions unanswered, but at this point, you must find an answer to these. Let's assume the initiative you're starting in Accelerator 2 is an operational excellence program. In Accelerator 1 this program was branded as a crucial initiative in this year's portfolio. However, that strategy was set 18 months ago and the current annual plan only mentioned that the operational excellence program had to begin this year. In a situation like this, there will probably be many outstanding questions at the start of the initiative. These must be addressed before you organize a big kickoff and start doing your analyses. Examples of such outstanding questions are: What is the desired outcome of this operational excellence program? What links of the value chain do we need to tackle first? In which divisions and business units do we want to begin?

We are sticking with Kaplan and Norton. Kaplan and Norton's work laid the foundations for this part: translating your big strategic goals into goals for each individual initiative.[131] To apply this, let's continue with our example of an operational excellence program. We could decide that this is a must-win battle. It needs to deliver 10% greater efficiency, a 7.5% increase in productivity and a 5% boost in customer satisfaction. After all, better business processes lead to greater reliability, leaving more time to devote to offering better service.

5.1.2 Identify the main issue

Your goals point you to the dominant issue. If they're front office goals, like increasing your market share, revenue per user and customer satisfaction, the dominant issue is how you can improve and renew the strategic, tactical and operational processes that further these objectives. If your main objective is to increase your market share, you will probably want to do something about your sales strategy and your customer segmentation, your before and after sales service, and your delivery. You'll also want to take a close look at the kind of behavior that is appropriate for these strategies and processes, at your management structure and at all of the job descriptions for your salespeople and your support team. So, there are quite a few subsidiary aspects to a single sales issue. In strategy execution, however, simplicity is key. Therefore, you want to identify the issue that is critical to achieving your goal. In this example, the main issue may consist of two or three subsidiary aspects.

5.1.3 Choose an appropriate method and expertise

It's at this point that the risk of unprofessionalism is greatest. There's nothing wrong with relying on good old common sense. But in a world where distinctiveness is fading faster than ever, turning to specialized methods is a way to achieve real breakthroughs and to boost and bolster that distinctive character. Every issue requires its own appropriate, specialized method. You can't fix a broken arm with a band-aid. Likewise, an operational excellence issue in the supply chain can't be tackled using the same expertise you'd rely on for a sales effectiveness problem. And obviously, a synergy analysis in the due diligence phase requires a different method and specialism than an overhead value analysis.

It is possible, of course, to outsource expertise by calling in consultants, but every business needs to have the basic methods, specialized people and knowledge in house to deal with the issues that most frequently occur. Osterwalder and Peigneur's Business Model Canvas offers an extremely useful and successful format for innovating business models.[132]

Download #4 from Appendix 5 lists the most common strategy execution issues: Post-Merger Integration and Synergy, Sales Effectiveness, Lean, Corporate Culture and Conduct, and Structure and Governance. The download #4 from Appendix 5 leads you to a document that lists the main principles governing each of these big strategy execution issues. These principles are highly practicable, ready to use how-to's.

Avoid falling into the trap of quickly settling on a random method or even designing your own hobbyist method in a misguided attempt to keep things manageable.

A method or tool is a means to an end, not an end in itself. Methods and tools should be based on specialized, proven knowledge and experience. Think hard about the method you choose and why. Even consider whether a combination of methods would be better. I'll give you an example, and it's one that MBA nerds will love—just saying. Let's look at what method you'd choose for elaborating a Type 3 (radical innovation) issue. Professionals can get incredibly passionate about what to go with. Some will argue for Eric Ries's Lean Startup method, others for Change by Design by Tom Brown et al. Supporters of the Lean Startup stress that there's no better way to innovate than by basing your process on leaps of faith; you create a prototype and develop it through validated learning, with short cycles of iterating the prototype as suggested by direct customer feedback. Proponents of Brown's design thinking, by contrast, feel that Ries's approach is so clinical and systematic that it overlooks the real breakthroughs and creative solutions. They don't have any qualms about quoting Einstein even, who once said that imagination is much more important than knowledge. Unlike knowledge, imagination has no limits and gives free rein to progress and evolution. So, don't stifle the imagination, they say.

But maybe the best approach is to combine the two methods. Go for the best of both worlds.[133]

Analyze innovations in the market. You should bank on your own innovative capacity and originality, but don't be afraid to help get these kick-started by analyzing others' innovations. Every organization should be aware of the new business and revenue models that are out there, both in their own industry and beyond. For this reason, we have provided an overview of innovative business and revenue models in Appendix 5, download #7. This appendix lists Type 3 innovations (new business models) and links to an online list that is periodically updated (seeing as Type 3 innovations have a high failure rate and many new innovations are introduced every year).

5.1.4 Analyze

Gone are the days when business analysis was a viable topic for a PhD dissertation. In the past, it would take months of analysis before anyone dared decide on a direction to take in search of a solution. These days, that's neither necessary, nor possible. It's unnecessary because analysis methods and skills have come a long way. And it's impossible because speed and agility count if you want to survive. The new creed is: rigorous where necessary, practical and fast where possible. Analyses for their own sake are pointless. Sensitivity analysis 13c, variant 2, has nothing on number 4 and merely causes cramping and "analysis paralysis", as I once heard a McKinseyan say. It can even lead to a quest that lasts until a reason is found to do nothing, or "death by analysis". Also, the obvious need not be proven; so yes, water is wet.

Avoid false precision. I've lightheartedly confronted many a consultant about their false precision by citing a story (probably apocryphal!) about a battle between native Americans and U.S troops back in the 1860s. At one point, the Sioux had an Army outpost surrounded. Their chief wanted to know how many soldiers were garrisoned there, so he sent a scout to spy on the fort by night. When the scout returned to camp, he went straight to the chief's teepee and reported on his findings:

"1,016 Army soldiers there, chief" he said.

"How do you know their numbers so precisely, scout?" the chief asked.

"Well, chief," the scout replied, "the fence around the fort has four watchtowers and on each of them stand four guards. So that makes 16. And I estimate that inside, there are about 1,000 more troops."

Analyze the key processes and the aspects of the business model that make or break the goals. The best way to do this is by working with "as is" and "to be" hypotheses. "As is" hypotheses analyze existing facts, such as problems and strengths. "To be" hypotheses analyze opportunities, for instance by doing market research to assess the market potential of new prospects. Hypothesis-oriented analysis is the only way to quickly get a grip on problems and opportunities.

Figure 23 provides an overview of the types of issues, insights, frequently used analyses and methods. Good analytical instruments are key. I have seen quite a few good customer interview formats get turned into structurally applied instruments. There is no bigger compliment for your work.

Analyze your soft capabilities for each initiative by using a hard analysis tool. Analyze culture and conduct in relation to the goals you set for the initiative, just as you did in Accelerator 1 for the entire organization. Use the SECA.NU tool for this purpose. This will reveal your soft execution capabilities. You can use the results to organize a couple of qualitative sessions, in which your current culture is analyzed in relation to your current and new goals.

Successful Application of Building Block 5, MUST-HAVES

Case study: Two Dutch broadcasting companies in the run-up to their merger
Breakthrough: Their ambition was to become the largest broadcasting company in the Dutch public broadcasting system while implementing the cutbacks demanded by the government. Joint integration teams were tasked with fleshing out this ambition and forcing a break with the past. Each integration team was given a specific, synergy-oriented stretch target. These gave them the bearings and handles for making sound design decisions.
Impact: The integration teams' work led to an integration and reorganization plan that enabled the new company to realize both its quality programming and financial goals. Among the goals achieved was a 39% FTE reduction in overhead functions and a 25% cut in primary staff positions. Since then, the new broadcasting brand has carved out a prominent place for itself in the Dutch public broadcasting landscape.

Figure 23 — **The type of issue is all-important.** Ensure that you apply the right kind of analysis, method and expertise to each issue.

	Issue	Affected parts of the business model	Insight	Analyses and Methods	Type of Strategy Execution
1	**Strategy**		Market	Porter, Ansoff matrix	2, 3
			Product portfolio	SWOT, BCG matrix	1, 2
2	**Business model, innovation, sales**		Sales Effectiveness, Revenue Per User, market appeal	Value proposition, PMC matrix, Pareto (revenue, costs, profit), Customer Journey Mapping, Churn, BMC, OGSM, Massive Transformative Purpose (Singularity), Lean Startup	1, 2, 3
3	**Operation (delivery, logistics, sourcing)**		Efficiency and effectiveness of primary processes	Value Stream Mapping (VSM), Waste Analysis, Sawtooth Model, Swim Lane, Time allocation	1, 3
4	**Overhead processes (Finance, HR, IT, Purchasing, Facility Management)**		Efficiency and effectiveness of secondary processes	Overhead Value, VSM, Sawtooth Model, Swim Lane, Time allocation, Vendor Management	1, 2
5	**Knowledge & data**		Knowledge use and application	Knowledge management of the Value Chain	2, 3
			Performance history based on data	Hypothesis-driven Big Data Analyses (from correlation to machine learning)	2, 3
6	**Synergy**		Synergy targets and other partnership goals	100-day Method, Synergy sample book, due diligence of type of integration	2
7	**Structure & Governance**		Management Efficiency and Effectiveness	Overhead value, Business Performance Management, Balanced Scorecard	1, 2
			Financial Structure	DuPont	1, 2
8	**HR, culture & codes of conduct**		Organizational Norms and Values	Cultural Analysis and Development, Assessments (MBTI, MD, ID)	2, 3
9	**Leadership**		Leadership Style	Leadership Style Analysis and Development	2
10	**Overall execution**		Strategy Execution, Project and Program Management	MSP, Prince, LeSS, Agile, Scrum, Kanban, SECA.NU, Design Thinking	1, 2, 3

Source: Tjalle Hoekstra, Turner, 2016

5.2 Building Block 6: BREAKTHROUGH

Content matters. It's the backbone of any initiative. The Minimum Viable Product (MVP) you develop in this building block must be based on at least one innovative breakthrough. To identify your breakthrough customer value proposition, you take a series of methodical steps. I'll touch on creativity, Customer Journey Mapping, the need for simplicity, and your design's consequences for your organizational structure.

5.2.1 Methodical steps

To recap, at this point you have clear goals and priorities; you have identified the main issue you need to address; you have selected an appropriate, specialized method and expertise to do so; and you have analyzed the key processes and assessed your organization's soft capabilities. Now you can get down to business. Your next move is to take a set of generic steps and apply some basic principles, namely the timeless basics of problem analysis and decision-making.

The methodical steps that will get you from good design to Minimum Viable Product (MVP) every time, in every initiative, are:

- Systematically gather ideas.
- Identify the breakthrough customer value proposition.
- Design, redesign and simplify.
- Determine how the new processes affect your organizational structure.
- Integrate indispensable soft capabilities into your design.
- Write your draft business case and goals.

These steps deserve some explanation. In my explanation, I apply these steps to an initiative aimed at renewing or innovating customer processes. Ultimately these are the most important processes. If you were designing a different initiative, like a post-merger integration project, the steps and principles would of course be different, just as they would be different in a sales effectiveness program, etc. Appendix 5, download #4 lists the most common types of issues and links to a downloadable list of the main principles of each of these issues.

5.2.2 Systematically gather ideas

Create the physical and mental space you need to foster creativity. This may strike you as paradoxical, because creativity and stress do not mix and I keep emphasizing the need for speed—after all it should take only 3 to 5 weeks to complete this accelerator. Yet fostering islands of creativity in this phase is a must, and it can be done. If you take the approach explained in this book, you will be creating a climate of continual improvement, renewal and innovation. This means there will be a pool of ideas to choose from. It's more productive to select and harvest ideas that were proposed long ago and have been germinating than it is to hope for a miracle during a short afternoon workshop you crammed into your schedule. That's why you should set up a suggestion box where everybody can leave ideas. This provides you with a wealth of ideas to choose from during this phase.

Generating ideas should be possible anywhere, anytime. Creativity must be part and parcel of Running the Business. It is a continuous process just like delivering value to your customers. If your plan says the brilliant idea has to result in a rollout in Project Week 3, you are trying to force something that can't be forced. It also makes it more likely you miss out on some great ideas. If the flow of ideas is constant, all you need to do is cherry-pick. That's a whole lot easier than muzzling creativity when there is no initiative happening and then turning the tap back on when you suddenly do need ideas.

The selection of ideas is a balancing act. It is the same type of process as the selection of portfolios (Accelerator 1), which I described in Chapter 4. Essentially, you want to strike a balance between ideas for Type 1 Change (Improvement), Type 2 (Renewal) and Type 3 (Innovation). Another way of looking at this is to create a balance between ideas that have a high chance of success in the short run (Type 1) and those whose chances are lower (Type 3). Type 2 is right in between. The high uncertainty of Type 3 (radical innovation) forces us to draw up a list of 20 ideas and then select no more than five of them for actual experimentation. Incidentally, this selection process is one activity that should definitely *not* be done in a top-down way! Research by Stanford professor Justin Berg shows that managers and board members are the worst predictors of which ideas are going to prove successful. Lower-level peers are much better at this. That's good to know before someone suggests inviting the Board of Directors to take part in the selection of ideas. Don't forget that it was board members who rejected both Harry Potter and Star Wars.[134]

Don't stifle serendipity. Penicillin was discovered by accident. There are ways of increasing the odds of such fortuitous accidents. One of the most important is knowing which way you're headed. The better your sense of direction, the more receptive you are to other ideas that pop up along the way. It's a flexibility that makes you comfortable with being out of your comfort zone.[135]

Critiquing ambitious and creative ideas that can lead to a breakthrough is healthy. However, it's dangerous to do that too soon. Generating ideas is a different process than selecting ideas. Marty Neumeier, an expert in innovation and design thinking, has identified six factors that can stifle the imagination during brainstorms: an unfounded conviction, a lack of technical know-how, a rigid mental model, cafeteria behavior (this, but not that—stripping an idea of its coherence), fear of failure, and a fixation on the right answer.[136]

5.2.3 Identify your breakthrough customer value proposition

Think from the outside in. The outside equals your customers. Keeping your focus on the outside means focusing on your customers first and foremost, and on the value proposition you have for them. If there is one pitfall you need to avoid at all cost, it's letting your initiative fall prey to an inward perspective. Our research showed that the one thing most successful strategic projects had in common was a consistent outward focus. In all analyses and solutions, everything everyone did was driven by an awareness of the need to consistently think from the outside in.

Link every solution and design to your customers and stakeholders' goals and needs. Keep reasoning from the outside in. That's the hallmark of successful projects. To ensure that you maintain this type of reasoning, remind your team of these goals and demands at the beginning of every design and progress meeting. Project managers might find this hard to do, but they are usually praised later on for their perseverance. A refreshing way of reminding the team of these goals is to set up a customer panel. Customers like to give honest feedback, particularly when they know their opinion will be taken seriously. Just going through the motions of asking for their feedback will not work and can even backfire. It is also important that the feedback process is modern and professional—both in terms of method and communication. Both B2C and B2B customers are used to participating in renewal initiatives and radical transformations. Organizations such as Dell and Salesforce.com rely on collaborative design.

You are looking for a breakthrough customer value proposition. Identify the customer processes and solutions that can lead to a breakthrough. There are often many possible solutions, but exhaustiveness is not your goal. You need to find solutions that have the biggest impact on your goals, make the biggest difference and can therefore lead to a breakthrough. Many solutions have already been tried. It makes little sense to beat a dead horse. The question is which new solutions (or combination thereof) is going to make the difference.

Identify your customers' hidden needs. Digital innovation enables you to radically change and improve how you anticipate existing and latent customer needs. The basic drivers of customer satisfaction are: the quality of your product or service; quality of delivery and service (in full and on time); and value for money. These factors determine your customer KPIs: customer satisfaction (NPS), revenue per user (ARPU) and customer (lifetime) value (CLV), cross-selling, customer retention, conversion, revenue and EBIDTA. But what levers does digital innovation give you to create a unique value proposition? The key is to improve not only how you meet existing customer needs, but also how you are going to meet hidden or future needs—as strange as that may sound. Research shows that every 10% improvement in customer satisfaction results in a 2 to 3% increase in revenue.[137] Download #5 from Appendix 5, Identify Your

Customers' Hidden Needs, shows how digital innovation can radically change and improve the way you meet customer needs.

Customer-perceived value is based on overall experience. What companies ultimately deliver is not just a product or service. Products and services are at the core of an overall product or service experience which begins with the consumer's first exploration and lasts until the final customer service experience. This is true whether you like it or not, and if you fail to take this to heart you'll be outdone by a competitor whose product or service might be inferior but whose overall customer experience outstrips yours. That experience increasingly consists of digital elements. Social media messages on behalf of a product or service are not just media messages; they have become part of the product experience itself. These days, every object is surrounded by a cloud of information and services. That relationship is valuable. In short, digitalization requires multidisciplinary cooperation on customer experience—with more interactive moments, which create more opportunities.

Create a logical customer journey. Customer Journey Mapping has been around for a long time, but its popularity has rapidly increased thanks to digital innovation. The traditional marketing and sales funnel (Attention, Interest, Desire, Action), which steers customers to your product, hardly even exists anymore. Brand loyalty is no longer something you can count on.

According to McKinsey, your customers' decision-making process is a circular journey (end-to-end) with four phases: orientation; active evaluation (research) shortly before purchase; the purchase; and post-purchase evaluation to determine whether or not to buy the same product again next time.[138]

In these new dynamics, customer journey mapping helps you to put and keep yourself in your customers' shoes. The key advantages of this method are that it gives customers top priority, helps to identify latent customer needs and hence chances of growth, while also identifying potential synergies between (digital) channels. In addition, its highly visual nature makes it simple and easy to explain. Customers find it just as recognizable as employees do, which is always helpful in strategy execution. If you decide to use customer journey mapping, keep in mind a few important principles:

- Users are user archetypes who, taken together, represent the relevant customer segments.
- You use customer journey mapping to analyze and innovate customer processes, aka service concepts. Doing this means scrutinizing the

entire customer journey. Continually looking from your customers' viewpoint, you go through every stage of the journey, from identifying your customers' needs to your customers sharing their experiences. In between these two ends of the journey are other typical customer actions: research, selection, purchase, reception, use, change and service.
- In essence, the customer journey map is always the same, regardless of segment and channel. But to ensure that you sufficiently segment your customers and differentiate before- and after-sales concepts (or rather, processes), you map your customers' journey using personas.
- You analyze every touchpoint through every channel to judge whether this is where customer satisfaction is made or broken. By putting yourself so completely in your customers' shoes, you are sure to expose any inconsistencies in your service and between channels (web/mobile/social media/phone/store). Figure 24 depicts the Customer Journey Mapping process.

Figure 24 — **Customer Journey Mapping: (digital) process innovation that puts the customer at center stage.**

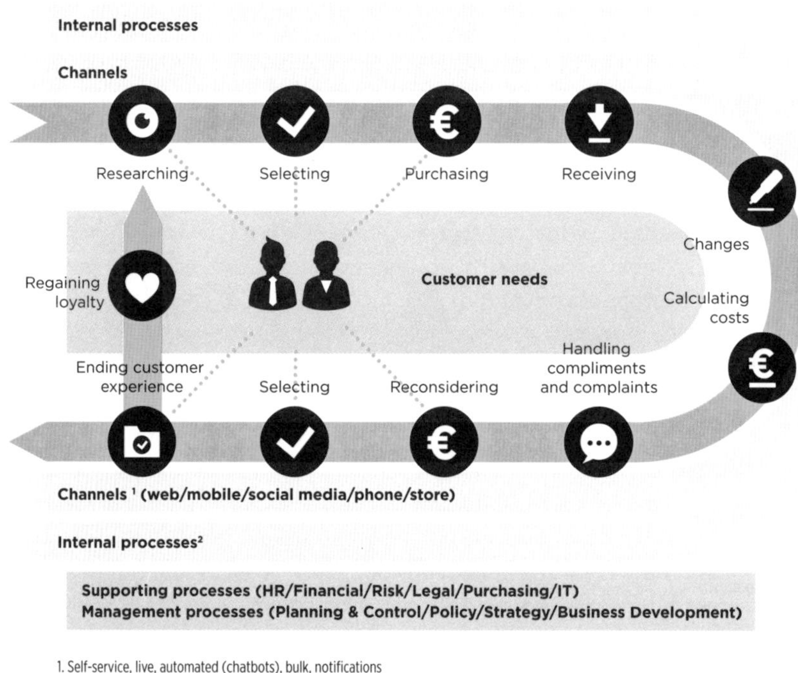

Source: Bas van Rooij and Patrick Eppink, Turner, 2016

Doing this systematically and actively seeking customer feedback allows you to identify the moments of truth, or points of delight. Obviously, you want to find the points of delight with the biggest impact and uniqueness, while removing the points of pain. There are two takeaways here. One: ensure enough peak experiences that deliver on the brand's promise and meet the most important customer needs. (Keep in mind, by the way, that 20% of your customers' needs usually determine 80% of their satisfaction. Which means you really need to pinpoint which 20% these are.) And two: your customers' final experiences during the final touchpoints largely determine their memory of the overall experience.[139] Figure 25 shows which touchpoints in the customer journey have the biggest positive and negative impact.

Figure 25 — **Customer Journey Mapping clarifies which touchpoints have the biggest positive and negative impact.**

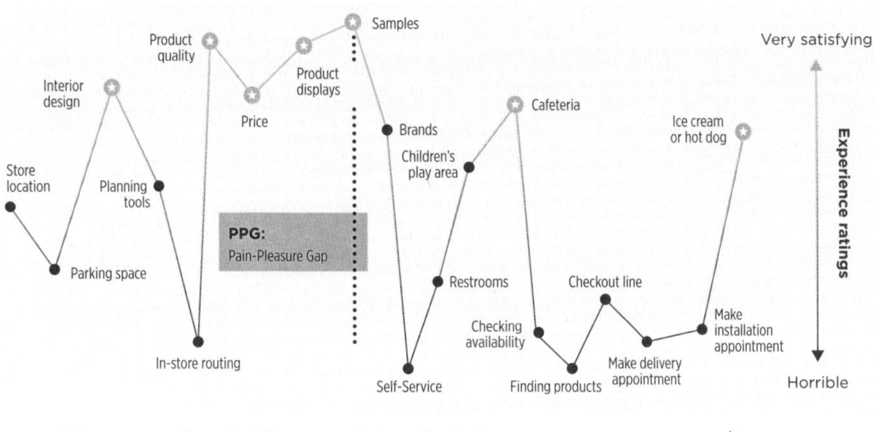

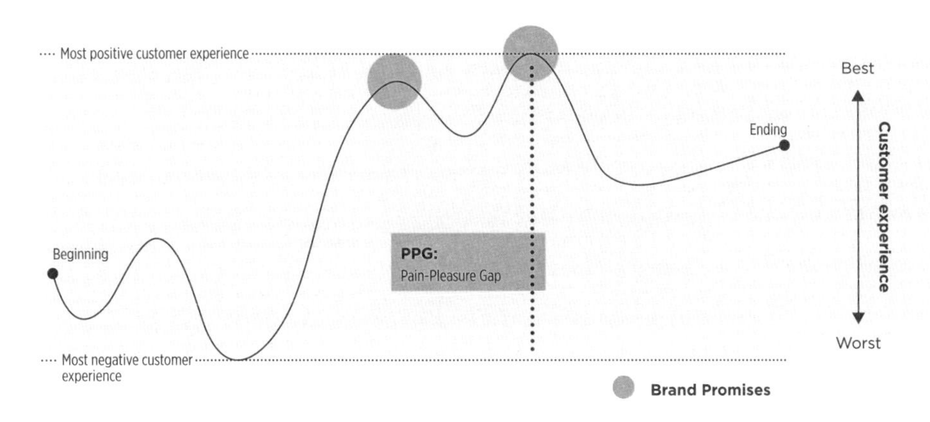

Source: Ikea Customer Journey

Customer processes *are* the customer value experience. In digital business processes, the customer journey is the main driver. McKinsey consultants always base their key conclusions on a firm foundation. They prove that you can significantly improve the customer journey by digitalizing processes. Their clients report increases of up to 20% in customer satisfaction. But the best thing is that they also see 10 to 15% revenue growth and cost reductions of 15 to 20%.[140] Greater customer satisfaction results from new and better ways of fulfilling customers' needs. The customer journey must drive all processes, but especially when digitalizing these processes. Every process must contribute to the customer value experience. Well-thought-out and well-executed digital innovation satisfies customers' deeper needs, builds community and enhances the perceived value.

What's happening here is fundamental. Customer perception determines your product's value and hence *is* the product. The traditional marketing paradigm was all about creating customer loyalty by keeping them in the cycle. In essence, this is a negative approach in which the company drives up switching costs, diverts customers' attention from alternatives and pushes customers towards those needs the company can meet. In the new marketing paradigm, you take a deep breath and accept that customers have, and deserve, the right to switch providers any time they please. Organizations have to anticipate this as best they can and seize any opportunity they see. A customer journey as shown in Figure 25 is the perfect foundation for this new approach. One promising fact is that in the digital era, the number of interactions with your customers increases significantly, in some cases from three to 11. The trick is to devise new revenue models that can capitalize on the opportunities this opens up, because creating value is not the same as monetizing value, as Henk Volberda, Erasmus University professor of Strategic Management, has pointed out.

Customer-oriented thinking is a hot trend in new businesses, and that's a positive development. Businesses ask their customers for (digital) feedback all the time. It's become so ubiquitous it might be going too far and could actually start to annoy customers. But let me give you an example of successful customer-oriented thinking. Knowing its non-digital processes were its Achilles heel, an organization with a new online retail business model decided to monitor these processes particularly closely. The business informed its suppliers they were going to apply a three-strikes rule. After two warnings of service mistakes, suppliers had one last chance. The business also introduced a stop button, enabling it to immediately remove a product from its website if a supplier failed a third time. These measures ensured customers did not have a bad experience caused by failing suppliers. The company enjoyed growth rates between 30 and 250% per year, making them a textbook example of how to assure quality.

5.2.4 Design, redesign and simplify

Identify key processes you can leverage to achieve your goals. Amid all the business processes, you need to identify precisely which ones can make or break your initiative's objectives. Those are the key processes you need to start working on in order to forge a breakthrough to a new business model. Ideally, these key processes consist of no more than 10 subprocesses at operational level.

Business process orientation is fundamental to strategy execution. One of the good legacies from the heyday of Business Process Redesign in the 1990s, is a lasting orientation towards customer and business processes in analyzing problems and reengineering processes.[141] This is an objective way of ensuring that you remain focused on reasoning from the outside in. After all, processes have no bias, unlike politically charged top structures, management and leadership issues, job descriptions and cultural analyses. The only value judgement you can place on processes is the question whether they achieve the company's goals. And that's exactly how it should be.

Business processes are also a practical peg for dealing with a number of elementary matters. They are useful for determining precisely where an organization's strategic capabilities need strengthening, for limiting the scope of an initiative, for setting, analyzing and designing priorities, and for objectivizing discussions. In addition, they are helpful for determining which dependencies need careful managing in order to guarantee logical coherence. By keeping your organization's process model ready and up-to-date you ensure that execution is happening with one eye on the big picture (see Figure 26). A Business Process Map the size of a placemat helps to get and keep an overview. They are made to be printed out and pinned to a wall, so you can roll up your sleeves and get to work and use that timeless business process orientation to good effect. Use your business processes as your basis, because these are objective. That placemat-sized business process diagram is an ideal peg.

Train yourself to think in processes. Realize how many processes every organization has. Any company that operates largely autonomously has more than 150 processes (see download #8 from Appendix 5, which lists 153 business processes). If we categorize these, there are 29 processes at the general value chain level. Beneath them, we find 40 primary processes, 36 secondary or support processes and 32 management processes. Plus the 16 change processes that are the subject of this book, of course: the four accelerators and their corresponding hard and soft subprocesses. These are the processes defined down to Level 3. IT development and standard operating procedures (SOPs) are down at Level 4, and have numerous subprocesses and workflows at even lower levels. Clearly, this is fodder for those looking to criticize an organization for its complexity. But I challenge anyone to identify an unnecessary process among those 153 processes! Obviously, you should try to keep processes simple by standardizing and automating them as much as possible. But that doesn't mean they don't exist. In short, this is a realistic count.

IT functionalities are usually set at Level 3, while SOPs for core primary processes are Level 4. It's a fallacy to think that only IT projects need a process architecture. On the contrary, every issue should be approached with the same objectivity and consistently be driven by your customer and business processes. Figure 26 shows the importance of business process orientation in strategy execution. Appendix 5, download #8 provides a further breakdown of each of these processes.

Figure 26 — **Business process orientation is fundamental to strategy execution.** A placemat-sized Business Process Map is a good peg.

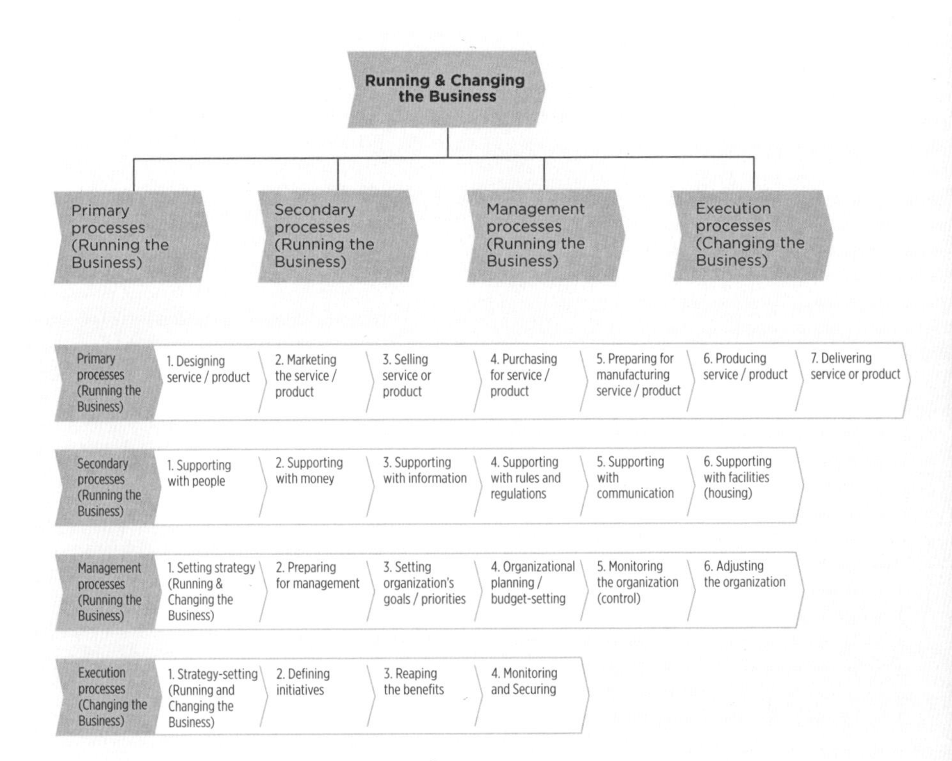

Source: Jurgen Frumau, Turner, 2016

To recap, this section was intended to establish the importance of business process orientation, enabling you to identify the key processes for each initiative.

Redesign your key processes. The creative solutions you selected in the previous step have empowered you to identify a breakthrough customer value proposition. Now it's time to elaborate these ideas as design principles. Examples of such timeless principles are:

- Eliminate any non-value adding step.
- Introduce proactivity (lay the groundwork before you start building).
- Integrate horizontally (preceding and subsequent processes).
- Prevent peak production, or design counter-cyclically.
- Segment and differentiate (as a rule of thumb, you need 3 to 5 process variations; fewer than 3 leaves you not enough to differentiate; more than 5 makes execution too complex).
- Apply the 80/20 rule.
- Use predictable or observable customer or product signals.
- Do things right the first time.
- Automate standardizable process steps.

Start by designing free-hand. Model later. By free-hand I mean that the medium doesn't matter at first. Some of the best designs I have ever seen started out as comic strips. But at some point, you will need to model your design into an architecture in order to achieve execution at scale. Hence, you'll need to select and apply some sort of process architecture method.

Simplify. Simplicity is so important that simplification deserves to be a separate step. Any new operating procedure will affect your current processes and require you to adapt those to accommodate the new process. Processes are like algae: they grow, but they never shrink. That's why you should simplify every project, regardless of whether it pertains to existing or new processes. Because no matter how creative or brilliant a design, it will usually be too complex rather than too simple. As management thinker Robin Sharma said: "The key to excellence is simplicity. Construct your life and your business around a few vital priorities and focus, almost single-mindedly. Distraction obscures what you're good at. But don't overdo it." On the same note, people often quote Einstein as having said: "Everything should be made as simple as possible." What they leave out, is how he continued: "...but no simpler." [142]

5.2.5 Assess the implications for your organizational structure.

The next step is assessing what implications your redesigned processes have in terms of management, HR, behavior, knowledge and resources. A brand-new process won't work at all if you don't implement the necessary changes in job descriptions, management and IT. Let's return to the sales effectiveness issue we discussed earlier. Let's assume you have come up with a new customer segmentation and designed the corresponding before- and after-sales service processes. Usually this will also require changes in management, conduct, support, and resources. Those may seem like minor, practical adjustments, but they are really important. A good conversion from design into organi-

Figure 27 — **A clear understanding of your business context and model is essential.**

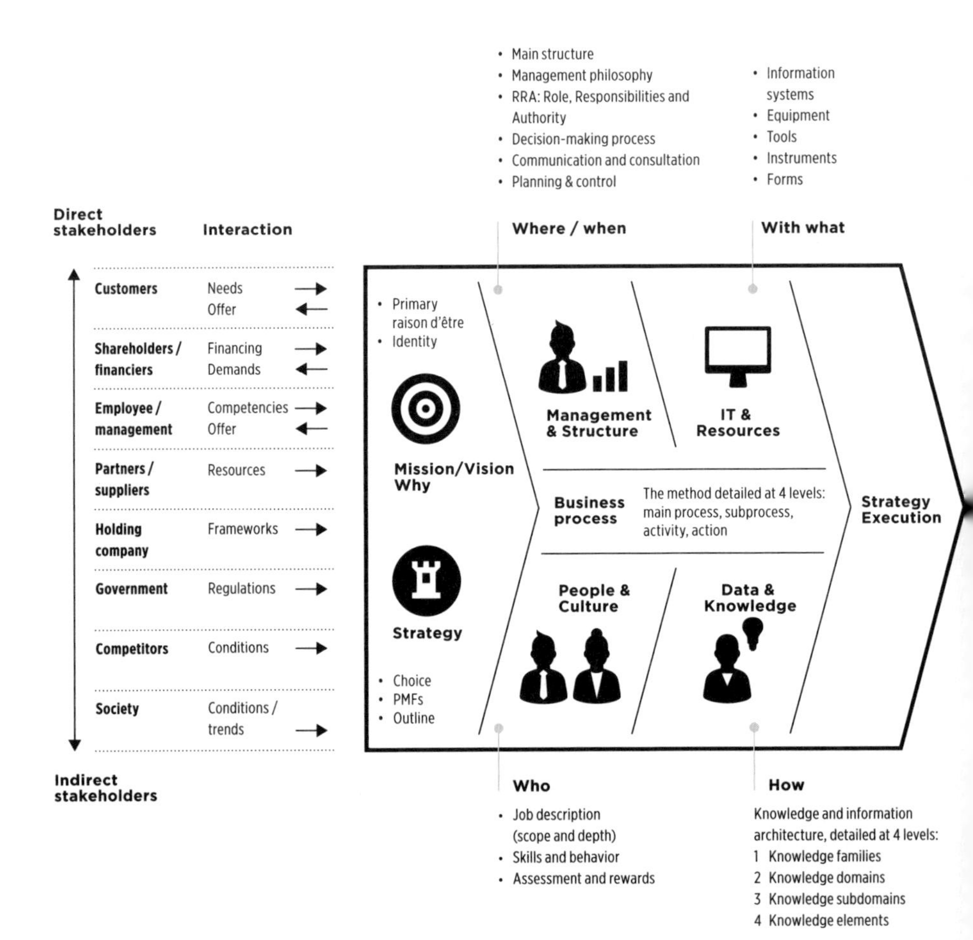

Source: Turner, 2016

zation ensures that the new process will take hold, creating a "retooled culture," as I once heard someone call it. This conversion is a matter of great precision, as illustrated by Figure 27, which shows how many facets of the business can be affected by a new business process. This is something you can't afford to ignore. Without a proper conversion, your brilliantly designed process will be unbalanced and not anchored by competencies, behavior and resources. Your new processes will be wobbly, like a bent bicycle rim.

5.2.6 Design the soft side

New processes, systems and structures are not enough to create lasting change. Corporate culture needs to change too.

Employee conduct is determined by several factors. Carrying out targeted interventions can help foster desirable conduct. This pertains to cooperation, leadership, responsibilities, communication, and confronting co-workers about unwanted behavior or the need for new behaviors. But how and when do you decide to intervene?

Edgar H. Schein argues that the only way to achieve cultural development is through the development of actual behavior.[143] According to him, behavioral development is useful only if you choose specific behavioral themes that have a direct relationship with specific goals and business processes. In other words, cultural change works only in context.

Attempts to change culture and conduct work only in conjunction with content, or your hard goals. Soft design needs to be integrated into your overall design by defining the actual behavior people need to display in order for a designed process to take off and by choosing interventions that are conducive to it. Forget those inspirational plaques with your organization's core values. They have zero bearing on the day-to-day, or on innovation. Here's how you design the soft capabilities in two steps:

1. **Select a maximum of five behavioral themes.** Each theme describes a type of conduct and the shift in behavior that will reinforce your goals and develop the culture. Your description must clearly connect the behavior to your hard goals and specify where in the overall design—in which business process—the behavior in question needs to take place. Behavioral themes must have a one-to-one correspondence with your strategic objectives.

2. **Select a maximum of ten interventions.** Defined as a conscious stimulus or activity related to a behavioral theme, an intervention is run parallel with the hard activities of a particular initiative to foster the

behavior necessary to achieve your hard goal. To ensure impact and focus, attempt no more than two interventions per behavioral theme. Otherwise, your approach runs the risk of degenerating into a general cultural program.

Let me give you two examples of an effective behavioral theme that is content-based and connected to hard goals.

Example 1. Positive reinforcement of entrepreneurship

1. **Goal:** Sales +10%
2. **Reason why you need a soft intervention:** In terms of content, your initiative is well-designed and solution-oriented. But you notice a lack of inspiration. The initiative needs something, an intervention that ignites a spark in the salespeople executing this project.
3. **Behavioral theme:** Entrepreneurship
4. **Possible intervention:** Dragon's Den. Although slightly hackneyed, this is an effective format requiring professionals to pitch a new idea before a panel. Doing this systematically normalizes the point that ideas are necessary and welcome, and that they're critically assessed before a decision is made to run with them or reject them.

Example 2. Positive reinforcement of overall excellence

Quality in little things = great professionalism.

1. **Goal:** Excellence, or going for 0 mistakes
2. **Reason why you need a soft intervention:** Spelling errors, not keeping small promises, not sticking to agreements; all of these tendencies have a disproportionally negative effect on customer satisfaction. And they can all be avoided, which starts with awareness.
3. **Behavioral theme:** Excellence
4. **Possible intervention:** Set a good example by ensuring all internal communication is excellent and free of misspellings. Raise awareness of the need to pay more attention to detail by lightheartedly but consistently monitoring the number of days without spelling errors and other minor mistakes. You don't want to breathe down people's necks, but you do want them to take excellence seriously.

These are just two examples. Don't hesitate to contact me for more examples of interventions aimed at modifying behavior. Be aware that soft interventions can be a huge pitfall. Every organization has its share of people who forget to connect soft interventions—aimed at individual and team development—to organizational goals. They get carried away and go for all sorts of spiritual and esoteric formats. Let me warn you:

avoid letting yourself get suckered into vague personal development courses. Choose your interventions wisely, because they are the foundation for the next building block, Excellent Start. To create a balanced MVP, you need both hard capabilities (processes) and soft ones (conduct, leadership and collaboration styles).

5.2.7 Create a business case and set goals

Create a concise MVP for a single goal and a single theme. Concise in this context means with the minimum necessary specifications, the bare necessities, the essence. Elaboration and sustainable concretization will follow later. At that point you will need to begin guarding against overcomplication. As I said before: take no more than five weeks for this phase.

Do not develop anything beyond what is necessary to start the first wave of execution, and limit the number of goals and processes in the initiative. The initiative might have three goals and involve five processes, but limit your MVP for the first execution to a single goal and a single theme.

Get your MVP ready for execution. Embrace agile principles. The term Minimal Viable Product (MVP) comes from the world of digital innovation, but has made its way into the world of strategy execution in

Figure 28 — **Design a Minimum Viable Product (MVP): a limited, yet complete initial design for a single goal and with a limited scope.**

Source: Turner, 2016

established businesses. Note that minimum does not mean sub-par. Instead, it means designing a high-quality product for a narrowly defined goal and a manageable scope, and getting it ready for execution. It is meant to bring about the minimum necessary customer experience, goals and functionalities. Don't forget the 80/20 rule: 80% of the effects result from 20% of the causes.[144] Though it does not always hold true, this principle is frequently applied in business administration, both in relation to problems (80% of complaints are lodged by 20% of your customers) and to positive effects (20% of your customers generate 80% of your profits). The 80/20 rule also comes in handy when defining solutions and that's how it's used here. When designing an MVP, focus on the 20% of functionalities that have the greatest impact on customer experience and your goals (see Figure 28).[145] In Accelerator 3, you will learn how to scale and iterate an MVP, using agile and Scrum principles.

The concept and principles of the MVP are universally applicable to Types 1, 2 and 3 Change. Obviously, an MVP intended for improvement (Type 1) is different from an MVP intended for innovation (Type 3), but their essence is the same: the design should not be overly detailed. You don't want a fully developed blueprint because you want to move on to execution as soon as possible. This is the same for any type of change, whether it is a Lean project focused on eliminating back office mistakes (Type 1), a post-merger synergy project (Type 2), or split testing a digital product innovation with groups of customers (Type 3).

Test whether the MVP will achieve the business case. You've set your goals, done your analysis, and decided what solutions will get the job done. Now you need to add metrics to the design. You have to define what you're going to measure during execution and how. That's always hard because you need to measure execution in isolation in order to get a clean reading. How much incubation time is necessary? Where do you draw the line between direct and indirect effects?

Proceed as rapidly as possible to the next building block: Excellent Start. You learn most from testing your ideas and solutions in practice. An ideal wave takes five weeks, which means its timebox exceeds the recommended duration for Accelerator 2. But this is where we cross over into Accelerator 3, which is all about the rollout. The execution team defines concrete sets of tasks and divides up the work.

Make value creation and achieving goals your top priorities. These are the same priorities you had in mind when you selected this initiative in the first place (when you were assembling your strategic portfolio in Accelerator 1). The same principles apply at initiative level: prioritize by value and urgency. Matters that are less important to value creation or goal achievement can be dealt with in later waves. That's how you ensure you get around to every idea, which is important because ideas with no follow-up just erode valuable brain energy.

The big difference between this and other methods is that you stop analysis and design (thinking) far sooner, and start executing much earlier. Your aim is to put your design to the test as quickly as possible, so you can see what works and what doesn't, and why. The sooner you start to experiment, the sooner you can adapt your MVP and start a second wave. So, yes, you're less certain of the final design of your product, but at this point in the process certainty spells a lack of imagination.

Agile for business processes. This way of working bears a strong resemblance to agile and Scrum, which have been popular in the IT industry for years. In agile and Scrum, waves are called sprints. Meanwhile, these methods have found their way into other industries, too.[146]There is also some overlap with the Business Model Canvas in the sense that this way of working is radical and practical.[147]

Successful Application of Building Block 6, BREAKTHROUGH

Case study: fonQ sparks off Dutch online retail revolution
Breakthrough: Much like Amazon, online retailer fonQ replaced the traditional brick-and-mortar department store in Dutch consumers' hearts and minds in no time flat. The company—with a name that sounds like the word spark in Dutch—offers a product range that it adapts daily to changing tastes and fads, while its same-day or overnight delivery brings products to customers' doorsteps in about the same time it would take them to go to the store. Getting to this point was not all smooth sailing. The company had its share of problems and hard choices to make. The business model is top heavy with details and conditions. But in digital business, experiment is the operative verb. The difference is made in operational experimentation based on facts (real data), prognoses (seasonal / pattern recognition) and customer traits (not segment characteristics, but unique markers). That's the arena where companies are continually looking for new breakthroughs in performance.

Impact: fonQ's strategy is execution. The company's development is not a straight line. It is continuously developing an even better paradigm based on a combination of hard data and its sixth sense about what the next trend is going to be. The story of fonQ's development is unique in that its implementation and strategy went hand in hand. The spark grew into a blaze: small got bigger, and practice made perfect. Failures equaled lessons learned. The business was based on a single basic application: a balancing act with a big impact.

The soft building blocks in Accelerator 2: EXCELLENT START and PSYCHOLOGICAL CHECK-IN.

As you know by now, every accelerator consists of two hard and two soft building blocks. Having dealt with the two hard building blocks (MUST-HAVES and BREAKTHROUGH), it's time to tackle the two soft building blocks in Accelerator 2: EXCELLENT START and PSYCHOLOGICAL CHECK-IN. In **Building Block 7, EXCELLENT START**, you draw up an execution plan that reflects the goals and priorities of your initiative and you implement your MVP. In **Building Block 8, PSYCHOLOGICAL COMMITMENT**, the Execution Lead (project or program manager) and other key actors in the vanguard commit to the initiative and its objectives.

5.3 Building Block 7: EXCELLENT START

Use the execution cycle (see Figure 29) to draw up an execution plan that reflects the goals and priorities of your initiative and implement your MVP. Execution is the name of the game now. In this first execution wave, your priorities are fast failure and success. Your aim is to do a quick experiment to see what works and what doesn't, and then to repeat this pattern, as a succession of short waves helps you progress faster. You are also looking to institute new habits and behaviors in the organization that will help to maximize the odds of a successful implementation.

5.3.1 Start executing

Execution begins with the writing of a concise plan. If your initiative has clearly defined goals and priorities (as it should), your execution plan links the actors to the goals, describes who is going to lead the execution and what the execution will look like. It's about *who* is going to mobilize the troops and exactly *how* they are to go about it. Based on the Accelerator 2 Fact Sheet (see Appendix 5, download #10), a good plan informs and motivates. At the same time, its importance should not be overestimated and writing it should definitely take less time than it used to in the old days. More important factors are who is involved in drafting the plan and how they go about it. I may be stating the obvious, but if the presumed lead and the key actors behind the execution are the ones to write the plan, they already half own it and are well on the way to the full engagement needed to fulfil their roles. It goes without saying that the Chief Execution Sponsor of the initiative is also involved at this point. In short, the plan must definitely be a co-creation.

It is essential to carry out the first execution wave with the people who were involved from the outset. The crux of modern strategy execution and change management is that one and the same group of people sets the goals, does the analyses, designs the process, writes the execution plan, and prepares the first execution wave. You may want to put together an execution team, because execution requires different skills than process design. But you definitely need an overlap between your design and execution teams. The hand-over and periodic coordination between the design and execution teams should be structured, parallel and iterative. The first blow is half the battle, so make sure it's on the money. Modern strategy execution is a healthy, high-pressure process. Think forward and start executing. Go for speed wherever possible and rigor when necessary. That is the divide that you as a leader need to straddle and embrace.

5.3.2 Carry out the first execution wave

Your main focus is execution. Because, as you are well aware by now, this is your first chance to test your strategy and prove it delivers. Strategy = execution. You will deal with iteration and scale-up in Accelerator 3. But right now, in Accelerator 2, it's time to start executing. This will teach you a lot about which scaling method might work best. So, let's dive headlong into execution and start executing your MVP with the help of the execution cycle (see Figure 29).

In essence, the execution cycle operationalizes standardized key moments. The 10 steps in the execution cycle are key moments. During every execution wave, you carry out a number of standardized steps. Figure 29 shows this execution cycle and the steps you need to repeat during every wave and for every target group. In between these key moments, everyone involved does a lot of hard work with as much professional autonomy and freedom as possible. But at those key moments, everybody gets together and you all take the next step according to a fixed format. Don't change the format. If you do, you are in effect thinking up a new method every time.

This execution cycle is not the latest fancy change management jargon. It's a clear-cut process that follows a fixed set of steps. Remember, standardization is a success factor, because it creates time and space for flexibility and creativity.

Figure 29 — **The execution cycle is acceleration operationalized.** These steps are repeated during every wave and for every target group.

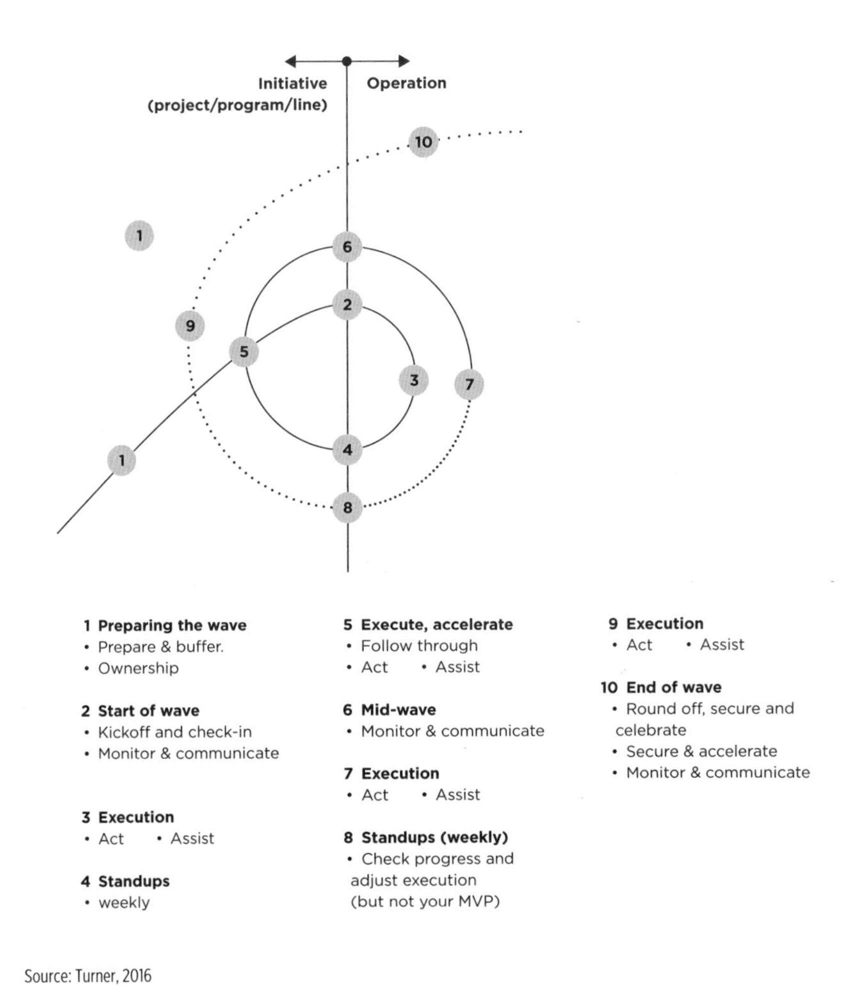

Source: Turner, 2016

These 10 steps have a clear beginning, middle and end. It's also easy to see the balance between give and take. The vertical line running straight down the middle of the figure marks the border between your project or program activities and your line organization. The execution's center of gravity is firmly located on the line side of the equation.

Essentially, every action of the cycle is executed in, for and by your line organization.

At the start of the first wave, your team lives and breathes the MVP. The key actors check each other's expectations and roles to make sure everyone is reading from the same script. Halfway through the wave, it's time to check progress. Things that need tweaking are tweaked, larger issues are put aside until further notice (or "sent to backlog" in Scrum terms[148]) and adjusted separately by your design team either simultaneously with the wave or at a later stage. At the end of the wave your team assess the results, your MVP and the execution. SMART agreements are used to adjust your MVP and the way it is executed before the next wave starts. Between start and finish, you need a few fixed points, such as weekly or even daily standups, to quickly check progress. Keep the agenda short: (1) what has been achieved so far, (2) what has not yet been achieved, and (3) what do you need? In between these key moments, everyone works autonomously, but not in complete isolation. Progress is shared among team members using up-to-date graphic and communication technology.

The most frequently occurring verb in the cycle is "to act," or in other words, "Go for it!" This pertains to your goals and the behavior necessary to turn the new process into new work habits.

Communication is an important aspect of the cycle. Those involved in the rollout should communicate directly with their co-workers and the people who will be asked to join them in the next wave. That's how you ensure that the first execution wave rolls right into the next one, which is far more effective than creating test panels, focus groups and brand ambassadors.

Resist the urge to adjust your MVP during the first wave. You will be tempted to adapt your MVP during the execution cycle, but don't do it. Stick with your design for the duration of each wave, otherwise you will lose track of what you're testing and learning. Adjustments are made at the end of a wave, before the next one starts. That's the way to iterate.

Short waves travel furthest. That's how my father once explained why I was able to listen to Radio Moscow in the Netherlands. In terms of the scope, a good rule of thumb is to include the same number of people in the first wave as have been involved so far. So, if 15 to 20 employees were part of the analysis, design and redesign process, then that is a good number to involve in the first wave. This usually equals one or two teams, or one department. Timebox your waves and limit them to six to eight weeks. Keeping them short guarantees maximum effectiveness.

Failure is a core competency. The motto "fail fast, fail cheap, fail often" definitely applies. People generally aren't afraid to try something and fail. What they're afraid of is the blame game that follows. In truth, the adage "to err is human" is often preached but not practiced and usually someone gets the blame anyway. We need to turn that around and say "to err is necessary." Failure is bad—and costly—only when it doesn't happen fast enough and when no one learns from it. Failure is fuel, and without it innovation comes to a standstill. One manager who was attacked for failed innovations responded cheerily, "Don't worry. I have at least ten more failures planned." Fostering a culture in which failure is seen as a precondition for progress is not easy. The Netherlands-based company ASML, the world's largest chip-manufacturing equipment firm, does a good job of sending the message that failure is fine, with a motto of their own: "You win some, you learn some."

Of course, the call for failure is not the same during a risky post-merger integration process as it is during radical innovation. In the former case, it is vital to control risks and prevent customer and employee attrition. In the latter, it's adventure time: you are exploring and experimenting and hence failing some of the time.

5.3.3 Foster new work habits

Soft capabilities are actually hard capabilities: you want people to develop new habits. Fostering new habits may well be the hardest thing to do. Your MVP has introduced a new business process. You have integrated the necessary behavioral changes into your design and have included KPIs so you can measure performance and hold people accountable. The execution cycle discussed above, and the scaling methods to be discussed in Accelerator 3, maximize the odds that your implementation will be effectively and sustainably staged. That is the goal you are shooting for.

In order to be an effective strategy execution lead, you will need to understand how behavioral change works. Nir Eyal is a successful young entrepreneur who has earned a lot of money from his own startups and who now lectures at Stanford. He publishes and speaks publicly about the interaction of technology, psychology and business and how this brings about behavioral change in customers and employees.

In his blog "The Strange (But Effective) Way I Stick to Hard Goals," he first cites a definition given by psychologist Benjamin Gardner from King's College, London: "[H]abit works by generating an impulse to do a behavior with little or no conscious thought."[149] So habits are simply what the brain learns to do without having to weigh its actions deliberately. Not all behaviors become habits. Eyal then gives a few good tips on how to develop new behaviors. For one thing, learning new habits is not rocket science. If you want to eat a healthier diet, don't buy unhealthy food; that's the best way to avoid another misstep the next time you feel like having a midnight snack. "Don't put yourself on temptation island," he writes.

Eyal also talks about writing a book. Writing is hard work that requires a lot of discipline every day. If you wait for inspiration to strike, you probably won't be seeing that book of yours in print any time soon. But you can give yourself a helping hand by planning your writing for set times each day.

This has big implications. Forming new habits is very different from following a ritual. For starters, you need to accept that new behavior is not learned through discipline.

Take discipline out of the equation in fostering new behavior. If the behavior you are trying to encourage among your employees requires too much conscious thought, it is unlikely to become an ingrained habit. Eventually, everyone will revert to old behaviors. The solution is to ensure that new behaviors don't depend on employees' discipline. An IT platform, for instance, can require people to complete certain steps before they can proceed. At Turner, you don't receive a billing code for writing billable hours until you have entered every last detail of your new client's data. As you can imagine, data entry is not an easy thing to get highly educated professionals to do. Still, this example illustrates an important characteristic of many new business processes, which is that IT plays a big role, albeit not an exclusive one, in reinforcing new behavior.

New habits also need to be reinforced by your culture and management. Cultural norms and values are a powerful tool for influencing behavior, but they also tend to be entrenched. If you've been insisting on risk control for years and now you suddenly want to encourage more risk-taking in innovation, it will not be easy. Management, too, should foster new habits. In my research, I encountered many situations where the need for more alignment between sales and operations was addressed by setting up multidisciplinary customer teams consisting of both sales and marketing employees.

Some behavior will depend on discipline, though. Some behaviors will never become habits, but are necessary anyway. These are your indispensable rituals and routines. Every new process comes with a number of tasks that do require new behavior, but will never become a habit.

Like it or not, every process includes a few unavoidable routines; for instance, writing billable hours or filing progress reports. This must be managed, to ensure it gets done. Self-management works best, but senior managers need to check on it too. No one likes checklists and policing people, but it is what it is. Chores are part of the deal.

Successful Application of Building Block 7, EXCELLENT START.

Case study: empirically seeking breakthroughs at Würth
Breakthrough: Würth is a German supplier of fixtures and fasteners for the construction and other industries. Its customer-oriented business model that truly puts the customer first, was stretching the back office very thin. This was the case in both category management and delivery. Meanwhile, margins were getting smaller and smaller. The company really needed to buckle down, but couldn't afford to start any big portfolio or customer segmentation programs that would cause major upheaval and interrupt daily operations. Change would have to take place in the line organization, where employees would use normal operations as their testing ground.
Impact: Practical improvements in the primary process improved revenue. The existing business processes were analyzed and simulated. That proved to be an excellent start. Experiments with the prototype and the new way of working during execution generated information about what worked and what didn't. Suggested improvements had to be easily implementable (in a matter of days). These ideas were then run through a computer simulation and if the simulation proved to be positive, they were implemented in practice at account, assortment or delivery level. Small changes were pivotal and were easy to monitor for their practical effect, even by employees from other departments within the company.

5.4 Building Block 8: PSYCHOLOGICAL CHECK-IN

This building block is about having the Execution Lead (Project or Program Manager) and other key actors in the execution coalition check in to the initiative and its objectives. The Lead, acting in concert with the Chief Execution Sponsor, will need to show change leadership so that other members of the execution coalition and beyond will also check in and show that they've taken ownership.

5.4.1 Write a story

In Accelerator 1, I explained the importance of a story to go with the strategy. Just as you need a Big Why and a Small Why, you also need a Big Story and a Small Story. Write the story for each initiative, preferably in the shape of a one-page letter of credence or as a one-minute video message. It should roll right off your tongue, or flow easily from your pen. If you can't come up with an appealing story to accompany the initiative, something is wrong. Any initiative that's key to a strategy and which people in the organization have explicitly committed to, must have a story. Your story about an optimization initiative in the IRS back office must be just as persuasive as the one about a "sexy" post-merger integration project following a spectacular takeover that dominated the front pages of the *Financial Times* for months.

5.4.2 Execution Coalition: Build Execution and Benefit Ownership

Essentially, you want to foster ownership. That's why you need to ensure that the key roles that are vital to a particular accelerator's main focus are filled by excellent actors.

In Accelerator 1, we demystified the phenomenon of ownership and made it more manageable. In that phase, the Chief Execution Sponsor and Co-Sponsor roles were most essential. In Accelerator 2, the focus has mainly been on the role of the Execution Lead. The lead must take full responsibility for the execution. Ideally, the lead is someone in the line organization who will also be responsible for the realization of the benefits at a later stage. The lead picks a small team of just a few key actors with whom to execute this phase. These Execution Team Members are jointly responsible for the execution. Execution in this phase means delivering the results of Accelerator 2, that is, an ambitious but feasible design and an MVP. Figure 30 shows the five key initiative roles and their relationship to ownership during Accelerator 2.

The execution is led and carried out by the Execution Coalition. Leading the execution, or change leadership, consists of forging the execution coalition for the specific initiative from the portfolio that is now beginning. This might sound touchy-feely, but teambuilding and cooperation for the duration of the execution is a non-negotiable factor for success. And execution starts now, so this is your only chance to get it right. The execution coalition's strength depends on its members' commitment level. McKinsey has shown that if professionals truly take ownership and have sufficient autonomy, the odds of success are 79%. Compare that to the typical 60 to 90% failure rate! Behavioral psychology corroborates these findings: if we choose to do something out of our own free will, we are five times more committed than when we are made to do something. "Wanting to" is much more motivating than "having to."

But intrinsic motivation alone is not enough. In this accelerator, change leadership also means that the Chief Execution Sponsor and the Execution Lead work together to reach out to people outside the coalition and secure their commitment too. You need engagement anywhere in the organization where you will eventually want to scale up. It's hard work, but well worth the effort to optimize engagement through communication and co-creation with external stakeholders. The same McKinsey study cited above reveals that organizations that do this are four times more successful than those that don't.[150]

An execution coalition maximizes your chances of success because it can secure not only alignment between Running the Business and Changing the Business, but also horizontal alignment across disciplines and vertical alignment across value chains. In this accelerator, alignment is mainly about aligning the various dependencies that exist between parallel initiatives with closely related goals and/or scopes.

Figure 30 — **The Execution Coalition: Execution and Benefit Ownership in Accelerator 2.**

1
Chief Execution Sponsor

- Forges the execution coalition and enables its constituent individuals to take ownership.
- Communicates with the principal sponsors who have a role in executing Accelerators 3 and 4.

2
Co-Sponsor(s)

- Helps the principal sponsor in kick-starting the strategic initiative.
- Coordinates with other initiatives in terms of content, change management and out of political/strategic considerations.

3
Execution Lead (usually a program or project manager)

- Picks a small team of key players who will jointly execute this phase.
- Prepares the decision-making process in conjunction with the principal sponsor.

4
Execution Team Member(s)

- Make(s) a clear commitment to spearhead this initiative// be part of the vanguard.
- Commit(s) to their specific role(s) in the initiative.

5
Benefit Realization Manager

- Envisions what ownership of benefit realization and the accompanying responsibilities should entail.
- Decides how the initiative is going to deliver the benefits.

Source: Turner, 2016

5.4.3 Have every Execution Coalition member personally check in

There is no ownership without commitment and vice versa. It's crucial that everyone involved feels ownership toward the execution and the objectives it is meant to achieve. This goes for all five roles in the execution coalition. A sense of ownership determines whether your strategy execution is led by one genius with a thousand helpers—which won't achieve a thing—or by a leader who understands that results depend on everyone in the coalition feeling personal ownership. Solid commitment also tends to cause some friction, though, because every professional who really commits to something also has a strong opinion about it. I have learned to appreciate that, but I have to admit that it can also be a bit of a pain. This is one of the toughest divides leaders need to learn to straddle; you know that you need to set a clear framework and assign clear tasks, yet you also know that things will only work if a potential lead is intrinsically motivated. And a lead's motivation depends on how much autonomy they have to carry out the task. A lead who commits to a task will treat it like their own business, and that's exactly what you're after. This requires time and effort on your part, though. You can't just call a potential lead from your car on the day before kickoff and say: "We'd like you to lead an important project. I know it's kind of short notice, but we really want you to do this. Can you be at the kickoff tomorrow? Oh, and can you address the team then too?" This, of course, is bound to fail. As one professional put it: "Dear manager, if you put more time into deciding which Aston Martin to buy than you spend clarifying the role you would like me to play, then I am not interested." See also the practical tips at the end of this chapter: the commitment café.

5.4.4 Expand ownership beyond the Execution Coalition

Increase external ownership through feedback, communication and interaction. In the old day, this would have come under the heading "communication," but as we established in Accelerator 1, communication is one-way traffic and as such too non-committal, particularly when your goal is to garner execution and benefit ownership. Communication is just one of the tools you need to build ownership. You'd better get used to this multitool approach, because it's something that will come in handy in the other accelerators too.

This accelerator is about paving the way for the inclusion of more key actors at a later stage. To this end, you should choose and organize activities with your current key actors and use the scope of your initiative to assess which groups, teams or departments will be affected by it later. This is how you lay the foundation for involving more people in the execution later.

In so doing, you need to make some clear-cut decisions. What target group do you want to reach, when, with what message and for what interactive objective? And what information, resources and formats are appropriate for this? Particularly the latter question is crucial. The whole crux is to come up with the right mix of activities that balances broad and narrowcasts, and one-way communication and interaction. You can use the menu in Figure 19 on page 117 to help create the right mix. This figure shows which formats and resources are appropriate for building ownership for each goal and target group.

Tone and format are just as important as the contents of your message. The activities you select for building ownership must reiterate and reinforce your objectives. Participants must immediately understand why they've been invited, what they can expect to happen, and what the anticipated outcome is, so they can take a position on the initiative from the outset. In this way, they can prepare and ask questions and express any doubts they may have. Only then can they take ownership. You also want to make everything personal. Use a variety of personal, social and structural influencing techniques to achieve lasting behavioral change. During each activity, test for motivation and ability. As David Maxfield has shown, successful change managers systematically use various sources of influence.[151] Let's look at a few examples of appealing ways you can involve people in debate and get them to change their behavior.

Gamification is part of organizational reality now. This is especially true in the realm of HR, where it offers a refreshing new dimension to traditional types of training. Traditional training has not lost its value, mind you, but it does have to be geared to the digital age. Generic training is pretty pointless. Gamification makes training more specific and execution-oriented . It works particularly well because people retain information they learn in a playful manner more fully and longer. This is of course a highly relevant quality for use in strategy execution and change management.[152]

If the laws of change have taught us one thing, it's that lasting change is hard to achieve. To illustrate some of the laws of change, here is something you could try at a kickoff meeting for a renewal project. Split the group into pairs and have the pairs face each other. Ask them to turn around and change five things about themselves. Then ask each of them to turn back and name the changes the other has made. This exercise shows it is hard to let go of the familiar, and harder to make radical changes than incremental changes. It also demonstrates how quickly we tend to revert back to our old behavior, because as soon as the exercise is over, most people quickly remove their Jimi Hendrix headband and restore their necktie to its proper place under their shirt collar.

Live the process. My final suggestion for influencing people's behavior is to use video. Record the old process, then set up a simulation of the new process and shoot that too. Then pretend to be a lab analyst and closely study the differences while asking the big question: "Have we achieved a breakthrough?" This analysis and your initial design will help you assess the impact of execution.

Successful Application of Building Block 8, PSYCHOLOGICAL CHECK-IN

Case study: Utrecht University of Applied Sciences, Department of Nature and Technology
Breakthrough: Process improvement teams within the educational programs checked in. In an effort to halt the decline in the faculty's educational outcomes, several process improvement teams started by actively engaging the teaching staff to get them to commit to improvement. In this way, everyone involved coalesced around a shared idea of the problem's causes and the solutions that could lead to greater teaching success, as well as clarity about the ways in which team members were expected to contribute.
Impact: In all educational tracks in the department, staff collaborated on improving student results. The process improvement teams were intrinsically motivated to increase the number of students who graduate.

Useful Tips from Successful Leaders

Every chapter concludes with several proven, practical ideas that have helped leaders and professionals make a difference in real world situations. You can also use these as mini case studies and learning points.

1 **Look at what others are doing.** As a strategic advisor to a Board of Directors told me, "Usually, people's fundamental analyses are fine. That's not a problem. But their analyses tend to be too linear. I always arrange for a couple of field trips to other businesses or institutions in a totally different field or industry. The idea is to see how they do things there and get some inspiration. More often than not, we come back with interesting new perspectives that can lead to refreshing breakthroughs."

2 **Analysis Menu.** In the words of one program manager, "Eighty percent of the analyses we do are very similar, yet people kept reinventing the wheel. I'd had enough, so I had them draw up a menu of frequently used analyses. Picking the analyses we need from that menu literally saves weeks of time."
3 **Database of ideas.** "One fool can think up more ideas than a dozen geniuses can implement," a COO once told me. "But the point is you want to select them and space them out. They often evaporate. So, I've set up a repository for ideas, which acts as a buffer. It has a calming effect on the organization. Putting an idea in the database gives people the feeling they get a mental receipt."
4 **Best practices and next practices database.** Another manager told me he set up a database for best practices and next practices. It's important to distinguish between these two, he emphasized. Next practices don't exist yet, which directs your attention to the next renewal instead of just circulating existing best practices.
5 **The MVP room.** It's pretty much universally recognized that it makes no sense to design comprehensive blueprints. An MVP is the best way to start testing your idea in the real world. Even so, an MVP is often still an abstraction because it exists only digitally or on paper. "Execution works better if you first bring the MVP to life in a special space equipped with physical design tools. In that MVP room, you can draw, shoot or paint the customer process, or really do anything that contributes to the verisimilitude of the scenario," one professional told me.
6 **The smart kickoff, Predictor 1.** If the signs are not positive, stop the process. Never waste a kickoff. A program manager once told me that when she discovered she had to battle for the time and resources for a good kickoff, and was supposed to be happy with the meager attendance at the event, she called it off. If the kickoff was going to be her party only, then there would be no party at all. These days, she even cancels if the chief sponsor and other key players from the line organization aren't showing enough engagement. "A smart kickoff is a huge opportunity to make progress in terms of your hard goals, and for laying the groundwork for ownership and engagement in terms of soft goals. The first blow is half the battle. Presuming it's on target."
7 **Commitment Café.** The most important thing is that people take real ownership and commit to the execution and its goals. Wanting to is much more effective than having to. As one senior manager worded it: "I put a lot of time into that, and I try to make it fun too. My favorite way is what I call 'commitment café'. I invite every key player, one-by-one, to go out for drinks with me. I order a plate of appetizers and we seriously talk about the challenge we're facing. I want to find out whether that key player wants to seize the opportunity and what they need to get the job done. If I notice a lack of engagement, I retract the offer."

All these ideas call for valuable, but time-consuming involvement. To a great extent, time expenditure is what effective strategy execution is all about. "How would our time be best spent?" is a question well worth asking.

And finally, Building Blocks 7 and 8 are universally applicable to Type 1 Change (improvement), Type 2 (renewal), and Type 3 (innovation). However, it is not one size fits all: you do need to differentiate, tailor and tweak, of course.

6

ACCELERATOR 3: HARVEST

A kitchen makeover costs $38,769 rather than $18,658 / the lone nut / eyes on the prize / vanity metrics / the two-pizza principle / a Baby Welcome Box distributor

When is this accelerator relevant, and why?
Let's be honest: Accelerators 1 and 2 are fun for most managers and professionals. Both require curiosity, creativity, innovative capacity and conceptual ability. But in Accelerator 3, which is about how to concretize and execute your design, a lot of people lose interest. That's unfortunate, because at this stage people need to be engaged. Otherwise, you won't get to the execution side of strategy execution. That's why Accelerator 3 is where the real change leaders surface.

Recommended maximum time/resource allocation for this accelerator
Timebox for each strategic initiative: five weeks to elaborate the design and five weeks for every execution wave.

Although this chapter is shorter than the ones describing Accelerators 1 and 2, don't be fooled. This is the accelerator you need to spend the most time on. In fact, this is the biggest factor determining your odds of success: spending 80% of your time and resources on pure execution.

And that's not surprising, because now you're getting down to the nitty gritty. This is where you have to show resolve and actually execute your plans, rather than thinking up new ideas while your earlier brainwaves haven't yet had a chance to produce any benefits.

The hard building blocks in Accelerator 3: BENEFITS and CONTINUOUS DEVELOPMENT

Every accelerator consists of two hard and two soft building blocks. The first two building blocks in Accelerator 3, **BENEFITS** and **CONTINUOUS DEVELOPMENT**, are hard. In **Building Block 9**, BENEFITS, you begin monitoring and reaping the benefits by taking your MVP through its first execution wave. In **Building Block 10**, CONTINUOUS DEVELOPMENT, you adjust your MVP based on customer feedback and practical considerations.

6.1 Building Block 9: BENEFITS

Now that your MVP is in its first execution wave, you can start monitoring and reaping benefits. This building block deals with the difference between goals and potential for improvement; the importance of benefit realization management; the need for a practical measuring method to monitor execution; how metrics help validated learning; and how to measure and harvest correctly from the very first execution wave.

6.1.1 Take benefit realization management seriously

There is an elementary distinction between an initiative's objectives and its potential for improvement. Don't get these two notions confused. Potential for improvement is an absolute and refers to the best possible outcome you could attain. Your objective is of a different order; it refers to the part of the potential improvement you want to achieve by a certain date in your execution. Determining potential improvement helps you to distinguish between levels of feasibility, which in turn enables you to set your goal based on urgency and feasibility. Such goals, set for your team or individuals, are often called targets.

This distinction between potential improvement and targets is not only an important difference in terms of substance, but also for managing expectations. Once people in the company hear and start sharing rumors of some extremely high potential improvement without mentioning that it is not the execution target, you'll never get the genie back in the bottle. People will see the lower, more realistic execution target as an initial setback. They might even deliberately frame it as such, if they have something to gain by that.

The best targets are quantitative first, and qualitative second. If you focus on the qualitative aspect of target-setting first, you run the risk of overlooking the quantitative aspect. Therefore, it makes sense to start with the hard numbers and then find a way to make them qualitative.

Optimal targets are 10% higher than the optimum. You don't want to set targets too high, because that will discourage anyone from trying. But you shouldn't set them too low either, and for exactly the same reason. You do want to build in some stretch, some tension between what people consider optimal and what you will ultimately be satisfied with.

Watch out for the planning fallacy when forecasting your benefits. Nobel Prize winner Daniel Kahneman calls it the planning paradox: the tendency to overestimate the benefits and underestimate the costs. An interesting 2012 study showed that Americans on average expected their kitchen makeover to cost $18,658, while in reality the average price tag came to $38,769. Analogously, many C-suite executives count their chickens before they hatch, assuming their projects will deliver far greater benefits than they actually do. At least, that's what they do privately. When communicating with the Board of Directors and analysts, they tend to build in some slack.

Benefits and benefit realization management. Benefits are the measurable, planned changes that result from a strategic initiative and are seen as beneficial for stakeholders.[153] Benefits are net results: what is left after the costs and negative benefits (which are not the same thing as costs) are deducted. Costs are things like investments in a program aimed at enabling the business to achieve the benefits. Negative benefits, on the other hand, might be the loss of revenue as a result of pulling out of a particular market.

In strategy execution, benefit realization management refers to the establishment, operationalization and use of a benefit measuring system. This is also known as business case management or target monitoring. But what's in a name? These are all synonyms for using metrics to measure the results of strategic initiatives. I use the term benefit realization management. Generally, this is called business performance management, which is about measuring the results of day-to-day executive management (Running the Business) and of improvement, renewal and innovation management (Changing the Business). You can determine how these translate into your KPIs in terms of customer and employee satisfaction, revenue, profit, etc. But tracking your improvements (Type 1), renewals (Type 2) and innovations (Type 3,) in their own right is much harder. And yet that is exactly what you want to do.

You will need to put more and more resources (time, money, and energy) into improving, renewing and innovating. After all, the results will enable you to better compete and survive. But then you do need to know exactly what works and what doesn't, and you also need to differentiate between Types 1, 2 and 3. Measuring an improvement project (Type 1) and drawing conclusions based on those data is not the same as measuring progress and interpreting data in a radical innovation project that results in new business models (Type 3).

The benefit tree structure. Look long and hard at the KPIs you decide to use for obtaining metrics on benefits. Not all performance indicators are suitable for measuring whether you're getting the desired results. Sometimes you need to use sub-KPIs that you can later combine to measure your final KPI. Add to that the fact that many KPIs are interrelated and you get the picture: this needs careful consideration. During the design of the prototype in Accelerator 2, your metrics team and your design team can already map out most of the variables, including the relationships between them, in order to get a grip on the whole system of variables. For example, more hits on a website convert into more requests for a quote, which convert into increased sales. Ultimately you want to build a KPI tree structure that includes all your final strategic goals, your benefits, your KPIs and the relationships between them. Download #9 from Appendix 5 gives an overview of commonly used KPIs, or metrics.

Plot the benefits against the stakeholders too, and mark the intersections between them with a code that indicates whether a benefit has a positive, neutral or negative impact on your stakeholders. You may end up with a pretty lopsided relationship where there are plenty of green marks in the shareholder column, too few in the customer column, and none in the employee column.

Benefit ownership is key in benefit realization management. If there is one key aspect to benefit realization, it's ownership of specific benefits. This needs to be worked out well. Find someone who you think qualifies early on in the game and give them an opportunity to personally commit (check in) to this benefit. This maximizes your chances that they will really go for it. In the same vein, you need to break down the overall benefit accountability into sub-responsibilities at team and individual level. Are all the right people worrying about the right responsibilities, or is it all on the shoulders of one lone nut? This makes the difference between a whole team celebrating the realization of the benefits, or just one individual.

Keep your eyes on the prize. Keep checking whether your initiative's goals and benefits are in keeping with the overarching organizational objectives. Every initiative must contribute to "the prize." But keep an eye out for side effects, too, like serendipitous benefits. A friend of mine set up an international advertising platform for the gaming industry, and in the process acquired huge amounts of data about that industry. That data proved more valuable than his advertising commissions-based revenue model. Fortunately, he had the presence of mind to embrace those unforeseen benefits and integrate them into his business model.

Benefit realization management can be hard. It can be difficult to determine how much of your increased revenue results from your sales effectiveness project because it's hard to isolate that project's contribution from other variables such as unexpected market fluctuations (other than normal seasonal fluctuations), the return of your top salesperson from a sabbatical, or the immediate impact that quarterly economic indicators have on consumer spending. Some people get so paralyzed by these factors that they decide not to measure anything at all, but others have the guts to make assumptions, objectivize the subjective to the best of their ability, and to be transparent about how they're doing that. They then come up with scenarios and conduct sensitivity analyses, enhancing their ability to isolate and take the measure of a project's contribution. I highly recommend taking the gutsy approach.

Appoint a separate benefit realization manager/team, but ensure close contact with your project and program managers. Benefit realization management provides direct input for action, risk and progress management. If you are dealing with a complex program, it makes sense to set up a small metrics team. But the team must stay in close contact with the program management office because the metrics people and the program manager need to confer regularly about what needs to be done. If you consider combining benefit realization management for Running the Business and Changing the Business, make sure the responsibility for both lies with one and the same person.

Benefits must not get in the way of other benefits. Sometimes a project really takes off and achieves great benefits far more quickly than expected. Even so, your primary processes must always remain your top priority, because the day-to-day of Running the Business must continue at all costs.

6.1.2 Set up a practical measuring system

Use a simple measuring system. Once you've translated an initiative's maximum potential for improvement into a concrete execution target, you need a way to size up how well you are doing. Your analysis and design should be based on a quantitative foundation expressed in a number of substantial spreadsheets. For instance, a program aimed at cutting costs and improving back-office quality by means of effectiveness and efficiency targets definitely needs some strong independent analyses and benchmarks. Ultimately, those need to be condensed into a number of summaries that give a concise overview of the objectives, analyses, designs and business case at a glance. These summaries are often what you use to define a target for each process and, of course, to link this to the appropriate execution and benefit owners.

Measure! The key is to start measuring right away on the initiative you are executing. Effective leaders monitor the progress of the entire portfolio on a quarterly basis, and current initiatives every month. Better face the devil than fumble around blindfolded.

As we saw in Accelerator 2, you set goals at both strategic level and initiative level. If your goal is to realize 10% growth in a consolidating market, you will probably need to combine all three types of change initiatives. All leaders know how to forge growth targets by approaching them from several angles at the same time. Let me give three practical examples:

Sample Type 1 initiative: improvement project aimed at winning more contracts and thus increasing revenue from existing markets and customers. Type 1 Change (improvement) tends to focus on single goals and is executed in a single process within a single discipline. Its clarity of scope makes such an initiative easy to measure. In this example, a professional service organization implemented a Lean project to improve its tender conversion rate. Before the initiative, their conversion rate was one in seven. A process improvement team analyzed the situation and identified some quick wins and some minor and major improvements to be made in the sales process. The improvements had to do with optimizing the translation of customers' request into deliverables; incorporating time for iterative consultation with the customer (instead of pretending that a single discussion is a good enough basis to make a tender); and explicitly formulating a vision on the customer's request rather than simply copying the request.

By making these changes, the company improved its tender conversion to one in five in just three months, and one in four after six months. Without erring on the side of false precision, the process improvement team had made a baseline measurement and set up a clear-cut measuring system with three simple corrections built in: one for seasonal fluctuations; one for organic growth and what the day-to-day of Running the Business contributed to this; and one for employee turnover (the organization was growing and hiring new people). The team also introduced several objective measurement points. Once a month, the improvement project's contribution to the growth target was measured. Obviously, the team also took care of the change management basics (the soft capabilities). Many people find this hard to do, but it's simply a matter of involving all your sales professionals, especially those who were not involved in the first analyses. It really is as simple as that, so don't overcomplicate it.

Sample Type 2 initiative: a post-merger integration project aimed at sales synergy. Type 2 changes (renewal) tend to focus on achieving several objectives simultaneously and often affect multiple processes, disciplines and departments. In this example, the integration project followed the takeover of one wholesaler by another wholesaler. Mergers and acquisitions are often called mergers and scourges because of their notoriously low success rate in creating actual synergy. Obviously, the main reason for this failure is a lack of post-merger integration effort. This is often foreshadowed by the absence of a post-merger integration section in the due diligence report preceding the deal. In this example, however, both the goals and the post-merger integration mandate had been clearly defined. There were explicit goals in terms of sales synergy. The two wholesalers asked themselves what markets and customers they could jointly serve more efficiently, and how. Mergers often cause short-term customer churn because the businesses are too inwardly focused, but in this case, there was a plan in place to prevent this. One of the measures was to create a red carpet treatment plan for both wholesalers' top ten accounts by dedicated account teams from both organizations. Another common post-merger problem is a talent drain. To tackle this, the new organization had rigged up an actual talent management process. They had identified the top 50 employees in both businesses and arranged for each of them to have a personal interview with an envoy from the new board and their new manager. This was quite a feat, considering how long it can take for a merged business to come up with a new top 100. However, the new organization made it a top priority to complete the process in less than two months. And even in cases where things had not quite crystallized, the interviews simply went ahead anyway. Although the goals of this post-merger initiative affected strategic, sales, marketing and HR processes, they were kept measurable.

Sample Type 3 initiative: innovation project aimed at creating new revenue and business models that must make a measurable contribution to the organization's growth targets. At its most extreme, Type 3 Change (radical innovation) does not affect any existing process, discipline or department. It is essentially the creation of a new business model, after all. However, measuring its effects is not so simple. As I mentioned in Accelerator 1, it makes a lot of sense to use Eric Ries's Lean Startup model for radical innovation. This is not only an excellent innovation method, it also explains very well how to measure execution. Ries warns against vanity metrics and recommends creating real innovation accounting in reference to digital business models. Vanity metrics measure the total number of registered users and the total number of customers. These are not useless parameters per se, but actionable metrics are also needed.[154] However, real innovation accounting involves setting up a disciplined system to determine whether we're achieving what we are aiming for by validated learning through experimentation. Investment firm Andreessen Horowitz has drawn up a list of 32 startup metrics, intended specifically for digital innovation (Type 3 Change). These metrics range from financial and business-related metrics, to product and engagement metrics. This list—included in download #9 from Appendix 5—is well worth studying.[155]

6.1.3 Use validated learning

Validated learning in Type 3 innovation projects is showing proof of progress while facing the uncertain conditions in which most startups operate.[156] Validated learning is the process of collecting practice-based evidence of truths about your current and future customers. It is much more concrete, accurate and faster than market prognoses or classical business planning. It is all about learning. Anything other than learning from your users is eliminated. In other words, validated learning is learning based on your organization's actual development and is supported by real customer data. A startup should conduct experiments that enable the organization to learn and successfully navigate through uncertain waters.

Convert your leap-of-faith assumptions to a quantitative model.[157] Innovation accounting consists of the following steps: One, use your first MVP to collect real data about your baseline. Two, try to fine-tune your engine right from the start by tweaking your MVP. Three, iterate your MVP to optimize it through validated learning. The closer to the optimum you get, the faster you can decide whether to persevere or pivot.[158]

Split tests and cohort analyses are two of the most important tools in the Lean Startup method. Instead of looking at a cumulative chart of your revenue or number of views, you look at separate groups of customers (cohorts).

Metrics are what enable you to measure progress. Metrics need to meet three requirements. First, they must be actionable. They have to show a causal relationship, e.g. views per day. Second, they must be accessible. Only then can they be analyzed, and if they aren't accessible they are a waste of your time. Third, they need to be verifiable. You have to be sure they are accurate and timely. Any metric that does not meet these three requirements is a vanity metric, a metric that is not actionable.[159]

Avoid vanity metrics. A large scientific publishing company was careful to avoid the pitfall of vanity metrics. The organization had a balanced portfolio of innovation initiatives. Knowing that successful innovation is far from easy, the company religiously applied Eric Ries's Lean Startup principles. Their exemplary portfolio showed a wide and extensive exploration of ideas throughout the entire company; a selection of ideas based on customer value and opportunities; and experimentation. The number of experiments they carried out was based on a simple calculation: how many experiments do we need in order to end up with enough successful ones? What can we handle and what is measurable? The publisher also made sure there was a balance between internally generated innovation experiments and startups, spinoffs and acquisitions. See Figure 15 on page 109 for a reminder of how to organize radical innovation. The publisher in this example used metrics to monitor the progress of innovation experiment execution.

6.1.4 Measure and harvest

You started your first execution wave back in Accelerator 2. This is worth its weight in gold for your main goal of realizing your strategic objectives, but also for feeding your learning and measuring process. You find out what works and what does not. And you learn how to measure effectively (see Figure 31).

Figure 31 — **Measure the business case realization of initiatives, independent of the contribution your day-to-day management makes to your strategic goal.**

	Goals	Contribution that managerial excellence makes to goals and progress	Execution format (project/ program/ M&A)	Contribution that execution excellence makes to goals and progress	Rating
1	**1 EBIDTA margin: +2,5%, 20 => 22,5%**	1%	Commercial excellence project	Goal: 1.5%, progress at 25% of execution: 0.5%	
2	**Innovation: 10% revenue from products < 2 yrs., 5 => 15%**	None	Innovation projects	Goal: 10% increase, progress at 10% of execution: 2%	
3	**Customer satisfaction: NPS 8 => 9**	0.5 NPS point	Commercial excellence project	Goal: 0.5 NPS point, progress at 35% of execution: 0.2	
4	**Delivery reliability +10%, 85 => 95%**	None	Supply chain program	Goal: 10% increase, progress at 75% of execution: 8%	

Source: Turner, 2016

Apply the basics of performance management. Performance management is a well-researched topic. Most of the information available is about performance management systems in regular Running the Business environments. Most of the success factors from this system can also be used to measure your execution, but some apply uniquely to the Changing the Business environment:[160]

1. A realistic discrepancy between ambitious and feasible goals. Rule of thumb: ensure that four to five of your 20 to 25 KPIs are really stretching it, while the rest are realistic.
2. Experientiality of the selected KPIs: you don't want a paper tiger.
3. Specificity and SMART-ness (however cliché this may seem), both in terms of content and timing of your targets. "A few" is not a number and ASAP is not a fixed date.
4. The leeway to cross discipline and department boundaries.
5. A healthy balance in goals, which requires you to have at least two goals. Even a cost reduction program should have a continuity goal and a renewal goal, so that cuts are made with a view to keeping talent and capabilities for future growth.
6. Define your targets from your stakeholders' point of view and from the outside in, and think their consequences through.
7. Keep it simple, not only in terms of executionability, but also of metrics.

8 Think. And think again. Even target debates are often too superficial.
9 Align your targets with the current KPIs and targets of your existing performance management system.
10 Set up your system as a dynamic one; the whole point of measuring is to enable yourself to make adjustments.

Successful Application of Building Block 9, BENEFITS

Case study: International bank: visible benefits help "sell" change
Breakthrough: Short-cycle reaping of benefits. In various divisions of an international bank, several change projects have been initiated that need to be rolled out in all countries where the company is active. The changes involve a new Target Operating Model (TOM) and a program aimed at breaking down silos to generate maximum customer value (PRIME). Although IT tends to be a key enabler in the financial services industry, the bank has decided to implement non-technological solutions only, simply because an IT development project would take too long. The program is led centrally, but the mandate lies with the line organization in the individual countries. Hence, that is where the benefits are realized as well. There is a rollout schedule for the various clusters of countries.
Impact: An enormous boost in the realization of strategy. Using international benefit tracking, the team visualized how the incentive for taking part was directly proportional to the envisaged benefits. Even though benefits in one country do not mean anything for the chances of success in another, measuring the benefits is key to cue the branch offices' willingness to change. The program measures both direct and indirect effects, and both quantitative and qualitative indicators of customer satisfaction, cost reduction, and simplification. Program management has designed a worldwide transition dashboard that shows both the change effort (in time and money) and the metrics per country. Weekly reviews and a focus on the demonstrable correlation between effort and effect have moved the program smoothly forward. The team is achieving excellent operational results; every six months it cuts through the banking world like a hot knife through butter.

6.2 Building Block 10: CONTINUOUS DEVELOPMENT

In this building block, you are going to work out the details of the resources you need for implementation and set up a business case monitoring system. Continuous alignment with other initiatives and disciplines has to become second nature. You are going to continue to develop your MVP based on customer needs and responses. Topics covered in this building block are getting your MVP ready for implementation; aligning your MVP; your execution resources; and further developing your MVP using agile principles.

6.2.1 Concretize and align your MVP

Your MVP is not ready for large-scale execution. This is true of all initiatives, regardless of whether they are Type 1, 2 or 3. There is still a gap between your MVP—your first design of the solution and your prototype of the new business process—and execution. The level of specificity needed to involve larger cohorts of employees after your initial execution wave is often higher than what was achieved in Accelerator 2. And your goal is different too. In Accelerator 2, your goal was to get concrete enough to be able to start execution and to do a first experiment with a small group of users. Once this has been achieved, your next goal is to get your concise design, or MVP, ready for the next wave of execution. The punctilious people on your team will seize this opportunity to do more in-depth analyses and draw more detailed conclusions. The flexible and expeditiously inclined people will see this as the time to dive headlong into execution. It's up to you to bridge the gap between the two. Trust me, there is a golden mean to be achieved!

6.2.2 Work out the details of your execution resources

Traditionally, organizations have treated execution resources as strategy and execution's poor cousins. A concretized MVP does not become executionable by waving a magic wand. You need resources to execute it. This is crucial, because you don't want to have to rely on oral instruction only. It's true that people do the actual executing and, for this reason, oral and personal execution are the most important formats, but execution should not entirely depend on these formats. Your MVP also needs to be legible in its own right and should in fact be so well written that it cues most of your execution capacity. It should be so inspirational that the people who read it are just dying to get involved in the next execution wave!

In terms of execution resources, you need both content-based and change-oriented resources: a practical digital checklist for a new process; a mini-protocol with a simplified version of all processes involved; a letter of credence in video format; a personal manifesto format; and a Q&A database.

One indispensable execution resource is the Execution Tool Kit. It is designed to present the whole design and MVP on a silver platter to anyone who is new to the initiative. This tool kit needs to both informative and tempting. Its structure—head, tail and body—must be well thought out. It consists of: a crystal clear ten-pager detailing the initiative's who, what, why, where, how, and with whom; a convincing letter of credence from the Chief Execution Sponsor, preferably in video format; and a carefully balanced summary of content and the analyses that led you there. In short, it should contain a mixture of hard goals and soft, change-oriented elements.

6.2.3 Continue to develop your MVP

New or redesigned business models are digital by definition. As we saw in Accelerator 2, continuous development of your MVP is relevant to any type of rollout, but most definitely to cases where the MVP and its business process are heavily IT-dependent. This will often be the case, because these days, almost all processes are data-intensive and digitalization is spreading like wildfire through existing and new revenue and business models.

Continuous development ≠ scaling. Developing new versions of your MVP (1.0, 2.0, 3.0) is altogether different from scaling a single version. The latter will be discussed in the second part of Accelerator 3 (on soft capabilities). Here, we're dealing with the former. How do you continue to develop your MVP into new and better versions? The key is to use customer data for agile iteration.

Do not try to reinvent the wheel when it comes to picking a development method. What I am referring to are development methods that are known to deliver increasingly successful renewed or innovative business models (Type 2 and Type 3 change in our lingo). Agile development encompasses many different methods, of which Scrum is the main one. The following section provides an overview of key concepts from agile development in general, and Scrum in particular.

6.2.4 Know your way around agile

Agile is an influential school of thought. Its manifesto was drawn up by a group of software developers in Utah in 2001:

- Individuals and interactions over processes and tools
- Working software over comprehensive documentation
- Customer collaboration over contract negotiation
- Responding to change over following a plan

The 12 principles behind the Agile Manifesto

1. Our highest priority is to satisfy the customer through early and continuous delivery of valuable software.
2. Welcome changing requirements, even late in development. Agile processes harness change for the customer's competitive advantage.

3 Deliver working software frequently, from a couple of weeks to a couple of months, with a preference to the shorter timescale.
4 Business people and developers must work together daily throughout the project.
5 Build projects around motivated individuals. Give them the environment and support they need, and trust them to get the job done.
6 The most efficient and effective method of conveying information to and within a development team is face-to-face conversation.
7 Working software is the primary measure of progress.
8 Agile processes promote sustainable development. The sponsors, developers, and users should be able to maintain a constant pace indefinitely.
9 Continuous attention to technical excellence and good design enhances agility.
10 Simplicity–the art of maximizing the amount of work not done–is essential.
11 The best architectures, requirements, and designs emerge from self-organizing teams.
12 At regular intervals, the team reflects on how to become more effective, then tunes and adjusts its behavior accordingly.[161]

Agile development is based on increments rather the traditional waterfall approach in phases. Each increment delivers a realized part of the ultimate business model or MVP. The first increment is your MVP, the second your first iteration and so on. An increment is never a stable end stage; all it ever is, is the basis for your next iteration and innovation.

In contrast, a traditional phase delivers an interim result of the envisioned end product measured against time and cost criteria. For example: design, preparation, realization, implementation. An increment, on the other hand, is the time-boxed delivery of the customer's functionalities with the highest priority. Every increment also consists of design, preparation, realization and implementation. This might look like a minor semantic difference, but the impact on the customer is immense.

There are some excellent books that describe Agile development and project management, such as Jim Highsmith's *Agile Project Management*, Ken Rubin's *Essential Scrum*, and Andrew Stellman's *Learning Agile*.[162] A good Dutch source is *Managen van agile projecten* by Bert Hedeman, Henny Portman and Ron Seegers.[163] This book gives a clear overview of the types of agile management, their interrelatedness and their key principles. It also includes a clear overview contrasting the traditional waterfall model of (IT) development projects and the agile model (see Figure 32):

Figure 32 – **Differences between the waterfall model and the agile model.**

Waterfall Model	Agile Model
Management and control by project manager	Self-managing teams
Sequential development	Iterative development
Progress based on % of activities done	Progress based on % of product done
Milestones when work is done	Timeboxes with interim product assessment
Phases with interim results	Increments with delivery of partial product
Control of time, money and quality	Control through deliverable functionalities
Results are delivered at the end of the project	Results are delivered in increments
Project Manager directs	Project Manager facilitates

Source: Hedeman, Portman & Seegers, *Managen van agile projecten*, 2014

Having replaced the original term "software" in the table with "product," you can see that agile principles are equally applicable to the (iterative) development of non-IT projects. Projects can pertain to marketing, operational or innovation processes, because actually agile principles are applicable to any project or program where:

- project or program members and the line organization have to collaborate right from the start in order to achieve sustainable results;
- a "big bang" is impossible or poses too much of a risk of the wrong outcome or of failure.

In Appendix 5, download #5 provides an overview of the key operational elements of agile and Scrum, which can help you with the selection and setup of such a development approach.

Successful Application of Building Block 10, CONTINUOUS DEVELOPMENT

Case study: Medium-sized University of Applied Science in The Netherlands.
Breakthrough: Class scheduling had been a challenge for this fast-growing university for years, but later became a major problem and ultimately a full-blown crisis. Its impact was huge, because scheduling problems led to increasing dissatisfaction among students and teachers. At the start of the project, the business case made clear what improvements were required. The most important goals were that the schedule would contain fewer mistakes and changes and that the scheduling process would be better controlled and less hectic. The realization of these goals was monitored at key moments. After each important step in the scheduling process, the stakeholders examined how the goals had been realized and what changes to the process were necessary.
Impact: The capacity utilization of the classrooms is now over 80%. The ongoing focus and regular updates on the main goals, especially during execution, have given the main stakeholders (students and teachers) immediate insight into which improvements were made and which bottlenecks remained. Scheduling has become a calm, panic-free process. The realization that the problems were of the institution's own making because people did not provide correct data, has really sunk in at every level and may have been the key breakthrough. The sponsors were kept well informed throughout the project and knew exactly how much of the mission had been achieved at every point in the execution.

The soft building blocks in Accelerator 3: SCALING and BRIDGE-BUILDING

Each accelerator has two hard and two soft building blocks. The soft building blocks in Accelerator 3 are **SCALING and BRIDGE-BUILDING**. In **Building Block 11, SCALING**, you select, concretize and operationalize the scaling and rollout methods most appropriate for your initiative. In **Building Block 12, BRIDGE-BUILDING**, the change leadership and the execution coalition remove obstacles and celebrate any successes achieved so far. This is all about adding value and fostering positivity.

6.3 Building Block 11: SCALING

Now it's time to select, concretize and operationalize the scaling and rollout methods most appropriate for the initiative. You may need to scale up from 15 to 1500 employees at this stage. Just be grateful not all 1500 of them were involved in the initial analysis and design. Topics in this building block are the need for a modern mindset regarding change management; various scaling methods; and how to organize feedback from your execution team, customers and employees.

6.3.1 Spread the gospel

Promote a modern mindset in change management. Many change management schools of thought regard scaling and rollouts as cardinal sins. In their view, every employee is supposed to tackle their own process improvement. That may have worked once upon a time, but it won't any longer. We need to see bottom-up change and the taboo on detailed, planned execution for what they are: outdated dogmas. As a leader, you have to make a case for a more modern take on strategy execution. Your call to action should include the following elements: First, everyone is involved in both running the business and changing the business. So, everyone already contributes to executing and improving their job and the organization as a whole. Second, in terms of changing the business, your role may not always be the same. Sometimes you play first fiddle and are involved from day one in the analysis and the design; at other times, you play second fiddle and are asked to join in only in the execution phase. Thirdly, if you happen to play second fiddle, just do what you need to do. Refrain from trying to create elbow room for yourself. You can assess whether the first fiddle's work is thorough enough and ask questions, but only ask questions to seek clarification. It's not your job to cast doubt on everything and look for loopholes and wriggle room.

Realize that this call to action does not turn you (or me) into Don Quixote. It's human nature to want to have influence and I'm not trying to invalidate that. But in the digital age, organizations that pray to the god of bottom-up change won't survive.[164] The "not invented here" syndrome is incompatible with ambitious organizations looking to be efficient, effective and agile. There is plenty of room for influence without needing to reinvent the wheel as a matter of principle.

E = Q × A is still valid, but the A is changing. It's a powerful notion and a classic equation in change management: Execution equals the content's Quality times the degree of organizational Acceptance, or E = Q x A. Even today, this formula still holds true. But in light of your call for a modern mindset, you need to look at the Acceptance variable differently. Generally, professionals no longer accept the absence of a clear framework; they see this as a sign of negligent leadership. And when they are leading an initiative, they don't take well to peers who fail to make useful suggestions but instead waste their time with vague questions about "what you would like." They get annoyed when someone claims to have "deliberately refrained from providing too much detail to leave room for interpretation," while it's clear to everyone in the room they simply haven't done their job.

In most organizations, it's impossible for everyone to be involved in every initiative from the get-go. And that's fine. But you do need a clearly defined execution method, for two reasons: First, it signals a healthy urge to start executing and second, experimentation provides quick feedback that proves what works and what doesn't, enabling continuous development of your MVP and subsequent versions thereof.

6.3.2 Widen your execution

It's important to decide which chunks to execute, and in which waves, because small can be big. In Building Block 10, you learned what it takes to concretize and develop your MVP further. This section discusses different scaling methods, selection criteria, and how to fill in the details.

MVP development methods are inextricably linked with scaling methods, but should not be confused with one another. The distinction is perhaps artificial to some extent, particularly in Type 2 and Type 3 (digital) change initiatives. Usually, a new version, or release, of your digital product or service has also been tested and implemented by all your new customers. But this is not the case in the lion's share of Types 1, 2 and 3 initiatives. Usually, a new business process has been developed with a select group of customers and employees and this needs to be scaled up and rolled out to the wider customer base and all the organization's employees—and often to all those in the supply chain and in partner organizations too. That's why it's good to have a look at the various scaling methods out there.

There are many proven scaling and rollout methods. Selection criteria always boil down to which scaling method ensures the fastest, most controllable and sustainable execution in waves of the envisioned result. Scale always boils down to the chunks of content that your design can best be divided into and executed. In making these choices, you have to consider questions like: For which groups of professionals? Which organizational units? And in which order? How do I combine an existing business process with a new one in a single wave? Does "the switch" need to take place within the span of a single wave? This is often the case in IT projects. I imagine some of you might think this is probably only relevant to huge companies with tens of thousands of employees. Rest assured, this is relevant wherever the original 10 to 15-person team has designed an MVP that eventually needs to be implemented by more than 100 employees.

Base your choice of scaling method on the following variables: execution capacity, urgency, ambition and risk of reputation damage. These are the factors that determine how fast you can scale up, in which chunks, and in which organizational units. Figure 33 shows six archetypal scaling methods. You need to make an informed choice, and that always involves picking the lesser of two evils. Or put more positively, it is about choosing the method that represents the optimum mix of these four variables. Remember that nine times out of ten, the more manageable your chunks and slices, the more successful your execution.

Method No. 1 is the Big Bang method. This is what you go for when urgency and execution capacity, or change capacity, is high. Method No. 2 is a sequence of shock waves, which you choose when your execution capacity is mediocre or uncertain and there are big differences between the organizational units where the changes need to be rolled out. Method No. 3 is the exponential scale-up. This is the one to choose when the design's potential risk or odds of success are unknown or when a lot has been left undecided and the prototype has to be concretized during execution. Depending on whether the prototype leads to positive results, the next increment can be bigger. Method No. 4 is the linear sequential method, or waterfall method, which is appropriate when your execution capacity is low or very uncertain and there are great differences between the organizational units where the changes need to be implemented. Each organizational unit requires great dedication to the execution. Method No. 5 is the hybrid method. This is similar to the waterfall method, but is appropriate for situations of heightened urgency that require acceleration for critical parts of the prototype. Method No. 6 is the delicate method. This is the most appropriate method if your execution capacity is extremely low and your design has a high risk of reputation damage. In this method, you cut up your prototype into two or more chunks. For example, a legal services provider wanted to roll out a new business process to more than 700 lawyers. The design differentiated between three distinct processes: a new sales process, a new method for handling legal cases and a new management process. Even though these three chunks varied radically in terms of complexity and odds of success, they were all part of one prototype. Their interrelatedness made this justifiable, but this is the type of situation that cries out for Method No. 6.

Every rectangle in these methods represents an execution wave and consists of the activities detailed in the execution cycle in Accelerator 2, Building Block 7 (see 154). Your choice of scaling method applies to a single version of your prototype. This selection process needs to be repeated at every new rollout of another version of your prototype. What happened in earlier scale-ups should have a strong bearing on your choice of method for the next scale-up.

Just as in Accelerators 1 and 2, this is the time to make use of SECA.NU. This tool will help you update your assessment of your organization's execution capacity, which is one of the main variables for selecting your scaling method.

Figure 33 — **Choose your scaling method carefully:** which chunks in which waves? Small can be big.

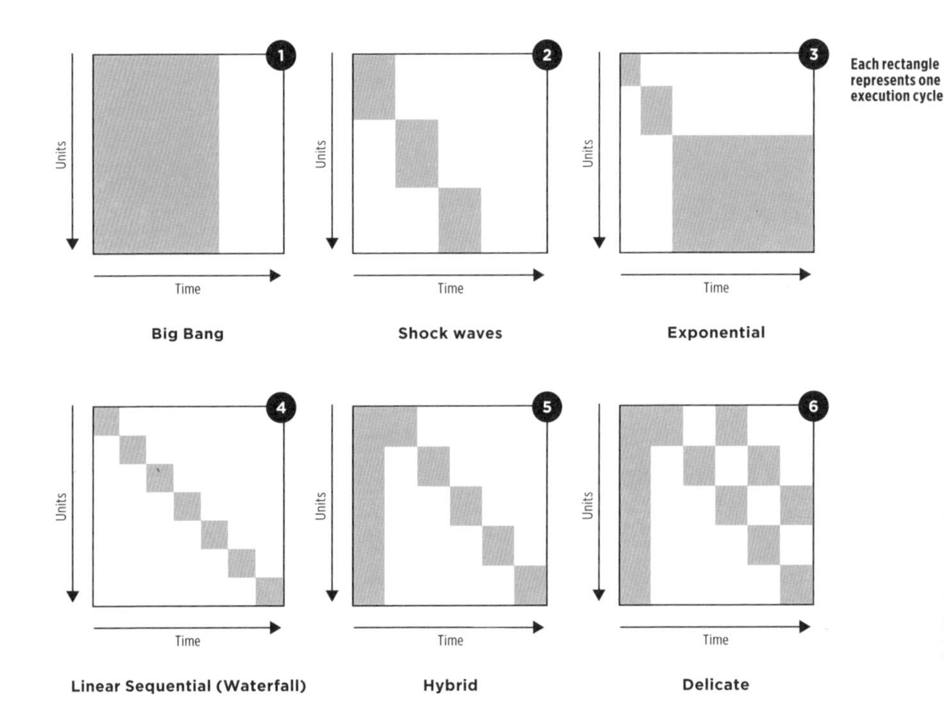

Source: Turner, 2016

The devil is in the details. Once you start scaling your prototype with the help of your chosen method, you'll find yourself programming activities in quite a linear way. What you're trying to do is find the best balance among several variables that are all vying for priority treatment. And that's okay. Let practice decide how to best apply theory.

In rollouts, "pull" works better than "push." I have seen more than once that a geographically removed division asks why they are last in line, because they've heard such great things about the first results. That's always a good sign. If you can do something about it by bumping this division up to a higher place, then do it. But if your hands are tied, you should carefully explain why this is the case. Keep them engaged and provide clarity about the process. The same can happen within a single location, where one department is later in line than another.

Sometimes, the cohesion of an increment needs to be disrupted because the execution requires smaller chunks. Even if a rollout seems to be going perfectly, it may still be necessary to cut it up into smaller increments. Let's return to our example from the legal services industry where the new business process boosted both effectiveness and productivity. Content-wise, these two goals were very harmonious, but because the rollout would have become too complicated, they were treated as two separate increments. So, effectiveness was tackled first and then the process was repeated with the focus on productivity.

Be sensible about recalibrating your scaling plans. Execution practice is your best teacher. For example, you may find it is possible to shift from Method No. 3 (exponential) to Method No. 4 (waterfall), but only if you have heeded the motto "small can be big" from the very beginning. Continue evaluating your chosen scaling method and change tack if need be. It's not just the design that benefits from this approach of achieving small chunks and waves of execution. The approach itself is a learning process, too. The method you initially selected can be adapted along the way. Depending on how fast and how well things go, you can speed up or slow down. But don't rush things. Despite all the careful timing and depth of analysis applied during design and redesign, people tend to get impatient in the implementation phase and rush the rollout, jeopardizing the end result. This risk is especially high in very decentralized and heterogeneous organizations, for example, a business with many different, highly autonomous subsidiaries and local entrepreneurs. In those cases, a Big Bang rollout (Method No. 1) is bound to fail.

Be discerning in how you apply the principles to the various issues and initiatives. One frequently asked question is whether this whole thing of cutting up the execution into chunks is really necessary. Surely this is useful only in very complex organizations with many divisions, business units or subsidiaries, where huge differences exist, right? My answer is: no. Cutting up your execution into manageable chunks is essential. Always. More than 60% of strategy execution fails. And rolling out too much too fast is one of the major contributing factors. Obviously, there are always some "binary" issues, such as introducing a new top tier or changing the management and legal structure after a merger or acquisition. Compare it to being pregnant: you can't be "sort of" pregnant. Either you are, or you aren't. But most issues can be cut up. Hard-earned lessons from decades of strategy execution have shown that this is the most effective way of going about it. Small can be big. Iterative development in short cycles has become commonplace anyway, especially in radical innovation (see also Eric Ries's Lean Startup model). As it turns out, this also works very well for smaller improvement projects (Type 1 change) and more drastic renewal programs (Type 2 change).

6.3.3 Organize and utilize feedback

Let's recap what has happened so far in terms of strategy execution. The execution cycle introduced in Accelerator 2 (page 154) details the steps you need to take to execute your MVP with your first set of customers and employees. The development method described in Building Block 10 generates better and more workable versions or releases of your MVP. The scaling methods from Building Block 11 enable you to bring every improved version of your MVP to full execution.

Scaling your new product or service to all customers and employees generates extremely helpful feedback for further adaptations and iterations. Here are ten best practices for organizing and using this feedback.[165]

1 **Create separate development and execution teams.** The former has a different focus and dynamics than the latter. Analysis and design are not readily compatible with down-to-earth execution. Many managers have asked me whether the same people can do both. My answer is 15% at most. Some can, but never simultaneously.
2 **Keep your teams small.** Five to seven people for development and the same for execution, too. As Jeff Bezos of Amazon put it, every team should be so small you can feed it with two pizzas.
3 **Create linking pins between your development and execution teams and organize a continuous feedback loop between execution and design.** The linking pin from your execution team attends the kickoff, the half-way evaluation and the final evaluation of your development team's sprints. And vice versa.
4 **Your execution team indicates what does and doesn't work in the MVP design or a later release.** This gives your development team, which also works with your customers, targeted input on what customers and employees find works, and what doesn't, in a new proposition or business process.
5 **Be practical.** For iterations that are not labor-intensive or technology-intensive, the development team can even make adjustments between scaling waves and make these available to the execution team.

6. **Proven execution and execution results over extensive analysis and design of the MVP.** It is all about the rapid creation of maximum value and agility; prioritizing the rapid, effective adaptation of your MVP based on feedback from execution takes precedence over your scheduling.
7. **Use short waves.** Keep your timeboxes for adjusting your MVP and the successive execution waves short. Remember, short waves travel farthest.
8. **Safeguard the balance between discipline and freedom.** The key here is disciplined execution of a strategic initiative in fixed, standardized waves. Within those waves, you should give the professionals who carry out the execution enough freedom to make their own choices about where to persevere, pivot or scale. Make sure agile development in short cycles is not used as an excuse for not analyzing, designing and planning.
9. **Learn lessons about content and change management, but also about project management.** Each wave teaches you about the amount of effort required of all participants. Use this to make subsequent waves easier to plan, control and manage.
10. **Cultivate the emerging execution culture.** This way of working is a breath of fresh air for both designers and executives, as many case studies have shown. Nothing is more satisfying than getting a good idea to work. This method gives people the best chance to do so.

Successful Application of Building Block 11, SCALING

Case study: NVWA (= Dutch equivalent of the FDA), regulatory and enforcement agency for food safety
Breakthrough: Huge ambition, small steps. In essence, a large-scale, complicated implementation was cut up into small chunks. The first waves had to prove successful before any scaling was allowed. This created an implementation and renewal engine. The real breakthrough came from a carefully selected number of slaughterhouses where food safety risks were highest: success in an area where it's least expected accelerated the rest of the operation.
Impact: Leiden University independently measured the results, which are substantial and sustainable. The approach is a showcase for large-scale sustainable renewal in the public sector.

6.4 Building Block 12: BRIDGE-BUILDING

In this building block, the change leaders clear away any obstacles and make sure successes are celebrated. The point is to add value and be a positive influence. The execution coalition and the professionals who've recently joined the effort become avid change ambassadors, helping to make the change irreversible. In this building block, you learn why it's important to widen the execution coalition and create broad ownership, and how to institutionalize agile methods by creating semipermanent strategy execution roles.

6.4.1 Analyze the growing number of stakeholders

First of all, secure the key roles in the execution coalition. The vanguard from Accelerator 2 still forms the core of the coalition. But a lot has happened so far in Accelerator 3. The coalition members are the main design supporters, but even they may differ in opinion and interests. Who is fully engaged and who isn't? That is the main question at this point.

In a typical scaling process, the number of stakeholders will now be growing fast. This is true of both the execution and benefit realization executives. Often, the process or program manager will really grab the reins of the execution at this point, but sometimes a reshuffle is called for. This might be the case if the execution lead for the previous phase was selected based on that individual's specialist expertise, analytical ability or process redesign competency. The person who is to lead the execution in the strictest sense should mainly be chosen for their ability to garner the necessary support to execute the design and make it a success. Only 15% of people are good at both. When dealing with execution issues that involve many people, it's best to have separate development and execution teams.

Generally, new key actors will join the execution coalition at this point. If possible, have them check in even more explicitly than your vanguard. The latter had the privilege of playing first fiddle. Your new echelon will by definition be playing second fiddle and will be there to implement the design. They may, for example, be line executives who will have to use the design to reach their targets. It's human nature to want to come up with your own design or redesign. But that is one of the greatest pitfalls and failure factors ever. That's why your newcomers' commitment and engagement is of the utmost importance to the overall success of your execution.

This is also a good time to update your stakeholder analysis. Organizations are full of people, above all. And all those people have a personality and a set of interests determining their attitude. So, before you start scaling, it would be wise to conduct a classic stakeholder analysis.

The stakeholder cube in Figure 34 is very practical and easy to use. Tape a copy of this cube to your flip chart and fill in the names of your people in each of its eight corners. Now add the actual behavior that was your reason for assigning this person to this corner. Determine who your main active proponents (backers) and main active opponents (blockers) are. Entire books have been filled on these topics, but in essence it's all about careful communication, personal persuasiveness, and an occasional intervention. It goes without saying that status and job titles have nothing to do with it. However, there are situations where hard choices need to be made, and that's the only time you would be justified in pulling rank.

Don't neglect your insignificant active and passive backers and blockers either. An analysis of these stakeholders provides valuable input for communication and reviewing activities. On the other hand, don't overdo it. Time is your golden resource, after all. You only get to spend every minute once.

It's always interesting to see that the names in this diagram cut right across your program and line organization. You may identify active blockers at the very heart of your program organization. This does not have to spell disaster. On the contrary, I always advocate bringing resistance to the surface and pulling it up close, in your program organization. A poignant detail is when your Chief Execution Sponsor ends up in the influential passive backer corner. You would expect him or her in the influential *active* backer corner, right?

A stakeholder analysis, or stakeholder relationship management, is not a one-off exercise, but ongoing hard work. You want to find out from your main opponents whether they're entrenched or likely to change their tune. But one manager told me: "That doesn't happen overnight." Bringing important stakeholders that are not part of your core team on board is hard work. That is exactly why the method in this book repeatedly emphasizes the importance of alignment. In practical terms, program managers need to spend at least a third of their time on stakeholder management. "But then I'll never get my job done," one program manager said. I'm sorry, but stakeholder management *is* your job.

Normalize critical stakeholders. I am always struck by people's surprise at the resistance some stakeholders feel. Sometimes they turn this resistance into a personal drama, asking "Why are they criticizing my plan? Why don't they try to understand it first?" It's very simple; in situations where stakeholders are kept out of the loop, you fuel your own fear. As one leader put it: "You fear your hypothetical blocker's hypothetical strategy."

Be humble without showing off. In my Strategy Execution Masterclass, I often refer to one seasoned and very successful program manager who systematically identifies his stakeholders and takes the trouble to visit them. One of his stakeholders—an influential blocker—once said: "I know what you're doing, and you can come talk to me until hell freezes over, but I'll never change my views. This project stinks!" The program manager continued to pay visits and repeat his good intentions, but more importantly he *demonstrated* his good intentions. And in a later execution phase, this stakeholder became one of his biggest ambassadors. The program manager was smart enough to stress that you should never be boastful about this.

Fostering execution and benefit ownership should never devolve into manipulation. I have been asked more than once at which point systematic stakeholder analysis stops being a sound practice and turns into plain old manipulation. That's an important question, because that's a line you do not want to cross. The reasons for that may be obvious, but I'll spell them out anyway. First and foremost, you don't cross that

Figure 34 — **Differences in attitude, interest and power determine stakeholders' impact.** The stakeholder cube.

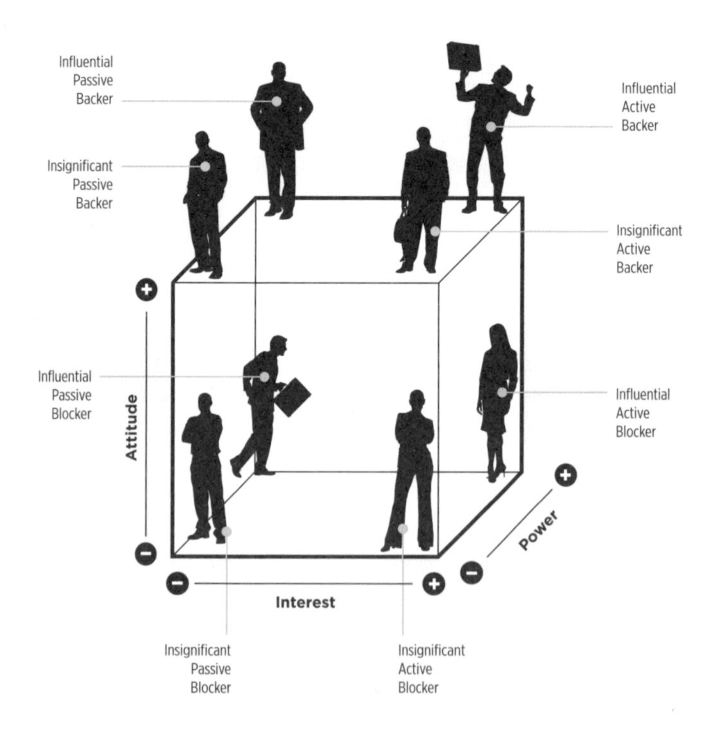

Source: Lynda Bourne, *Stakeholder Relationship Management*

line because you want to be ethical and act with integrity. Intrinsic motivation to show integrity is a personal matter. Second, because people know when they are being manipulated. Manipulation always backfires. You can count on it.

Monitor the influential stakeholders' commitment. I'm talking about constructive engagement here. In Chapter 2, at Success Factor 4, I already mentioned that too much effort tends to go into fostering generic engagement instead of looking at whether people's behavior matches their words and whether their engagement benefits your business. That is simply senseless. Some types of destructive engagement are so bad that you need to wonder, with friends like that, who needs enemies? Constructive engagement, on the other hand, is both critical and positive, and absolutely not "out to please." It definitely helps to improve things. You want to monitor your influential stakeholders' commitment and decide whether their engagement is constructive and translates into support and receptiveness. That tells you whether you are reading from the same strategy execution script and are working on achieving the same goals.

6.4.2 Execution Coalition: Expand Execution and Benefit Ownership

Pay serious attention to your execution coalition. In essence, you want to build ownership, and by this I mean ownership of each strategic initiative's execution and goals. That's why in every accelerator, you are prompted to reconsider how you've filled the key roles and what their priorities should be.

The execution coalition leads and executes. At this point in the process, the change leadership requires a lot of dedicated management to scale and simultaneously monitor whether the benefits are being realized. Make sure you give this your undivided attention. The Hawthorne effect (or observer effect) has proven its value time and time again. In times of Lean Six Sigma, value analysis has never been more precise—ranging from the optimal timing of breaks to the perfect place for the water cooler—but remember the essence of the Hawthorne effect is that no matter what you do, it is knowing that you're observed that improves performance.[166] Figure 35 shows the execution coalition during Accelerator 3 and the types of ownership and roles needed here.

The power of the Execution Coalition is that it aligns Running the Business with Changing the Business and increases an initiative's chances of success across disciplines and vertical chains. In this accelerator, alignment pertains mostly to the increasing number of dependencies caused by scaling. Those dependencies have not been specified on paper, of course, but do exist in practice. Although HR has been kept informed during Accelerators 1 and 2, the department may have taken a sort of "wait and see" attitude, but it now has to deal with the people affected by the initiative. Anticipate this and be proactive.

Accentuate the positive. Change leadership at this stage means removing obstacles and accentuating and celebrating successes. Like many other studies, our research has shown that accentuating the positive in execution further improves the initiative's chances of success. And it's just as important to dress up the boring truth as something sexy. That is, keep explaining why until at least 25% of your audience can't stand it anymore. If all you want is love and acceptance, you should have taken a job as a Baby Welcome Box distributor. By acting as a change leader, you cultivate execution. Change begets change.

Accelerate by storytelling. Systematically collect stories. There are plenty out there! You only need to show up near the water cooler or the

Figure 35 — **The Execution Coalition: Execution and Benefit Ownership during Accelerator 3.**

1
Chief Execution Sponsor

- Celebrates successes and acts as a role model;
- Helps the Execution Lead to scale execution. Expands from the vanguard to the first execution wave where new stakeholders need to immediately get on board, accept their role and take ownership;
- Keeps urgency alive and makes rapid decisions;
- Doesn't shy away from confrontation and presses ahead;
- Stresses the importance of perseverance.

2
Co-Sponsor(s)

- Helps the overall sponsor to scale up the initiative.

3
Execution Lead
(usually the Program / Project Manager)

- Devotes half their time to scaling up and onboarding new actors;
- Remains agile;
- Organizes interim meetings;
- Tightens up the execution plan;
- Keeps an eye on the necessary behavior and responsibilities.

4
Execution Team Member(s)

- The existing executive(s) act(s) as owner(s) and ambassador(s) and work(s) to widen ownership;
- Incoming executives make a clear choice to join this initiative's first or subsequent execution group.

5
Benefit Realization Manager(s)

- Actively explore how and when the initiative in execution is going to be ready for use in the primary process and what role they need to play in this.

Source: Turner, 2016

lunch table and you will hear the stories that matter. At the same time, it pays to use sociotechnology. It's a powerful tool that can help you gather a lot of input while guaranteeing participants sufficient anonymity and safety. Put the stories you gather in context and put them to good use.

A story needs framing to accelerate the execution of an initiative. If no one associates it with the initiative, it misses the point. So, your stories need a context and must consist of more than just a few random anecdotes. Just imagine you come across a crazy story about an A-account's complaint that was turned into a great opportunity (it happens, as we all know). Coincidentally, there's also a sales effectiveness initiative underway. It would be a real shame if you didn't use the link between the initiative and that crazy story you heard. You need to make that connection!

6.4.3 Consider setting up semipermanent agile development

More and more people agree that every organization should be permanently geared toward change. It's a widely held belief that change is the only constant. You can prepare for permanent change by adding structural or semistructural roles to the change side of your organization, separately from the day-to-day running of the business. Scrum-based tribes and chapters are a good example of this. But you can also institute more or less structural roles and organizational units higher up in the organization, such as a Chief Innovation Officer, Chief Digital Officer or Chief Change Officer. Often, organizations also spawn some form of internal change organization, such as Program Management Offices, Centers of Expertise, Centers of Excellence, and Business Development and M&A Departments.

The benefits of such roles and departments are obvious: you signal what is important and accord it extra weight. There are some drawbacks too. They create an excuse for people in operations and day-to-day management to lean back and shirk responsibility for changing the business. However, it's possible to enjoy the benefits without the drawbacks by filling the five roles of the execution coalition in a manner appropriate for every accelerator.

It is logical that businesses are increasingly deciding to institute these more structural roles. Improving, renewing and innovating—the three types of change distinguished in this book—have become a constant, everyday, structural responsibility.

At the same time, "structural" has become a relative notion. Even the day-to-day side of the business uses only temporarily fixed structures. High-tech firms like ASML work in partnerships on new technological developments. Their approach is highly structured, but temporary, because in a couple of years those partnerships are likely to include totally different partners.

Key roles in iterating the design. Since 2015, ING Bank in the Netherlands has adopted the agile methodology organization-wide. They work with self-managing, multidisciplinary and autonomous teams that have ambitious targets and end-to-end responsibilities, as the bank claims on its website. "In the agile method, everyone works in squads: self-managing, autonomous units with end-to-end responsibility for a specific customer-focused project. A squad brings together colleagues from all the disciplines that are needed to complete the project successfully. At the end of the project, the squad is disbanded and the members set to work in other squads. A squad works together in a shared space. To facilitate that and to offer inspiring work spaces, the ING head office in Amsterdam has been entirely revamped and so too has our office in Leeuwarden. No one at ING in the Netherlands has their own office anymore - not even members of the board. The squads form part of a bigger entity that operates along similar lines. Squads that are involved in the same area of work are part of an overarching tribe. In principle all activities are organised in squads, but we have created Centers of Expertise for scarce or specialised knowledge."[167]

ING modeled its organization on Spotify. Spotify shows how agile and Scrum methodologies enable a business to systematically organize innovation across the whole organization, using Scale-Scrum. In a great white paper, Henrik Kniberg and Anders Ivarsson describe how all of Spotify works agile.[168] The authors end their paper by describing the way Spotify worked in 2012. By the time you read this, their way of working will have changed. Even Agile is agile. Figure 36 shows how Agile works as a semi-permanent change methodology.

Agile organization is not a cure-all, even if some people tend to regard it as such. One of the senior managers I interviewed warned against this, saying: "Take a long hard look at what type of issue requires what type of method. Highly ambitious, high-risk issues that have an impact on several disciplines still require a well-balanced

Figure 36 — **Agile as a semipermanent change method: the Spotify model.** Tribes, Squads, Chapters and Guilds.

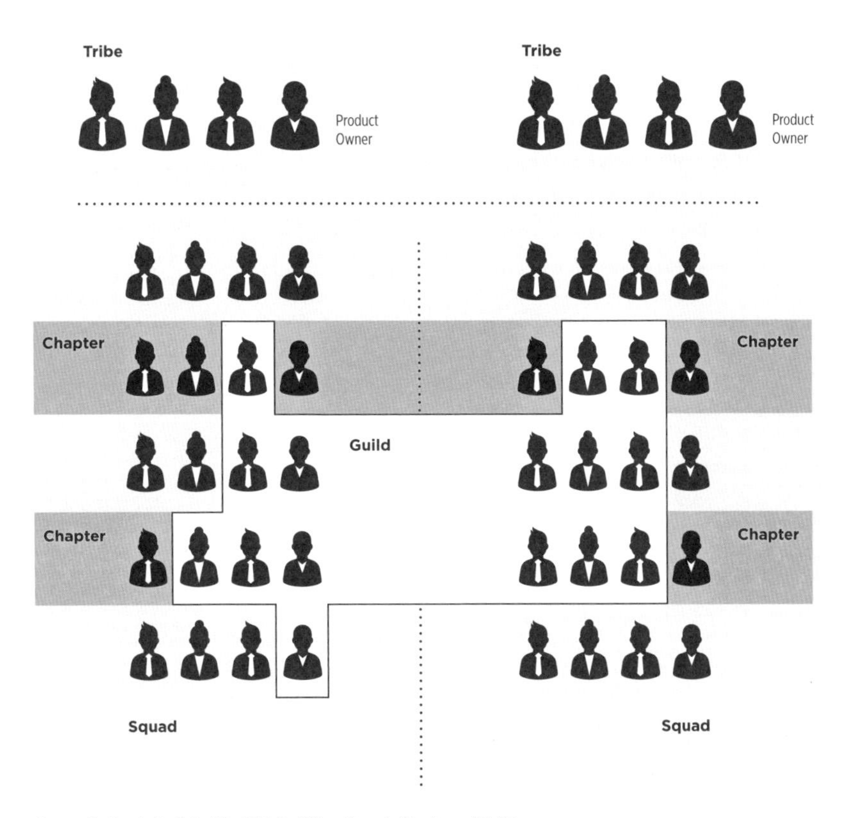

Source: Scaling Agile @ Spotify. With the Tribes, Squads, Chapter and Guilds
Henrik Kniberg and Anders Ivarsson, Spotify, October 2012

program or project approach, with a beginning and an end, predefined deliverables and a cascade of logical, sequential activities designed to achieve your goals. Just think of post-merger integrations, or becoming Basil II or III-compliant. There are organizations where it has become a taboo to NOT use agile-scale, because people are afraid to be called old-fashioned."

Appendix 5, download #11 gives an overview of how the roles in the various methods (Agile, Scrum, etc.) relate to the five roles of the execution coalition.

Successful Application of Building Block 12, BRIDGE-BUILDING

Case study: Arbo Unie [occupational health consultants] struck a sound balance between business sense and empathy
Breakthrough: Arbo Unie's occupational health professionals help workers to lead a healthy working life. Like any organization, this requires sound business practices. But many health professionals feel torn between business sense and empathy. Without effective management this leads to loss of revenue; activities are not always planned, planned activities are not always carried out, activities are not always recorded, recorded activities are not always billed. In 2012, Arbo Unie redressed this in a positive way. Changes were implemented based not only on a fact-based, hard analysis, but also by analyzing and discussing the underlying mindset of the professionals, who sometimes did not bill hours because "it was all part of the job" or did not bill certain actions because they and the patient "went way back." A team of local health professionals developed a new way of working, describing the behavior necessary to make improvements. Implementation of the new business process enabled this team to improve its productivity by 15%.
The real breakthrough took place when the process was scaled up to the national level. Arbo Unie used a dual change strategy launched by the COO. She came up with the framework and clearly explained the process (the why, the urgency, the scheduling). More importantly, she called for engagement. The change depended on the health professionals' participation. To secure their cooperation, the health professionals from the original team personally spoke with their colleagues in other teams. They talked about their added value and their impact on their clients, and asked them what made them decide not to bill a given service. They were given enough room—within the limits of the framework—to feel that they were taken seriously, which induced them to take ownership of the change. This method can evoke more questions and lead to repetitions which can cause delays, but the net result is still better. Creating more support and high engagement ultimately increases the rapidity of change.
Impact: By effectively removing a crucial, but difficult issue, the professionals' engagement increased. As a consequence, everyone felt better about the organization's capacities: "If we're able to overcome this obstacle, we can do anything." Moreover, Arbo Unie's clients appreciated the increased clarity and reliability of services.

Useful Tips from Successful Leaders

Every chapter concludes with several proven, practical ideas that have helped leaders and professionals make a difference in real world situations. You can also use these as mini case studies and learning points.

1. **Forget the Kickoff.** One senior manager discovered the value of the kick-through. "People get obsessed with the kickoff, but what really makes the difference is the kick-through." He secretly enjoyed surprising his people with his apparent indifference, which was in reality just a refusal to get worked up about the kickoff.
2. **Key Sessions with Key Actors.** When one leader had a gut feeling that things were getting bogged down, she managed to reinvigorate people by asking her key actors who they thought should get together to discuss things, and what they should discuss. Another manager calls this her weekly antenna-hour. Different name, same game.
3. **Alignment Lunch.** It is not my favorite idea, the alignment lunch, but I can immediately see why it would work. Leaders in strategy execution prove their worth by tirelessly working on drawing people together. Once a week, the person who coined the phrase "alignment lunch" buys lunch for two key players who are crucial linchpins in the execution. He is up-front with them about why he does this and says: "It should never come across as manipulative!"
4. **The A and B agenda of Balanced Execution Management.** The A agenda is about running the business, while the B agenda is about changing the business. This tip is so vital, I've included it as a fixture in Accelerator 1 (see also Section 4.2.4 on p. 107).
5. **Dosed Digital Sharing.** Organizations are overwhelmed by an overload of information. It is much better to try and get specific information to those who need it, when they need it. The CEO who gave this tip tries to be as sparse as possible with the information and communication about change programs. His motto was: "Don't do unto others what you don't want others to do unto you."
6. **Full-on Execution Weeks.** These are weeks devoted completely to execution—with the exception of customer-related work that must continue at all costs. The idea is similar to Spotify's sexy hack week, when everyone thinks for an entire week of innovative, sexy ideas (try this one during Accelerator 1). In Accelerator 3, it's not about generating ideas, though, but about execution.
7. **E2 (Execution and Energy) Sensor.** A highly successful CEO always draws two columns on a sheet of paper. The first column represents

execution progress (in terms of targets and deliverables), and the second represents people's energy level. Low levels of energy are not a reason to panic. After all, execution is sometimes like a trek through the Sahara. Tiredness is inherent, but should not be a permanent state. This CEO has become pretty good at predicting the energy levels per execution phase and has learned how to anticipate them. Be sure to avoid giving people the idea they should always be completely gung-ho about the process and pretend to be energetic. This puts unrealistic pressure on them, which is counterproductive to change.

8. **Script Check.** A colorful senior manager at a financial services provider regularly checks whether everyone is still reading from the same script. She knows that people's ideas and expectations tend to start diverging every three to four weeks. This is not necessarily bad, because it's a good gauge of whether the execution process is still on track, but it can go wrong if the focus on execution gets lost. "Taking an hour to check whether we're all still on the same page works miracles!"
9. **Consultation Doctor (aka Killer).** The person who thought of this idea has a dislike of meetings. "The list of action items just keeps growing, it never gets shorter." He blocks an hour in his calendar every quarter for what he ambiguously calls a "meeting consultation." It is a reminder to rigorously review all scheduled meetings and consultations and decide which are indispensable, which can go, and which must be held but need to be conducted more efficiently and effectively.

All these ideas call for valuable, but time-consuming involvement. To a great extent, time expenditure is what effective strategy execution is all about. "How would our time be best spent?" is a question well worth asking.

7

ACCELERATOR 4: SECURE

Comic strips are for lazy readers / communicate like President Obama / more micromanagement please / Neutron Jack / the Accordion Principle / Loose Ends Tuesday

When and where is this accelerator relevant?
This accelerator describes how to make this part of your strategy execution as impactful as the start in order to achieve full acceleration in strategy execution. After all, this is where you actually reap all the initiative's benefits, ensure full integration into your primary process and learn from your execution. This produces valuable knowledge that enhances your execution capacity for the next initiative.

Recommended maximum time/resource allocation for this accelerator
Timebox: Five weeks.

This is the shortest chapter in the book, but make no mistake: this accelerator is a vitally important piece of strategy execution, so resist the temptation to skip over it. This accelerator is about finishing, integrating and securing what you've achieved.

If you add up all the timeboxes for a relatively involved and complicated initiative, such as a large-scale transformative program in an organization with thousands of employees, you will end up with the following timeframe:

- Accelerator 1, strategy-setting: 5 weeks
- Accelerator 2, elaboration, for each initiative: 3-6 weeks
- Accelerator 3, scaling in ten 5-week sprints: 50 weeks
- Accelerator 4, securing and learning: 5 weeks

So, strategy-setting (Accelerator 1) takes 5 weeks, while full execution (Accelerators 2, 3 and 4) takes 58 to 61 weeks. You should see your initial results in the first three months. Traditionally, large-scale transformations used to be executed in two to three-year programs. It would often take more than a year before you started seeing results, and that's a generous estimate. Comparable transformations, when executed without the accelerators in this book, can take even longer.

Obviously, these timeboxes are averages. I've included this calculation to show that going all-out on execution affects your time and resource allocation, as well as your leaders' and executives' focus during strategy execution. "Show me your calendar and I'll tell you your priorities," as the popular saying goes.

The hard Building Blocks in Accelerator 4: ADJUSTMENT and OPEN ARCHITECTURE

Every accelerator consists of two hard and two soft Building Blocks. The first two building blocks in Accelerator 4, ADJUSTMENT and OPEN ARCHITECTURE, are hard. **Building Block 13, ADJUSTMENT**, makes the point that professionals need to be given room to manage their responsibilities. Self-monitoring is more effective than supervision. The business case monitoring method you've adopted will help them do just that. Make use of visual management as much as possible. **Building Block 14, OPEN ARCHITECTURE,** deals with the importance of a simple, open architecture. This makes it easier to institutionalize, monitor and adjust the new way of working (the design).

7.1 Building Block 13: ADJUSTMENT

This building block focuses on securing the benefits of your initiative, the importance of visual management and self-organization, adjustment during strategy execution and the specific characteristics of monitoring and adjustment in new organizations using digital business models.

7.1.1 Secure the benefits

This is where benefit realization managers make their last contribution within the context of the initiative. It pays off to create a good tool kit for those who will continue the work once the metrics team is disbanded. This is more important than you might think. Metrics and methods that make perfect sense to the metrics team and their users can be mumbo jumbo to those who are just climbing aboard. In fact, benefit management needs to be secured and integrated into your regular planning and control processes, because benefit management never stops.

Benefit Management continues beyond the scope of any project or program. If everything works according to plan, benefit management simply goes on. However, you don't want to accumulate new monitoring procedures in addition to your regular performance management system. So, at the end of each project or program, you should integrate the new monitoring mechanisms into your regular performance management system. This is a vital step, but one that is frequently skipped.

Reinforce the benefits. The soft elements in this chapter describe how to learn from execution and reinforce the benefits. The benefits ought to be the main item on the agenda of any learning and reinforcement session. But I can tell you that I've attended reinforcement sessions that were about all kinds of things *except for* these vital questions: How do we ensure the realized benefits are sustained and even improved upon? What is needed to ensure the benefits are permanent? What went easier than expected and what was harder? Why? What lessons learned from benefit realization management can you carry over into subsequent initiatives? Such sessions need to focus on assessing which benefits the initiative has and hasn't realized.

7.1.2 Visualize and monitor target realization

Design is everything: real monitoring is attractive monitoring. "Design is not what it looks like, design is how it works," Steve Jobs said. This is true not only of products and services, but also of strategy execution. In order to do justice to all the work that has gone into strategy execution, you need to do more than just measure whether your goals and targets have been met. You need to make it attractive, alluring even. So, don't just list and distribute your factually correct progress data, but package it in a format that grabs people's attention. This is not intended to disguise "bad data," but to improve the chance that people actually pay attention to the data you have. If your data is good, attractive presentation is the icing on the cake. This exponentially increases your chances of capitalizing and building upon it.

Use attractive presentation—not because it's sexy, but because it works. Ask anyone who has ever attended a change management conference. They can confirm that a picture is worth a thousand words.

People hear what they see. Computer and information scientist Michelle A. Borkin studied this phenomenon and found that visualizations that are memorable "at a glance" enable people to recall and describe their message in more detail.[169] The best way to get across what a circle is, for example, is to draw a circle. That works much better than giving the definition, that is: a circle is a two-dimensional geometrical shape in which a set of points on a plane are all equidistant from a center point. This is a lesson you need to take to heart in strategy execution.

Borkin and colleagues labeled and studied hundreds of visualizations and tracked dozens of subjects' eye movements when looking at those visualizations. They determined which components of the visualization attracted subjects' attention and which information the subjects encoded and retained in their memory. Their findings confirm and enrich what we know instinctively: "(1) titles and supporting text should convey the message of a visualization, (2) if used appropriately, pictograms do not interfere with understanding and can improve recognition, and (3) redundancy helps effectively communicate the message." Visualizations without the aid of any text are also capable of conveying a large part of the message. In other words, visual management is much more important than many leaders realize. But visualization does not supplant text. On the contrary, organizations ruled by the tyranny of visualization are the poorer for it. "Comic strips are for lazy readers," my father used to say. Yet, there are topics that absolutely require visual communication (see Figure 37).

Instill self-management. Getting visual management right helps you to instill a habit every organization benefits from: self-management or self-organization. Professionals don't enjoy being told what to do. Visual management is a much more direct way of communicating, which prompts action and self-management.

7.1.3 Adjust course

Think carefully about what and how you adjust. In a twist on theologian Reinhold Niebuhr's famous Serenity Prayer, I would say "Have the serenity to accept what needs changing, the courage to hold on to what needs to stay and the wisdom to know the difference." Depending on people's interests and views, there will always be plenty of arguments for one or the other. So, objectivize, take a stance and be prepared to defend your position. That doesn't necessarily mean you know for a fact you're doing the right thing. That's a certainty you'll hardly ever have. Objectivization starts with being explicit about your progress and how your insights are evolving. What have you learned about your targets and your MVP that you did not know in the previous phase? Gather data, do in-depth analyses where necessary, identify

Figure 37 — **In times of information overload, visual management techniques are crucial.**

Project Poster

Your high-level concept at poster size. If it doesn't fit poster size, something's wrong.

Execution

Execution in 10, 30 and 60 seconds. Good internal communication is structured like a pyramid: if you want to know more, you go deeper.

Execution Playbook

Graphically tight format with to-the-point content and hyperlinks that allow people to find all execution information in a maximum of 3 mouse clicks.

Infographics

Using data to create understanding.

Business Process Placemat

Using different colors to highlight various issues: bottlenecks, solutions, key processes, priorities, fragmentation.

Innovation Wall

Improvement, Renewal and Innovation Wall. An attractive and accessible way for employees to express their ideas and opinions.

Wailing and Rejoicing Wall

Analysis of the existing situation: what do customers and employees currently like and dislike?

Who's Who

A way to underline the fact that it is people who make the difference.

Dashboard

Short feedback loop between analysis, design and results. The more immediate the feedback, the stronger the ownership and hence the stronger the results.

Fact Sheets

Progress reports that invite you to study them.

Barometer

Every initiative should have only one main goal. Measure progress in this area in a spot that is visible to every employee.

Google Earth Navigator

Make it easy to navigate huge amounts of information.

Checklists

Everyone can use checklists at key moments. But don't overdo it.

Walk-the-Process Cartoon or Comic Strip

The more vivid a process analysis or design, the bigger its impact. Use animations, cartoons or comic strips.

Pictograms

Create one for every conclusion, solution and action.

Source: Turner, 2016

uncertainties about the whole initiative or part thereof, and clearly name your options and the decision criteria. Do this systematically and keep it up. This is how you create a stroke of luck, because "luck is just another word for tenacity of purpose," as Ralph Waldo Emerson said.

Reasons to persevere:
- The hiccup we're experiencing is temporary. We really need to keep pushing now. This is par for the course.
- Every problem and objection that is raised has been blown out of proportion by our detractors.
- The need to persevere has only increased.

Reasons to pivot:
- The hiccup we're experiencing proves that the MVP is wrong. Better to turn back while we still can.
- Even the people who were in favor at first, are now critical and worried.
- Urgency has been growing and we have generated better ideas to address these issues.

Choose your intervention with surgical precision. One thing that tends to go wrong at this stage in strategy execution is that it is unclear what needs adjusting and what doesn't. Communicate like President Obama, because even if the distinction is made, it will only be effective if every stakeholder perceives it as such. What counts is what people hear, not what you say.

Also, make sure that every executive committee or management team's agenda is set up to deal with strategy execution, and that it distinguishes between Running the Business and Changing the Business, and among the three types of change: improving, renewing and innovating. That is any leader's No. 1 job. I can't stress enough how practical and effective a standardized agenda is (see Figure 38 for a sample agenda).

More micromanagement please. One of the questions I get a lot is whether senior management needs to use such a practical, execution-based agenda too. Absolutely! In fact, the higher the level of management, the more pertinent. I interviewed a great many leaders who all deliberately use an agenda that is not just strategic and tactical, but also operational (see also the Unilever example I gave in Section 2.5.1, where the C-suite expects operational intensity at every meeting, at every level).

Operational intensity is crucial for introducing and maintaining an execution-oriented culture in your organization. The only thing that is different is the level of detail. Leaders must keep the bigger picture in

Figure 38 — **Tip: Use A and B management agendas in strategy execution.**

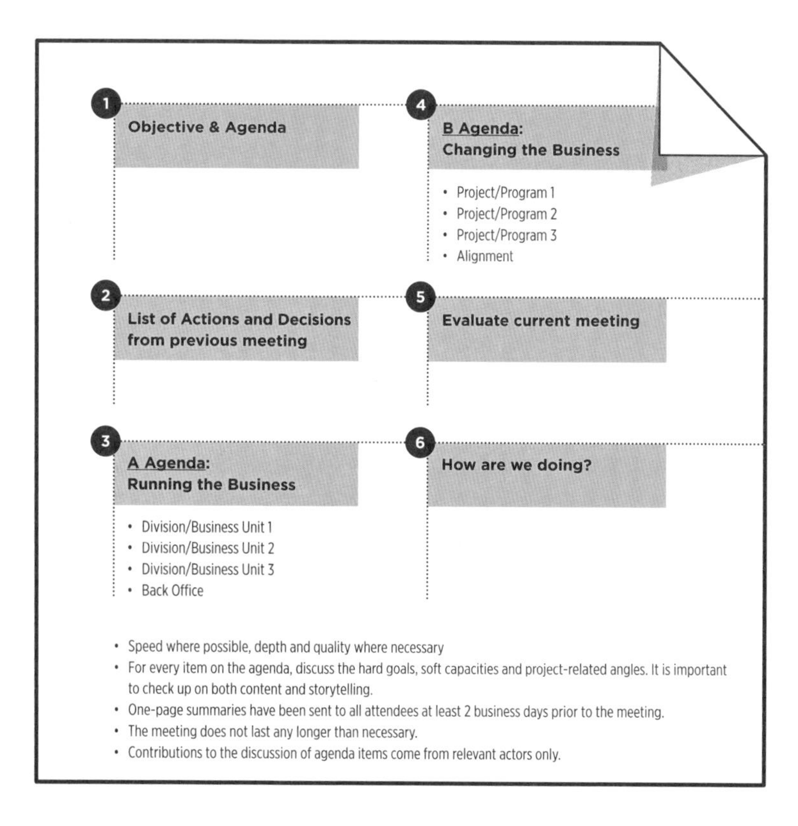

Source: Turner, 2016

mind at all times when making decisions about execution. They will always have to deal with objections from people who like to micro-manage and have a hard time distinguishing between important and less important issues. The key is to let that go. There will always be people like that. The only way to get rid of their mindset is to get rid of them. Which might not be a bad thing. Most micromanagers confuse the need to be specific and completist with nitpickiness, but trust me, those are two very different things.

Former General Electric CEO Jack Welch, aka Neutron Jack, is famous for the way he dealt with his employees. He divided his entire workforce into segments. Every year, he let go of the bottom 10% of his employees. This slash-and-burn method has been much maligned and can't be emulated everywhere because of labor rights, but essentially it's a positive principle that optimizes the workforce. And your workforce might be the most important variable in strategy execution. After all, "who" is more important than "what, why, when, where and how," as we saw in Chapter 2 about the six success factors.

Jack Welch also loves micromanagement, according to his blog. [170] Obviously, his blog does not celebrate overzealous micromanagers who prefer to do everything themselves, have nothing better to do, or don't trust anyone but themselves. Welch is also not talking about evidently excellent micromanagers who step in because their subordinates are not yet up to the task. That's all normal situational leadership. What Welch is talking about in his blog is the "accordion principle," or leaders who get in close to their people and the work when they know they can add something valuable and retreat when they know they can't.

How do leaders add value? They add value when they have knowledge, experience, connections or authority that can prevent unnecessary failure, or better yet, accelerate execution. This also sends an important signal: "I take this initiative very seriously and I'll do anything I can to play my part in making it a success!" This is how leaders help their organization and their people. They would be foolish not to do this. So, every time you feel tempted to move in, there is a simple question you should ask yourself: is this in the interest of the organization and is it ethical? The right answer should be obvious. Welch's use of the word micromanagement must have been provocative. What he is talking about is simply good leadership. And good micromanagement requires engagement. If you're engaged, you will know exactly whether you're barking up the wrong tree, or are right on the money.

Execution often fails because initiatives fizzle out precisely at make-or-break time. And also because at this stage, too little time and attention is spent on the learning process. This is one of those "black holes" of strategy execution, highly destructive gaps that need to be filled with strong interventions. This is confirmed by a recent wide-ranging McKinsey study into the most important leadership qualities. 189,000 respondents from 81 organizations were asked to choose from 20 leadership qualities. They showed a clear preference for typical execution competencies such as support, a strong focus on results, a continuous multi-perspective approach, and effective problem-solving. These are all qualities that count, particularly in the current accelerator.[171]

The next section will deal in more detail with how to manage Type 3 Change (innovation). Every leader we talked to struggles with this, so I figured it would be good to devote a separate section to it.

7.1.4 Monitoring and adjusting course in digital business models

New organizations excel in monitoring and adjusting course. Founders of successful new organizations are refreshingly different in the way they monitor and adjust course. They have an up-to-date grasp of their organization's objectives at every level and for every employee, both in terms of hard goals and soft capabilities, and steadfastly monitor whether things are still on track every week. This engaging yet unrelenting attitude is undoubtedly what Chris Zook and James Allen refer to as *The Founder's Mentality*.

This mindset feels like a breath of fresh air, without any of the apprehensiveness many established businesses feel towards managing in too quantitative or top-down a manner. In new businesses, employees accept the need for balance between quantifiable results and qualitative personal energy, and between top-down management and bottom-up input. This is a mindset you also see in people who've worked for both old and new organizations and know the difference. It opened my eyes to the fact that established businesses tend to seek this balance merely as window dressing or to project a politically correct image in the change management arena. They mainly want to avoid stigmatizing the management team as top-down, hard-ass managers.

I get skeptical when managers in established organizations claim they would do much better in a new organization. For this book, I talked to the founders of organizations that were once new, but are now big and established. These are businesses that currently employ hundreds of people in multiple locations. Despite the fact that these startups have grown into established businesses, their founders are still managing them in that refreshing way. This leads me to conclude that fresh management has as little to do with working out of an attic or garage as with a regular supply of brownies or donuts. The founders I interviewed are obviously able to sustain their leadership and management style, which means that "old" established businesses should also be able to adopt this leadership and management style. I highly recommend that you read download #13 from Appendix 5, which contains dozens of quotes from various senior managers. The first two are leaders of new, digital organizations whose remarks perfectly illustrate my point. Reams have been written about adopting a startup mentality, but its essence is the freshness I refer to here.

New organizations tend to use a narrow set of KPIs. Many use the Objectives & Key Results (OKR) model that originated with Intel and is also applied by Google and Uber, among others. The OKR model enables you to set and monitor clear objectives down to the level of the individual. A sample KPI Top 3: NPS, margin and turnover. And if I may turn this into a Top 5, I would add: repeat and ROA.

Monitoring and management in new organizations resembles High Frequency Trading. The frequency with which new businesses monitor and adjust their objectives may seem hectic to a manager in an established business, but feels completely normal to a digital entrepreneur. If you're a manager in an established organization experimenting with digital business models, you'd better get used to this pace. The new organizations we visited were managed almost in "real-time."

The No.1 asset of digital businesses is the speed with which they can adapt to stay competitive. These young managers monitor their operational targets on a weekly basis, and their strategic goals on a quarterly basis. They are right on top of their business's performance per category, channel, customer segment and product segment. Their motto is: know your ratios and know at any time, or at least once a week, how well you're doing. "If I can't monitor and adjust it on a weekly basis, it's useless," one young manager said.

However fast-paced the environment, the distinction between Running the Business and Changing the Business remains pertinent. In fact, most new companies don't even have the same people running and changing the business, although some who are involved in the day-to-day also participate in change projects. This is their way of ensuring that the right people are in the right jobs and that their focus remains firmly on running or changing the business. In our research, we found that in new companies with new business models, many running-the-business people participated in change initiatives. An average of 80% of people who worked in daily operations were also involved in change.

New businesses want to stay away from certain tendencies in established companies that are anathema to them. They are almost unanimous in their resolve to maintain their outward focus. There is nothing easier than analyzing your own database, but the trick is to avoid losing your outward-looking perspective. Another tendency they want to stay away from is the replacement of energy by resentment.

When I asked one young manager which typical characteristics of established organizations he wanted to guard against in his own organization, he said: complacency (no one can make a living off that), fact-freeness, figure-freeness, and endless, pointless meetings. He told me he used to randomly crash meetings and inquire whether they were necessary. This got a little overbearing, so he stopped, but he might resume this practice if he feels it's necessary.

Another entrepreneur said; "Before you know it, unwanted archaic practices sneak back in: complexity, officialdom, bureaucracy, rigidity and the absolute worst: a 9-to-5 culture. I'd rather see someone leave at 4 p.m. than at 1 minute to 5!" was his heartfelt cry.

It is great to have a working new business model and a modern business for the modern age, but the best thing might be that this is a chance to introduce modern processes, modern technology, a new management style and a brand-new culture. The latter in particular is an extraordinary luxury. Meanwhile, you can't forget about maintaining effectiveness, speed, simplicity and agility, of course.

There are operational basics that even new businesses can't do without. Let's put it this way: without these basics, they run the risk of descending into hipster hell. We spoke with the founder of a modern digital retail business who's back to asking and answering basic strategic questions. For example, what's our unique value proposition and which new products and markets should we target? He knows his organization can't compete on price with Amazon or Argos, because it's much smaller and doesn't have the same purchasing power. Other bare bones basics are regular analyses to stay abreast of where the business finds itself, what you're shooting for, and how you're going to get there. Get up on that soapbox every month and explain your vision and mission based on a solid management and leadership process, and solid HRM evaluation and remuneration processes. These are just a few examples.

Successful Application of Building Block 13, ADJUSTMENT

Case study: International tax and legal information publisher Wolters Kluwer introduces new service concepts
Breakthrough: The Legal & Regulatory division at Wolters Kluwer, a global provider of information services and solutions for legal and tax professionals, has implemented new service concepts for each of its customer segments in one of its geographical areas. This move was part of a transition to a more effective Go-To-Market strategy. The new concepts were intended to do justice to current customers' and prospects' value. The goal was to increase pressure on the market while drastically reducing the relatively high selling costs resulting from account managers' sales visits. Another goal was to improve the measurability of the company's sales efforts and results to get a firmer grip on the operation and to increase agility. These goals were achieved by introducing remote sales teams responsible for sales to customers in the mid to lower segments. The remote sales teams were also made responsible for account management in these segments. At the same

time, the publisher strengthened its online sales strategy and provided its sales teams with improved sales dashboards, virtual meeting rooms, and other digital tools.

Impact: The introduction of the remote sales teams led to an increase in customer coverage in the middle and lower customer segments from 40% to 70% in the first six months, at significantly lower cost. The portfolio value of the customers approached by the remote sales team is substantial and has kept growing. The real-time dashboards show figures like the total number of calls per day and the number of calls per employee, which are shared on large screens in the office. This enables the professionals to keep an eye on their own and their team's performance and make quick adjustments if necessary. This successful implementation has been rolled out to other countries where Wolters Kluwers' Legal & Regulatory division is active. Employees in these countries have been given a specific Go-To-Market Playbook.

7.2 Building Block 14: OPEN ARCHITECTURE

A simple, open architecture facilitates continuous development. It should be easy and self-evident to keep developing, updating and maintaining your design. This is how you secure, monitor and, if necessary, adapt your new way of working.

7.2.1 Maintain the content

It pays to find a format to record and maintain every idea and solution suggested for your earliest design and your original and iterated MVP. Although everything is subject to change in this digital age, you still need to maintain your design and make sure it is transferable and maintainable in the future. Aim high in terms of flexibility, accessibility and transferability. The best solution is to opt for a single architecture. Keep in mind that there are many options and that all of them are contested; whichever one you choose, some people will love it, and others will hate it.

Organizations have plenty of methods, techniques and tools to choose from. For example, an enterprise architecture model.[172] But ERP systems, too, can handle more than process automation and offer plenty of options for describing business processes. Plus there are many dedicated software options (cloud-based or otherwise) that support workflows.

In any case, it's imperative to choose one and apply it across the board. Any organization with more than 25 people will benefit from this. After all, if someone leaves, you don't want them to be irreplaceable. A single architecture methodology and tool ensures that any design and any process have a living backup, supported by a main architect and sponsors, or "godparents." They will remain responsible for maintaining the design long after its execution.

Create a living and closed maintenance loop. Make sure that the execution team maintains close contact with the MVP design team during and after every execution wave. The MVP design team and the execution team often overlap, but are seldom identical. In any case, designers and process owners need to coordinate their actions to ensure that the new processes are institutionalized in regular business operations and become part of a continuous improvement process.

Successful Application of Building Block 14, OPEN ARCHITECTURE

Case study: Alcontrol Laboratories (environmental and food analysis labs)
Breakthrough: To maintain and improve a new business process, the operational teams at Alcontrol hold daily standups and use a clear process architecture that gives them a consistent overview. That is the essence of a well-chosen architecture; it enables the organization to work from a position of overview and control. And those teams work hard! Every morning, every operational team in the organization holds a 10-minute standup with their team leader to learn from the work done yesterday and to plan what will be done today. Wherever possible, actions are directly assigned to one of the team members, while improvement initiatives are assigned to the process improvement team. If necessary, problems are escalated in less than an hour to the standups at department-head or management-team level. Improvement boards support visual management. There is a vertical improvement team that deals with continuous development at organization level and ensures that the process improvements developed by the various teams are institutionalized and integrated vertically. This vertical improvement team delivers a new release of the process architecture every six months and ensures the line organization implements this release.
Impact: Introduction of the standups has improved efficiency and effectiveness in the organization. Both individual employees and teams have more of an overview and more grip on their work, enabling them to reduce throughput times (96% of analyses are delivered on time), waste (5% reduction per year) and costs, and increase safety. The KPIs are different for every process and are in line with the objectives the

management has set. The process architecture provides a stable framework for maintenance and further development.

The soft building blocks in Accelerator 4: LEARNING and THE EXTRA MILE

Each accelerator has two hard and two soft building blocks. The soft building blocks in Accelerator 4 are LEARNING and THE EXTRA MILE. **Building Block 15, LEARNING**, shows how organizations seldom take the time to learn in detail from completed initiatives. This needs to change, because learning greatly increases your execution capacity. In **Building Block 16, THE EXTRA MILE**, you will see that successful institutionalization depends on how well the new processes are integrated in your line organization. Going the extra mile is the best way to ensure this.

7.3 Building Block 15: LEARNING

Learning is what enhances your execution capacity, but oddly enough, organizations seldom spell out the lessons learned from their completed initiatives. Organizations that do make that effort become demonstrably better at strategy execution after every initiative, because they apply the lessons they've learned in their next initiative.

7.3.1 Choose your teachable moment, method and format

It's now or never. Organizations seem reluctant to make use of this teachable moment. It is always last on the list, even though it is one of those rare opportunities that put you in a unique position to evaluate. The lessons to be learned are there *now*, right under your nose. You need to seize the moment. Three weeks from now it's too late, because you'll be swept up in the next initiative. That "aha" moment will be a distant memory and you will have lost the focus you have right now.

Leaders who take the opportunity to create a learning session will reap the benefits down the line, and their organizations will, too. Once you have decided to bite the bullet, and everyone has cleared a specific date on their calendar to evaluate and learn, try to make it a positive experience. An attractive agenda and positive jumping off points will ensure that this is not a chore, but an inspiration. Emphasize that you're there to learn, not to point the finger. Things will have gone wrong, obviously, and some aspects of execution will still be critical at this stage, so it is important to turn it into an appreciative inquiry, using a modern format.[173] It can also be refreshing to hold this learning session off-site, not in your regular office.[174]

Figure 39 shows a sample learning day agenda. The full benefit of this day becomes visible only when the lessons learned are applied directly in Accelerator 1, during portfolio-setting, and in Accelerator 2, when drafting each initiative's execution plan.

Figure 39 — **The ultimate learning day agenda: action-based learning.**

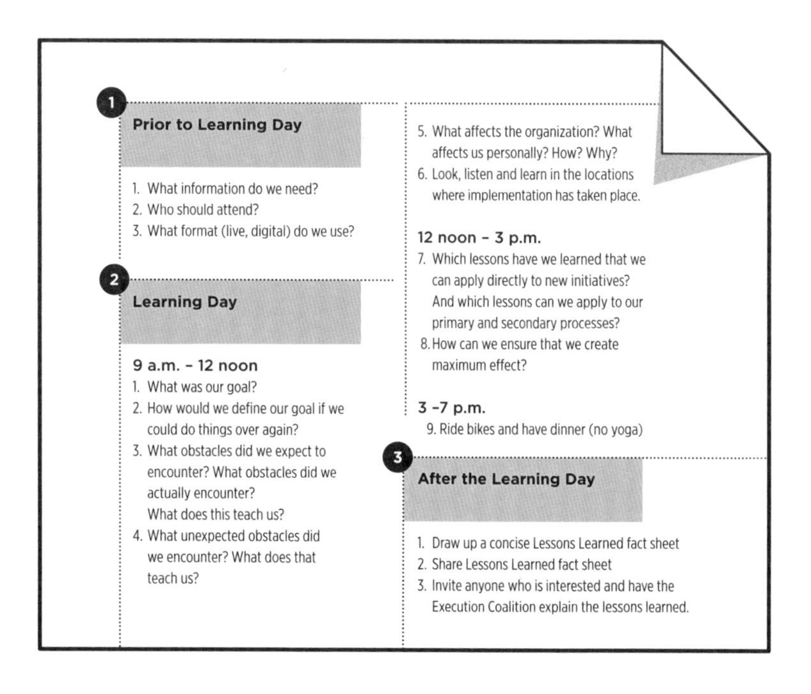

Source: Turner, 2016

Ensure that the learning process focuses on learning both hard, soft and project-based lessons to prevent everyone from zeroing in on interesting change management issues only. Avoid the path of least resistance. Don't just philosophize about where things went wrong. Don't focus on "them." Make sure you evaluate "us." Take the project management system used, your action management, and your progress report formats just as seriously as the hard business case system and the soft, cultural side of change.

Successful Application of Building Block 15, LEARNING

Case study: Royal Cosun, execution of growth-by-acquisition strategy
Breakthrough: Royal Cosun, an international agro-industrial cooperative that produces biobased products for food and non-food applications, has opted to pursue a growth strategy that is partially based on acquisitions. The takeovers are intended to make the cooperative grow in size as well as value. To this end, the business introduced a standardized M&A integration framework. Within this framework, recent acquisitions were systematically evaluated for how they were handled and how much value they added. The idea behind this evaluation was not to be able to "settle scores," but to learn from previous mistakes and apply these lessons to new acquisitions.
Impact: Royal Cosun consistently identifies, monitors and effectuates the main post-merger integration KPIs. For example, their goals are to realize 50% of synergy benefits in the first year after the merger; a customer and employee churn rate below 5% (the classic post-merger failure factors); 10% growth in specific markets, and so on. Structural evaluation of such KPIs serves two purposes: it tempers expectations of new acquisitions and it enables continuous improvement of the effectiveness of post-merger integration projects. Evaluation thus helps to realize the overall goal of 12% ROI.

7.4 Building Block 16: THE EXTRA MILE

Eventually, every initiative is handed off to the benefit realization managers in your line organization. They become the new owners of the goals and processes. Securement depends on integration into your primary processes. The best way to ensure this is by going the extra mile.

7.4.1 Embed benefit ownership

Benefit ownership and ownership of the new ways of working have to be integrated into your line organization. Every initiative should be finite and land in your line organization. Nothing is as risky as big programs and projects that start leading a life of their own and become little fiefdoms within a kingdom. Initiatives are selected and executed to improve, renew or innovate your core business processes. Eventually, the objectives of an initiative need to be subsumed into your organization's regular performance management system (in other words, the Running the Business side of the organization). If this has not happened organically along the way, the Execution Lead must make sure it happens when the initiative is completed. This integration into the line organization must encompass everything from management to budget to personally checking with the benefit realization managers to ensure they have realistic expectations. However, a word of caution is in order. The idea that it's time to hand off to line management can also come *too early* in the game, and can act as a false clap-o-meter, as I concluded on the basis of our study (see Chapter 9, Failure Factors). But once an initiative has been completed, it's time for the line managers to deal with it.

Note that the benefits realization managers in the line organization have to adopt not only the initiative's goals, targets and benefits, but also the new way of working and make sure this becomes embedded in the organization. Let's take an operational excellence program at a large Dutch university as an example. The program's goal was to increase efficiency in scheduling and planning, which would free up resources that would be used for teaching. A hand-picked team had analyzed and redesigned the scheduling and planning processes. They had periodically consulted with a carefully selected review and advisory group. No one in their right mind could call this an ivory tower approach. Yet, resistance could be expected from the education managers who had not been involved in the design, but who were now supposed to accept and apply this new planning and scheduling process. It would be unrealistic to expect smooth sailing. The "not-in-vented-here-syndrome" looms particularly large in this phase and you can't smooth it over by touting how you *have* consulted with future stakeholders, not even if you've played by the rules and religiously consulted, reviewed, enriched and communicated your design during Accelerators 1, 2 and 3.

The minimum requirements for successfully concluding an initiative by securing its institutionalization are a renewed psychological check-in, a foolproof tool kit, and management sessions. Each of the key roles must commit anew to the initiative in Accelerator 4. At this point, you need to ascertain that everyone is individually prepared to go the extra mile in order to bring the initiative to fruition. At this stage in the game, the Chief Execution Sponsor—and for a strategic program this is often the CEO—will have to revisit every benefit owner involved in the initiative. You want to make sure that every benefit owner feels ownership and takes it.

You'll also need a foolproof tool kit. You can't get away with quickly collating a few old fact sheets from Accelerators 1 and 2 to secure ownership. Instead, the program management office needs to provide the sponsor with a comprehensive tool kit that lays out all the program components on a silver platter, customized for each target group. This tool kit should look and read just as fresh and inspirational as when the initiative was about to begin. Some must-include elements are: ways to integrate the new way of working into regular management practices—performance management system, meetings, communication—and HR processes—recruitment, training, job evaluation. Your third must-have element is a series of well-prepared, well-organized and thoroughly followed-up management sessions to boost team spirit, unity and dependencies. The tool kit contains practical tools that help accomplish this. Excellent managers know this type of drudgery doesn't always lead to great acclaim, but they don't dodge systematically working through all the steps required to secure institutionalization. Excellent managers find a way to turn this into a celebration of the real benefits and their realization.

7.4.2 Execution Coalition: Finish what you started

If there was ever a moment when you are needed as a leader, this is it. Be hands-on and practical, and tie up any loose ends. While you are dealing with securing the execution, the execution itself is often still underway. If you were dealing with a big transformation in a large-scale organization, for instance, you might be starting to round off the initiative while Division No. 5, Business Unit 4, Department 5 is about to start scaling. Although it makes sense to want to apply the lessons learned at 80% of the transformation, don't forget that the remaining 20% is just as important.

Emphasize that the last wave is of equal value, or perhaps even greater, than the first wave. As they say, it ain't over 'til it's over. Whatever the hard goals and benefits, the "soft" effect of leaders who go the extra mile and actually complete the execution should not be underestimated. The following is a literal quote I heard during a large-scale transformation program at a temp agency: "Apparently, they're taking this very seriously, to the very end!" You see, the last blow is half the battle.

At this stage of acceleration, finishing the job is mainly a matter of removing any remaining obstacles. Those might come from closer to home than you would think. I once witnessed a board member create a big hullabaloo about kicking off a new project that largely overlapped with the initiative we were about to wrap up. Clearly, something had gone very wrong in the portfolio-setting in Accelerator 1, in the "soft" skills of collaboration and communication, in strategy execution management, and probably in several other areas.

Obviously, highlighting and celebrating your team's successes is an excellent incentive. Many stakeholders (both those involved in the program and those in the line organization) are probably exhausted at this point, while onlookers may have lost interest. It's up to the strategy execution coalition to organize the celebration. It's good to realize that the amount of energy professionals are willing to put into initiatives is proportionate to their opinion about how their organization executes and completes initiatives and whether they feel appreciated for their role in this.

And if this isn't reason enough, it also makes most sense from a strictly economic point of view. Many organizations fork out huge sums of money on large-scale transformations only to let the focus dissipate once these actually take off. They shift the focus exactly at the point when everything is finally up and running, when all the coalition needs to do is make use of the momentum and reap the benefits. Many opportunities are missed this way. Figure 40, about execution and benefit ownership during Accelerator 4, shows the five key roles of the execution coalition and the types of ownership in Accelerator 4.

Figure 40 — **The Execution Coalition: Execution and Benefit Ownership in Accelerator 4.**

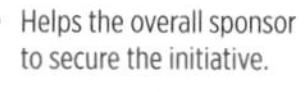

Source: Turner, 2016

The execution coalition leads and implements execution. At this stage, taking the lead, aka change leadership, is about capitalizing on what has been achieved, so that the organization learns, does better the next time and hence structurally improves its execution capacity and the hard and soft capabilities that go with that. You might think that this is overstating things, but it's true. Our study has shown that 70-80% of successful organizations learn from each completed initiative by making the lessons learned explicit in different ways. Concrete examples of improved capabilities are HRM competence and training requirements; new, explicitly mentioned and monitored conduct in the board room and the rest of the organization; tighter portfolio management; and improvements in the program management office.

The strength of the Execution Coalition is that alignment between Running the Business and Changing the Business, across disciplines and in the supply chain maximizes your chances of success. In this accelerator, alignment is mainly about coordinating dependencies in the line organization with the place in the organization where the initiative has been integrated. At the same time, these dependencies need to be aligned with possible new initiatives that are being prepared for execution, in accordance with Accelerator 2. Suppose, for example, that the completed project is a shared services center and that the board is currently discussing how to reap the synergy benefits of a recent merger. It would make sense to explore whether the business processes of the newly acquired business can be dovetailed with the new shared services center. At this stage, alignment is also about embedding the new way of working in regular processes and structures. For example, a radically different way of managing teams could be reinforced and consolidated by integrating it into the company's management development program.[175]

Successful Application of Building Block 16, THE EXTRA MILE

Case study: International law firm NautaDutilh, increases employee and customer satisfaction by institutionalizing continuous improvement
Breakthrough: A law firm is an organization built on professionals. Traditionally, the routing at NautaDutilh was content-based; professionals worked on legal questions from clients, delegated part of the work to colleagues and checked the results before delivering the answers to their clients. Possible optimization of these processes for both the professionals' and the clients' benefit, was not on the radar. Analyzing and monitoring these processes enabled the professionals to optimize

the results. To this end, the business processes were optimized to create added customer value (by way of Lean), and deliberately managed (legal project management) and enriched wherever possible with new technology. The institutionalization of these improvements in the organization is based on two pillars: 1. ensuring that the client is always involved and contributes to the improvements; and 2. the LEAN Academy, an internal training program in Lean methods. This has helped to embed continuous improvement in the organization, provided support for Lean projects and made it easier to initiate further steps. **Impact:** This new working method has led to verifiably higher margins, increased quality, increased job satisfaction and a better problem-solution fit for clients.

Useful Tips from Successful Leaders

Every chapter concludes with several proven, practical ideas that have helped leaders and professionals make a difference in real world situations. You can also use these as mini case studies and learning points.

1 **Execution Week.** Focus works. That goes for everything, as every manager and professional will tell you. Mostly, they refer to strategic focus. But some apply it to anything and everything in operational execution, with excellent results, which is of course strategic. After all, strategy equals execution! One tip you shouldn't skip is the Execution Week. One manager instigated this because he felt that this is not just a sequence of activities, but an intervention of monumental proportions. Spending a week not just minding the store, but really getting things done in Changing the Business has great impact. It creates focus and will be remembered for a long time. This week is a mix of hard goals and soft elements. Let's take a look at a sample Execution Week held during a post-merger integration program at a service provider:
   a **Institutionalization Monday.** By the end of the day, all the responsibilities have been fully, clearly and definitively transferred from the program organization to the line organization.
   b **Loose Ends Tuesday.** You're never completely done. Organize a 7 to 9 a.m. breakfast meeting with freshly baked croissants and fresh-squeezed orange juice to identify what's critically necessary. At nine sharp, work starts. Everyone is involved, from the mailroom to the boardroom. At noon, everybody takes a lunch break and shares updates. Then it's back to work, and from 6 p.m. to 7 p.m. you check things off the list together while eating some takeout. Attendance is mandatory. You need a *very* good excuse not to be there.

c **Learning Wednesday.** Discuss the lessons learned while everything is still fresh in mind. By dinnertime, you will know exactly what to do differently next time.

d **Extra Mile Thursday.** Nothing works better than raising the bar and keeping it very high. "You can't expect perfection," said the manager who swears by Execution Weeks, "but you can certainly expect people to strive for excellence." Therefore, one day in the Execution Week is reserved for going the extra mile. Make time to ask your top five customers what else they expect from the merger.

e **Celebration Friday.** Fortunately, the inventor of the Execution Week does not think celebrating means engaging in some horribly embarrassing team building activity like paintball, but an authentic day away from the office with room for athletics, creativity and games. In other words, a day that is melt-in-the-mouth soft and seemingly has nothing to do with organizational development, but which will actually deliver solid results because it provides time and space for the type of interaction that can really make a difference in people's engagement.

2 **Final Push.** This idea came from a COO who knew that any subsequent change would be taken seriously if people saw that current change projects were seen through to the very end. He came up with the idea of the Final Push, whose goal was to bring the same energy to the last stage of the project as to kickoff. This works very well. By completing the execution and embedding the changes, you achieve three things. You squeeze every last drop of result out of the project instead of letting the learning part go unused; you increase the odds that your changes will prove sustainable; and most importantly, you ensure that everyone involved feels taken seriously. The latter is not always the case at the tail end of implementations.

3 **Debriefing Dinner.** Not surprisingly, the manager who thought of the Commitment Café also came up with the idea of the Debriefing Dinner. These dinners are tough evaluations with every key actor from the initiative, ranging from the program manager and the various experts to the execution lead of the very last rollout. The focus is on what has been achieved, not only for the organization, but also in terms of personal development. The key is to do this in an informal setting, over a good meal.

All these ideas call for valuable, but time-consuming involvement. To a great extent, time expenditure is what effective strategy execution is all about. "How would our time be best spent?" is a question well worth asking.

8

PROGRAM AND PROJECT MANAGEMENT ARE INDISPENSABLE

Graham cracker crust / freestyling every day / the attention span of a goldfish / transcending Maslow / disdain is pathetic / speed dates and quality time / breaking the rules a little

Program and project management have been covered extensively by many authors. Without trying to redo their excellent work, let me summarize what managers and professionals consistently emphasize as essential for effective execution. Sometimes they even wax lyrical about it. That's hardly surprising, as professional program and project management plays a key role in almost every strategy execution initiative, whether it's about post-merger integration, outsourcing, development of leadership qualities or restructuring. This chapter covers the main points for each accelerator.

Effective project and program management has four functions. This holds true across all four accelerators. One, it's an engine. It gets the execution started and keeps it going. Two, it's integrative. It combines, aligns and integrates the hard goals and soft elements described in this book. Three, it's a monitor. It measures progress and manages risk. And four, it delivers. It ensures the technical realization of the project and program results, which is not a matter of leaning back and waiting for it.

A word of caution to prevent unnecessary resentment among project and program managers; this chapter will by necessity be somewhat technocratic. That's because the vital distinction between hard goals and soft, change-oriented elements in strategy execution has already been discussed at length. Therefore, all that remains in this discussion of project and program management is the technical angle. This is bound to worry any excellent project and program manager. They needn't be concerned or feel that I am ignoring certain things. I fully agree that any project and program management that disregards hard goals or soft change-oriented elements is pointless, an empty shell. Project and program management plays a pivotal, facilitating role in the combined and ongoing efforts of achieving results, instigating change, and aligning and integrating projects and programs into the line organization.

Many professionals and managers would prefer to "freestyle" every day and thoroughly dislike structure, action planning, progress reports and risk management. However, every successful professional and manager has discovered that they can't do without top-notch professional project and program management. You need that firm base. It's like the Graham cracker crust under my favorite New York cheesecake.

8.1 Project and Program Management During Accelerator 1: SELECT

8.1.1 Select a method and stick with it

There are various good methods, some more structured like tools than others. The trick is to choose just a few. One is not enough, as a complicated technology project obviously requires a different method than a small improvement project in your line organization. And you don't want to kill a fly with a bazooka. But limit your selection. Some good program and project management methods are Managing Successful Programmes (MSP),[176] IPMA,[177] Agile PM and Prince2.[178] And let's not forget the highly practicable and accessible Project Canvas, designed by internationally acclaimed management consultant Rudy Kor.[179] Like so many other business management domains, project and program management runs the risk of unprofessionalism. So again, it's important to prevent project and program managers from indulging their personal preferences at the cost of a central focus in the organization and its limited resources. Do not allow people to try random methods or to introduce a different method than the one(s) you have selected.

8.1.2 Develop people's basic competencies

Ideally, every employee at every organizational level not only has line responsibilities, but is also involved in at least one or two execution and change projects. Everyone can therefore be expected to have some basic project competencies. Again, this is not a matter of leaning back and waiting for it. Recruit people who have these skills and encourage your current employees to develop them. Accelerator 1, when you are setting your strategy and deciding on your portfolio of initiatives, is a particularly crucial time to analyze whether your organization has the necessary project and program management competencies and capacity. If necessary, you can tell your superiors that the acquisition of such competencies must be included as one of the initiatives in the portfolio. And don't forget that participation in strategy execution projects may be the very best learning curve available. Inexperienced but promising employees can learn from the project and program management stars. People learn more from one real-life situation than from ten theoretical training sessions. In creating the right conditions, you need to focus on the actual necessities. How many, and what type of permanent, in-house project and program managers do you need in order to forge strategy execution breakthroughs in initiatives organized outside of your line organization, in projects or programs?

8.1.3 Complex, multidisciplinary changes require a project-based approach

In many boardrooms, the "P words" are taboo. This is hardly surprising, as there are usually far too many ongoing projects and programs that are adding enormous pressure without delivering actual results, and that have sometimes even started leading a life of their own. However, it's unwise to let your line organization execute every strategy initiative just to avoid any project or program implementation. Most strategy execution initiatives are complex, multidisciplinary changes that can only be managed effectively as a project or program. And the whole issue is complicated further by semantics. Just consider who's responsible for carrying out projects and programs. Your line organization, of course. So, resisting the P words serves absolutely no purpose.

Selecting the appropriate type of project or program for your purpose is important. Type 1 initiatives that deal with incremental improvements need a light touch. The core team should be "anchored" in the business unit or department where the main issue resides and other disciplines can join as needed. The work can then be delegated to virtual, temporary working groups. However, ensure that the core team is a separate, visually recognizable and central coordinating entity. Other than that, normal project management principles should be applied, including choosing an appropriate action/risk/progress/project management method; taking a very structured approach; defining crystal clear goals, roles and tasks; and profiling the project as a short-term, clearly delineated endeavor—at kickoff, in communications and in every other respect. Type 1 projects should have a three month horizon at most. If by then you have not reaped the benefits, this is not an incremental improvement project. Those benefits should be subsumed into your primary process every quarter.

Type 2 initiatives (renewal) require a heftier project and program management approach. Let's say you're dealing with a post-merger integration project. Generally, this involves several disciplines in two organizations and the goal is usually to achieve some significant synergy. It's a no-brainer that this requires a robust project approach.

Type 3 initiatives (for radical innovation) require both modern project management methods and modern development methods such as agile and Scrum. If an initiative is set apart from the organization or treated like a startup, your project will become less complex, because there will be fewer dependencies on the existing organization that need managing.

By the way, strategy-setting in Accelerator 1 should be treated as a project in its own right. The discipline of the strategy consultancy involved will determine how well the project performs in terms of (1) time, (2) money, (3) quality, (4) information and (5) organization, and whether there's a viable balance between hard goals and soft change aspects.

8.2 Project and Program Management During Accelerator 2: INITIATE

8.2.1 Excellent start: Taking time to make an excellent action plan

Distinguish between getting started and being underway for every project or program. At the beginning, it's imperative to be thorough and arrive at a plan that's sound in terms of both content (hard goals) and change management (the soft, people-centered approach). Once you're on track, it is important to set an effective rhythm for both hard and soft activities.

Just as in strategic analysis and course setting at organization level, your planning at initiative level should neither take forever, nor be rushed. "Going slow to go fast" is essential. After all, you do want to execute the right things.

Select a format and stick with it. Many managers and professionals have a love-hate relationship with models and formats, templates, checklists and canvases (or fact sheets, as I call them in this book). You should realize, however, that these serve some really important purposes. First of all, anything longer than a single page has probably not been sufficiently thought through. Also, fact sheets improve people's focus. We live in a time when the average goldfish (I'm not joking, this has been researched) has a longer attention span than we do when casually skimming through a text. Therefore, a fact sheet enables your stakeholders to quickly ingest the essence of your initiative. In fact, every piece of information should come with a summary and be structured like a pyramid, so that readers can decide how deep they want to go. Also, fact sheets make the transfer of knowledge more dependable. Rather than relying solely on oral transmission, key actors who need to continue strategy execution, scale it, communicate it, review it, and make decisions about it, have a written source to refer to. And lastly, fact sheets contribute to the agility and iteration capacity of the strategy execution method I present in this book. Strategy execution is about targeted experimentation and scaling what works. In this fast-paced environment, keeping an overview is essential. Hence, it is crucial to update your fact sheets at key moments to keep them current. This will tell you where you stand, what you are doing and why, and what your main upcoming tasks are. If a main issue is not on your fact sheet, it does not exist. See download #10 from Appendix 5 that brings you to the downloadable project and program management fact sheet and the fact sheets for Accelerators 1 through 4, all of which focus both on hard goals and soft change management aspects.

8.2.2 An effective project and program management structure reflects both goal and phase

A project and program structure reflects and expedites your goal. Your carefully thought out structure is neither too large nor too small; it distinguishes logical elements that each have their own logical work package. Every key actor knows what their goal and role is and has a clear picture of how the total project or program structure is supposed to function.

The same is true of the project or program' s embedding and management. After all, a perfect project or program structure that is anchored in the wrong discipline or at the wrong level of the organization is not going to have any impact.

Just as in your regular organization, the structure you select must cover 80% of your work flows. Strategic projects and programs employ highly educated, autonomous professionals who spend the majority of their time working on their assigned tasks. They coordinate within and outside of their project or program when necessary. Ideally, 80% of their work is project or program-related. If not, there is something wrong with the project or program's main structure.

It is not at all strange to adapt your structure and management for each execution phase. When I suggest this, stakeholders often balk. "Do you mean to say my structure won't do anymore!?" My answer is: "Exactly! It's fine for now—until the end of this phase, but in two weeks' time, at the start of the next phase, it won't do any more."

One of the success factors our study revealed is seizing any and all opportunities to radically change the allocation of your resources (time, money and energy). And—surprise, surprise—this is facilitated in large part by project and program management. Management's monitoring and integrative role are precisely what enables a clear focus on this allocation of resources both during the initial planning stage and during the project at regular consultation and reporting intervals. At this stage of Accelerator 2, it is important that you are extremely concrete about the resources, money and capacity that the five key roles of an initiative need.

Expertise reigns supreme. Some program and project managers seriously believe that projects and programs can be run without any expert knowledge. Avoid those people. You might as well hire a robot or fill in forms supplied by online software. As our study has shown, excellent program managers always put knowledge and expertise first, and always refer back to that. They are great at consistently applying this to the change management side of things.

Program and project managers, if you stick with what you're good at, you'll be worth your weight in gold. There are program and project managers who are beyond technology, or who—inspired by spiritual courses and Maslow's hierarchy—might well be on their way to transcending it. They're not interested in managing technical basics such as progress and risk management or budget monitoring and action management, and would rather focus on the team and cultural development of the program or project they've been assigned to manage. They make the elementary mistake of thinking those basics are no longer relevant because *they* happen to be bored with them. However, it should be obvious that the basics need to work. Flawlessly.

When needed, supplement your staff with external hires who you hold accountable. Professionals in projects and programs used to come in two flavors: employees, and external business partners and suppliers, such as IT, strategic, management and HRM consultants. Recruitment and selection procedures were clear-cut and there was always some good-natured, or sometimes testy, squabbling between internal and external people. Collaboration between permanent, semiflexible and flexible professionals is the New Normal and it no longer makes sense to distinguish between flexible in-house professionals and external hires who work on projects. All internal and external professionals are selected based on skills and experience relevant to the project, and that's also what they are accountable for. But there's a paradox here, too. The more normal this situation becomes, the more important buying professional services becomes. Ensure that professional services are bought professionally, that is, based on value and accountability, and with remuneration based partly on a contingency fee, as Fiona Czerniawska and Peter Smith discuss in their excellent book *Buying Professional Services*.[180]

8.3 Project and Program Management During Accelerator 3: HARVEST

8.3.1 Agile and Scrum require project management too

Many people seem to feel—based on wishful thinking, I suspect—that agile and Scrum methodologies make project-based working superfluous. However, project management is indispensable for keeping agile and Scrum methods focused and to maintain the right balance between freedom and structure. Granted, this has changed the project or program manager's role. Project and program managers are no longer omnipotent doers who control the timeless, big five indicators—time, money, quality, information and organization—but facilitators who make their teams face up to their responsibilities and support them, particularly in agile and Scrum methodologies. Hence, that is also their role during Accelerator 3, which is about much more than simply tracking progress.

There were times when people showed disdain about project management and scoffed that "anyone can fill in a planner!" But nowadays, such contempt is considered pathetic. Professional program and project management is a vital and challenging field. Sponsors know that program and project management are the means to an end (execution), and recognize its exigency. They get justifiably irritated when project or program management is not in order, even when everything else goes right in terms of energy, engagement and results.

8.3.2 The crucial basics

Make sure you nail the crucial basics of professional project and program management. These must be part of every action plan and applied in the regular progress monitoring structure. Important basics include meeting formats, action and progress monitoring systems, fixed rhythms and standard agendas during execution.

Most professionals dislike meetings. You can count me among them, especially when it comes to meetings that last longer than an hour. However, appropriately chosen meetings play a pivotal, integrative role in strategy initiatives executed as projects or programs. Depending on the size of the project or program, make sure the following classical types of meeting are regularly scheduled:

- Sponsor meeting
- Steering group meeting
- Core team meeting
- Working group or work flow meeting
- Review meeting

More and more projects and programs affect production chains that extend beyond their structure. This is also reflected in their staffing. If the supply chain approach becomes a dominant characteristic, you should rebrand your steering group meetings as chain-level meetings.

8.3.3 Action and decision management, and progress reports

Every methodology contains a section on action and decision management. Rather than a bureaucratic trifle, this is elementary. Clearly, you can't expect to be praised for what is disparagingly known as "the checklists." They are obviously not the most inspirational aspect of a project or program, but these lists do deserve your attention anyway. Put on a red nose if you want to pretend it's fun, but don't skip this part.

Well-chosen progress reports have a pivotal, integrative function in projects and programs. Like effective strategy execution, effective initiative progress reports need to balance progress in terms of hard goals, soft change, and project and program management. Such reports should consist of a single page and consist of a short review and preview of the usual aspects: hard goals (realization, content); soft change-related goals (ownership, change strategy); and project progress (in terms of the well-known five parameters: time, money, quality, information and organization).

Progress reports are another one of those aspects of a project or program that few professionals love. But there are exceptions. Good professionals know that progress reports force them to take responsibility and create a zoomed-out overview of the project or program. That's crucial, because if you keep gaining momentum without ever stopping to see where you're going, you might overlook some threats until it's too late.

Keep it short. Sponsors and other stakeholders only want to read brief progress reports, particularly during Accelerator 3, which may last a while. Spare yourself the trouble of writing long-winded pieces, because no one wants to read those. However, be aware that it takes longer to write a good brief report than to write a bad long one.

8.3.4 Crucial standard agendas

Make sure that every meeting agenda keeps you focused on the basics. Fixed agendas list items that need to be discussed in meetings at regular intervals during the project or program. One of those items, all will agree, is progress in relation to your planning. Another important one is "people," where you check whether everyone is doing their part, without judging them. This is primarily about paying systematic attention to what is of paramount importance: your human capital. Obviously, not every fixed item on the agenda needs to be discussed every time; frequencies can vary.

Specific agendas list items that are relevant during a particular phase. For example, one item might be how to deal with conflict between two large projects with extensive dependencies in terms of content and change management. This can be a politically sensitive item, because the projects might be subject to a lot of exposure outside the organization, either in the market or among stakeholders. This can be the case in a public organization that has the government looking over its shoulder. However, a specific agenda is aimed primarily at dealing with unforeseen situations. Responding with agility to the unexpected is exactly what project and program managers spend most of their time on.

It is also useful to distinguish between short, quick items (speed dates) and longer, in-depth discussions (quality time). It's helpful to make this distinction visually recognizable on your agenda. A speed date lasts no more than 5 minutes and is intended to inform the attendees or to facilitate a quick decision. Longer, in-depth items require quality time. You do not want to be rushed when you are considering several angles and points of view. That might take anywhere from 30 to 60 minutes. Note, however, that this distinction does not say anything about the preparation necessary for each category. Every single item on the agenda should be well prepared.

8.3.5 Structure creates more time and flexibility

Fixed schedules carry the risk of creating a ritual that loses its authenticity, or so some people think. These people tend not to like structure either. Yet, a highly structured, fixed-interval approach is one of the very best ways to create time for tailor-made adjustments, creativity and quality time. It also allows you to make adjustments along the way (see also Success Factor 6 in Section 2.6, about the importance and usefulness of standardization.

8.3.6 Human Resource Management: A key topic from start to finish

Program and project managers know that people—or more technically speaking, human resources—are the main bottleneck in virtually every program or project. "Give me the right people and I can achieve any goal," a few seasoned program managers told me during their interviews. That's exactly where things get tough. Execution of highly strategic, must-win initiatives often winds up being shouldered by the same group of people. This is partly justified, because quality tends to rise to the top, but it's not entirely right, because other people's capacities tend to be underestimated.

Human resources have always been a bone of contention, and probably always will be. That's not to say there's no best practice. HRM is a key topic and process. Acknowledge this by turning it into a fixed item on the agenda for every important meeting. This helps you to avoid running into problems unawares and too late. For example, you don't want to miss how key actors are overburdened for too long and are struggling to fulfill their line duties as well as their duties in the two projects they're part of. That's how people get burned out, which is exactly what you want to avoid. Not realizing that an employee is being driven to the point of illness harms both the employee and your organization.

8.3.7 Mindset: Entrepreneurship

Talks with really successful program managers bear a certain resemblance to conversations with entrepreneurs. Regular program or project managers go to work and do a decent job. But excellent program or project managers give it their all and run their program or project as if it's their own business. They show commitment at every turn. They shed blood, sweat and tears along with everyone else, but keep enough distance to deliver at operational level and to think up and implement the appropriate tactical and strategic interventions. They break the rules a little, if necessary. Sometimes a bit of anarchy is the only way to get results. This mindset is especially crucial during Accelerator 3.

8.4 Project and Program Management During Accelerator 4: SECURE

8.4.1 Program and project management deliver the results

At the end of the day, the only thing that matters is whether you have realized the project or program goals. Pure professional pride ensures that project and program managers care more about this than anyone else. They are the conscience of strategy execution. There are countless examples of sales effectiveness improvement programs where the sales director and sponsor drop out as soon as enough benefits have been realized. It's even worse if they do this after the first (inevitable) setback. In both cases, the real benefit realization and securement have yet to begin.

Other, equally important questions are whether the benefits are sustainable and what lessons were learned from the execution. These questions need to be asked explicitly to significantly increase the chance of improving the way you tackle your next project or program. That's what Accelerator 4 is all about: securement and learning.

8.4.2 The program's role is not over until it's over

The relationship between programs and projects on the one hand, and the line organization on the other, has always been complicated. Don't waste your time fretting about this. Once you've settled on a program or project approach, there's a tendency to pass the endeavor to the line organization way too soon. Sometimes this happens right after the start and the first few steps. "It's time the line organization took over" is a risky statement. Of course, the people in your line organization need to do a lot right from the start, namely staff the project or program! But both the project or program and your line organization need to go all out throughout the execution.

Three generic principles remain valid from start to finish. One is that projects and programs are only a means to an end—the end being to improve, renew or innovate the going concern—and are therefore by definition temporary. Two is that your line organization is responsible for benefit realization right from the start, while the program is responsible for execution to the bitter end. And three, successful approaches recognize three stages in the coproduction of line organization and program, or line organization and project. The project or program is not dismissed halfway through execution, but plays a role to the very last day (see Figure 41).

Align, at every level, everywhere, all the time. The lion's share (about 80%) of any project or program should be carried by the structure you have chosen, regardless of whether it is about how your existing organization is structured or about what the structure, mandate and scope of your strategy initiatives should be. If this is not the case, you have chosen the wrong structure and have given people the wrong assignment. But even if 80% fits well, there is still another 20% that needs aligning. You need to stay nimble all the way through execution, if only because there are so many natural interdependencies between the various initiatives in an organization. Many process innovation projects require customized technology support, and hence alignment.

Alignment never stops, in part because you can't foresee every turn. It is also about constantly adapting your business model. For example, one interviewee told me how HRM stepped in at the tail end of an

Figure 41 — **The line organization / program coproduction has three stages.** The program's role continues to the very end of the execution.

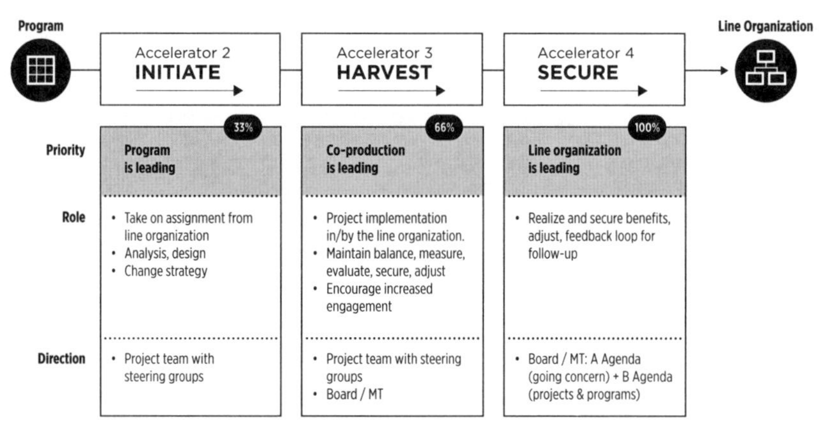

Source: Turner, 2016

execution project and restructured all the roles. This was a golden opportunity to include the HRM implications of the new way of working in the whole process and to adapt job descriptions and competency profiles to reflect the competencies and requirements needed in the new business process. If brand-new processes are not integrated into HRM—recruitment, selection, job descriptions, training, job evaluation—they will be hampered or may not work at all. Make sure that everyone knows who's responsible for alignment, both overall and for each workflow or working group. The most logical solution is to assign this responsibility to the project or program management team.

8.5 Project management is a whole ecosystem

Project and program management's role might best be described as a process, or ecosystem.[181] Project and program management not only connects and directs the hard goals and content of strategy execution, but it also links these with the soft, change-oriented elements. Project and program management needs to embrace good leadership in order for this ecosystem to flourish. And this is not the only balance that counts in this ecosystem. It is just as essential that there is an equilibrium between the initial strategy (Accelerator 1 and most of 2) and the actual execution (Accelerators 2 through 4).

Useful Tips from Successful Leaders

Every chapter concludes with several proven, practical ideas that have helped leaders and professionals make a difference in real world situations. You can also use these as mini case studies and learning points.

For Accelerators 1 and 2:

- **Stakeholder Map.** A seasoned program manager told me that one of her most important activities is to thoroughly map out all her stakeholders and their positions, interests, strengths and weaknesses—as people, that is. Based on this map, she selects her interventions. Programs are human endeavors. So, you need to understand what makes the people you are working with tick.
- **In Their Shoes.** The same program manager contends that mapping out her human capital is not enough; you need to go deeper. Sometimes the dynamics can be so complicated that it may take an hour of full-on sparring with someone in your program to really understand the people and dynamics. You need to put yourself in their shoes. That's not new age psychobabble, but sheer necessity.

For Accelerators 3 and 4:

- **Meaningful Progress Reports and Discussion.** One manager got frustrated with the empty routine of his monthly progress reports. "It takes hours to compile those progress reports, which are then barely even glanced at before the steering group meeting. I see empty looks everywhere." So, does that mean it's time to throw in the towel? No! You need to report on progress, but make it concise. This manager simplified the format, expertly balanced the hard, soft and project-related aspects and added storytelling as a marker of soft progress, asking: "What story from the previous month do we need to hear because it leverages implementation?"
- **Resource Allocation Map.** The notion that 80% of your resources should be spent on execution rather than analysis and design is widely endorsed, but seldom enforced. One manager at a publishing group deliberately focuses on this. He makes sure the analysis and design phase does not cost more than 20% of the available time and budget and monitors this.
- **Entrepreneurial Spirit.** One of the best program managers I know told me the secret of his success: "Make sure that program managers and their project managers look at the program as their own business." He cultivates this entrepreneurial spirit from day one. The fact that programs are run separately from the line organization for a time brings with it certain risks, but also certain opportunities. Make use of these. One of the advantages, according to my source, is that you can cultivate a strong subculture, in the best sense of the word—a "let's-get-things-done" culture, against the grain. One of his tips is to organize a Business Owners Meeting, where his people spar about issues like "What do I need to be successful? If this were my business, what would I need to get done? What's stopping me?"

9

FAILURE

Slush and whipping cream gone sour / nothing lamer than self-deception / conceptual top-heaviness / marshmallows / self-serving bias

This chapter focuses on failed strategy execution. In order to understand why strategy execution fails for 60% of organizations, we explore the reasons for failure in more depth than other analyses. Our research has revealed that failure is not just caused by the factors we're all familiar with, but at least as often by less familiar factors. This is why this chapter draws a distinction between familiar and less familiar failure factors.

Looking into failure only makes sense if we also ask ourselves what the price of failure is and answer the "so what?" question. The answer is simply that the cost is high and continuing to climb. It's become a life-and-death matter.

9.1 Growing Impact of Failure: It's Life or Death

When I give in-company presentations I always pose the question, "How good do you think you are at strategy execution?" Invariably, people think they're better at strategic analysis and course-setting than at execution. So, that's where the trouble starts. Everyone shrugs off the problem. There is only one thing more important than strategy-setting and that is strategy execution, and it's the hardest thing to do. Studies have shown that no less than 60% of strategies fail in execution.[182] Some researchers even cite a 90% failure rate. Part of the problem is probably due to people being people: always taking on more than they can actually handle. However, that does not fully explain such a high failure rate. In other words, there is a world to be gained by understanding the cause. In order to benefit from failing, you need to know what went wrong, why, and at what cost.

9.1.1 Failure costs

In times of increasing hyper-competitiveness and dwindling resources, failure is a high-stakes matter. It can be the difference between survival or bankruptcy. Failure costs are clearly identifiable, but tend to be left unspecified, both in quantitative and qualitative terms. Spelling out failure costs might seem superfluous, but isn't. Our research has identified the following types of failure costs.

Delayed execution

When strategy execution is delayed or flawed, your organization's strategic goals will also be delayed, or even thwarted entirely. This is true of both small, incremental goals and large, urgent breakthroughs. Operationally, delays have an impact on your objectives in terms of customer, stakeholder and employee satisfaction. Delays also have quantifiable negative consequences for your financial goals, such as projected revenue, margin and costs.

High direct costs

In any program or project, high costs may become a problem. The reasons for this vary widely, such as a wrong or overly broad scope, lack of monitoring and control, excessively long or misdirected analysis and design efforts, unsuitable people, and involving users too soon, too late or too little.

High indirect costs

Strategy execution costs money, and not just out of pocket money. If an initiative fails, there is usually no choice but to bear the costs, in other words write them off. This is usually the best thing to do, because you have to know when to cut your losses. However, the problem with strategy execution is that the costs tend to be structurally higher, because of investments in technology, for example. When those investments turn out to be worthless, the total cost of ownership has increased significantly without realization of a business case. As one of my clients once said: "This is how it tends to go: At the start of the project, I am promised a great business case that will contribute to my organization's goals at lower cost. But it usually ends with no business case and higher costs." Indirect costs also include a higher employee turnover rate due to frustration.

Overburdened and frustrated employees

Failed projects tend to frustrate the employees involved. They feel they are no longer taken seriously and their worker satisfaction plummets. One of the main causes is that they feel insufficiently supported during execution.

Untapped potential

Professionals and other employees are down to earth; much more so than many managers assume. They tend to be loyal to their profession and their organization. In exchange, they expect to be taken very seriously. Subpar leadership, unprofessional conduct and an unwillingness to learn from previous mistakes in strategy execution tend to cause dissatisfaction and may lead professionals to consider leaving.

Failure to fail, particularly in radical innovation

Failure is costlier when participants have neglected to learn from earlier stumbles. Success is not a one-time effort, especially not when you are dealing with radical innovation. Instead, participants need to learn from failure, and to fail fast and often, in order to increase their subsequent chances of success. Not doing so will drive up the price of failure.

New initiatives

When strategy execution fails, new initiatives will have to be started, at new costs. The envisioned benefits of strategy execution will only be realized later.

Growing social impact

Wastefulness and failure are no longer exclusively a concern for managers and shareholders. They affect everyone and everything, particularly now that many organizations have assumed social responsibilities or are in the spotlight because of their activities. We all know the headlines about failed technology implementations and gigantic budget overruns. Whenever public money is involved, it becomes painfully obvious what the price of failure is. And the worst thing is that these failed projects just keep repeating themselves.

You might consider this a nightmare. But you could also look at it and think, "What great potential!" We need to turn things around. We need to do better. Not only is it a matter of survival, it's also a chance to get an edge over your competitors in this new day and age.

9.1.2 A critical look at failure figures

All this attention to failure factors in strategy execution calls for a critical note. Every year some famous research institute or agency publishes another study on execution issues in general and into the reasons why certain strategy execution initiatives fail.[183] But how well-founded are these studies and how realistic are their conclusions?

Most sources claim that a very high percentage of strategy execution initiatives fail. Yet some researchers stress that these are estimates, based on outdated or incomplete information.[184]

In his *Harvard Business Review* article titled "The Execution Trap," Roger L. Martin explains that drawing a distinction between strategy and execution is often used to cover up a failing strategy. The argument is that the strategy was fine, but that the execution was all wrong. According to Martin, it is usually consultancies who tend to separate the two. This allows them to tell their clients that there was nothing wrong with their strategy, and that the client's execution is to blame for the failure.[185]

In addition, it's good to remember that failure analysis can become a self-fulfilling prophecy. The more we talk about strategy execution failing, the greater the chance that it will actually happen and the higher the failure percentage gets.[186]

Is 100% feasible? What do these studies actually measure? They are invariably based on the initiatives' stated goals. But the question is whether it's fair to set off the results against 100%. Is a perfect score even feasible? Organizations generally build in a 10% strategic stretch, which is a margin that must be subtracted from the goal before a failure percentage can be calculated. Strategic stretch is sort of a reality check. Organizations tend to aim high, in part because of the competitive market. Their goals therefore tend to be more ambitious than they can handle. This discrepancy—or strategic stretch—serves a purpose. But if it's too high, it won't work. Your goals are not credible and people won't buy it, regardless of whether you offer them an incentive of personal, variable remuneration. And if the stretch is too low, people won't get into gear.

Is the type of change taken into account?
A 90% failure rate is quite normal for Type 3 (radical innovation) initiatives. But for a Type 1 initiative (like a Lean project), this would be shockingly bad. And failure to increase your market share in a downward

trending competitive displacement market (such as ad sales in print media) is more pardonable than failure in a growth market with few competitors.

Even with a generous correction, there is lot of room for improvement. Additional research, based on a combination of input and output measurements, would generate far more reliable figures. The hypothetical 10% strategic stretch is not the only possible correction. It's not unthinkable that some research has a negative bias and primarily measures what goes wrong.

Still, our experiences and case studies prove that even after correction, the failure rate is high. A 50-60% failure rate is probably close to the truth.

9.2 Examples of Complete or Partial Failure

One of the requirements of our research was that it had to generate practical examples and insights. You can find these throughout the book, and in this chapter too. But while it's important to discuss failure, naming carries the risk of shaming. Therefore, I would like to preface these examples with a few words of caution.

In Northern Europe, failure in the (semi)public sector tends to be more widely known than in the private sector. We are much better informed about failure in the public domain than in private enterprise. However, that says very little about the failures in the private sector.

Failure is seldom absolute. Partial failure is virtually universal. Who could claim to have completed every restructuring operation 100% successfully? Just take Philips; over the past 40 years, they have at one time or another fallen into every category of possible failures listed below. Yet, they have recorded far more successes in that time period, too.

Failure is a must in innovation. Most innovations fail. And rightfully so. Wherever that's not the case, people are not experimenting enough. Just look at the number of innovative startups, or the early developers of smart watches. Only a very small percentage has survived. Large corporations tend to put a toe in the water more often and pull out immediately if their chances of success appear small. Those corporations can afford failure. Beyond that, we only hear their success stories, or what is known as the Steve Jobs Effect.

Important disclaimer. Bearing in mind the qualifications mentioned above, all the examples I give below were either "tough nuts to crack," partial failures, or even complete failures. For clarity's sake, I have not included this information in every heading. These examples are cases that I came across during my research. Some are single business examples, some are observations about an entire industry. I have categorized these examples into mergers, restructuring, cultural change programs, IT implementations and innovations.

Mergers and integration projects

An entire library could be filled with the books that have been written about failed mergers. This gives a skewed image, though. Governments can afford fewer failures under democratic scrutiny. Post-merger integration processes therefore take a lot longer in the public domain, with all the obvious pros and cons.

Private businesses

- Imtech. Many of this technical services provider's later acquisitions were never fully integrated in the core corporation. This led to fraud in its German and Polish branch, which ultimately led to bankruptcy in 2015.
- KPN. The biggest telecom business in the Netherlands (formerly a state-owned organization, privatized in 1989) bought up too many of its smaller competitors and grossly overspent on UMTS licenses in 2001. The company got into such deep financial trouble it needed a state bailout to stay solvent.
- Anything Microsoft touches turns to lead, it seems. Promising startups become lame ducks under its wing. The company structurally pays bloated prices, but stays afloat because of its cash cows Windows and Office.

Public and semipublic sectors

- Tergooi hospitals. Mergers in health care tend to produce dubious results. Two hospitals in the Netherlands that merged in 2006 found themselves mired in problems with incompatible IT systems. Rather than synergy, this led to chaos and job losses.
- ProRail. In the early 1990s the Dutch state decided to privatize its railway infrastructure. This has resulted in costly failures for several construction projects and huge budget overruns.

Restructuring operations

Public and semipublic sectors

- The Dutch Tax and Customs Administration. The Dutch counterpart of America's IRS implemented a restructuring that led to thousands of lay-offs. New computer systems were supposed to take over the work. But technology has its limits, it turned out, and the whole operation was very costly, in part because of an ill-conceived severance package scheme for older employees.

- Amsterdam Ambulance service. Even in a relatively small enterprise, such as Amsterdam Ambulance services—the result of an acquisition and merger in 2012—things can go wrong. The board did not keep a close enough eye on the change process; the members of the supervisory board and the workers' council only interacted superficially and the department heads did not get along. The restructuring did not deliver on the promised results and even harmed the going concern.
- Reconfiguration of the 12 Dutch provinces into five "clusters." Dutch politicians at the local, provincial and national level all had their doubts about this. Everyone feared the cure would be worse than the disease.

Cultural change programs

Public and semipublic sectors

- UWV. In 2009, the Dutch social security administration UWV had to turn back a partially implemented restructuring operation. Rather than serving its customers better, its benefit-awarding speed would only get slower, pilot projects showed. Instead of improving on its 85% timely decision rate, it dropped to 35%. The restructuring was called off and 1200 of its 20,000 employees who had gotten new jobs in the new organization had to return to their old jobs.
- National Dutch Police Force. Consolidation of local and national police forces into a single National Police Force was a prestige project championed by the justice minister and the top-ranking police commander, but things went badly wrong. In 2013, three years after kickoff, the goal had still not been achieved and the costs outstripped the original budget by 250 million euros.
- Dutch Central Agency for the Reception of Asylum Seekers (COA). In 2011, there was a lot of commotion about this body's poisonous corporate culture. Employees felt unsafe and their complaints were not taken seriously. On top of that, decision-making processes were as slow as molasses flowing uphill in January, which cost millions of euros in taxpayers' money.

Note: In my experience, free-floating cultural change programs without any hard goals are doomed to fail. Thankfully, this trend seems to be on the way out.

IT implementations

Private businesses

- McDonald's. In 2001, the fast food chain wanted to introduce a worldwide intranet. The project turned out to be overly ambitious, in part because many regions in the world lacked the required infrastructure. Total costs ran to 170 million US dollars.

- Banks: Van Lanschot Bank and Friesland Bank both had to take huge losses when implementing new software to automate their money transfer system.

Public and semipublic sectors

- Dutch Armed Forces. For decades, huge sums of money have been pumped into IT projects, with very little to show for it and enormous "surprise" budget overruns.
- Dutch Police Force. The Dutch police's IT systems have been called a "vale of tears." The technology was not user-friendly, made it hard to exchange information and the cost was tens of millions of euros higher than projected.
- Dutch IRS. Starting in 2005, the revenue service's IT system has had major problems, causing a loss of over 200 million euros.
- Mergers in the public education system have created unmanageably big schools.

Innovations

Private business

- V&D. This now-defunct Dutch department store chain is a typical example of a major player in the Dutch retail sector lagging behind in innovation, combined with a series of failed restructuring programs.
- Samsung Galaxy Note 7. This smartphone has batteries that can explode. In an unprecedented move, the manufacturer recalled all phones of this model (although it's a moot point whether this should be called an innovation. Many new smartphones are updates rather than innovations).
- bol.com. This leading Dutch online retailer was sold off too soon by Bertelsmann, its original owners. Their impatience cost them hundreds of millions of euros.
- WAP. In the early 2000s, WAP was hyped to be the next technical standard for mobile internet access. However, it turned out to be too expensive, too complicated and too difficult to learn. Ultimately, WAP was overtaken by the reality of mobile devices supporting HTML, CSS and so on.

Public and semipublic sectors

- Electronic Patient Files (EPD). Concerns about privacy and lack of cooperation in the Dutch health care industry made introduction of electronic patient files a slow process, fraught with problems. Finally, an American supplier who invested heavily in the technology caused a breakthrough, but the health care institutions are still struggling with its implementation.

- Introducing turnpikes in the Netherlands. In 2000, there were plans to turn the Dutch highways into turnpikes, but these were called off at the last minute for lack of political support. Because the minister had lied about the feasibility of an alternative pay-per-mile plan, the Second Chamber voted against the turnpikes. Note: as of 2018, no decision has been made either way.

9.3 Familiar Failure Factors

The cliché that strategy execution is bound to fail exists because it has often proven to be true. But if this knowledge is so widespread, why does the failure rate remain high? Partly because the analysis of failure factors tends to be too general and too superficial. And many failures are attributed to corporate culture. "The post-merger integration failed because the two corporate cultures were not compatible," is a commonly heard excuse, as if this explains every aspect of failure. Culture as a catch-all phrase is unsatisfactory and insufficient to serve as the findings of a thorough analysis. It's a fig leaf used to cover up everyone's shame.

9.3.1 Bad strategies

A vague or wrong strategy

No strategy execution can succeed if there is no good strategy to begin with. Bad strategies come in all shapes and sizes. For starters, a bad strategy is one without an appropriate doctrine. This is the case when hard decisions are avoided and leaders are unable or unwilling to define and explain the nature of the challenge they're facing.[187] Other frequently occurring problems are goals that are off-target, unclear, or unprioritized, or a strategy that is too broad and unfocused. A manager once told me: "A bad strategy feels like slush and smells like whipping cream gone sour. It bogs you down and it makes everyone turn up their nose in disgust." Another problem is caused by a clearly defined strategy that simply does not fit the organization's core competencies.

A detached or uninspiring strategy

Strategies that have been brooded out in solitude, away from the business, have little to no execution value. Unfortunately, this is the rule rather than the exception: lone operators who are convinced they are right, but are proven wrong. There is nothing wrong with a small group of good writers who come up with a good (clear, concise, easy-to-read) final product, *after* extensively talking with all the stakeholders. Then, the writing process takes only a couple of days. But that is something else entirely than doing the whole analysis and writing process in isolation.

Many strategies are made to look and sound dull. Every piece of written information must both inform and entice. People often fail to acknowledge that the seductive is just as important as the informative. As a consequence, your strategy might be exactly right, but dull as dishwater. Of course, your strategy document does not have to be a page turner or win a literary prize, but your stakeholders must at least be willing to read it.

Lack of support in the guiding coalition

Few things are as crippling as full-blown fights at the highest level. Mieke Bello, a well-known Dutch management consultant who has decades of experience advising boards of directors and supervisory boards, puts it like this: "Five inches of dissent at the top about what is and isn't important translates into five yards at the level just below. Any level below that and there is absolutely zero clarity about the organization's strategic direction." In his standard work on change management, John Kotter puts the lack of a sufficiently powerful guiding coalition at No. 2 on his list of reasons for failure.[188] Kotter states that organizational change can only be properly implemented when guided by a powerful coalition. Obviously, the people in the guiding coalition have to trust each other and be able to cooperate.

9.3.2 Picking the wrong people for key roles

Failing resource management: qualitatively and quantitatively

Not filling the key roles in strategy execution well, both in qualitative and quantitative terms, is one of the main reasons for failure.[189] Too often, incompetent people are assigned to important projects. Sometimes the people are competent, but lack some skills or specialist knowledge that is crucial for a particular initiative. When the initiative fails, the excuse is that the most competent people were already overburdened and that the "resource puzzle" was not put together properly.

This problem occurs not only at the start of new initiatives, but also along the way, because the strategy execution environment is never totally stable. Priorities keep shifting and new projects and programs are started that rely on the same resources. It requires monthly monitoring to identify what is going wrong or turns out not to be effective in practice. Too often, this has become a ritual dance in which project managers call attention to their resource problem in a steering group, while the responsible line managers nod and listen and then do nothing. It is the old bystander effect.

Unclear responsibilities, or the basics

Employees' operational duties have often been laid down clearly in a job or task description. Such descriptions clearly outline employees' accountability, detailed in roles, authorities, control and reporting lines in RACI tables. This tends not to happen in strategy execution projects and programs, even though it is at least as important to clearly define people's roles in that area.

9.3.3 Lack of alignment

At least 80% of the work spent on strategy execution must be carried out in the main structure where people work. It doesn't matter whether the initiative is delegated to the line organization, the department or the team people are working in, or whether it has been organized in a project. If 80% is not carried out in the main structure it was assigned to, it was probably a bad decision to choose that main structure. In addition, the people who execute the strategy also need time to coordinate and manage across other initiatives and disciplines (which takes 10 to 20% of the time spent on strategy execution). Plus they need time to report on progress, to manage escalations and maintain collaborations, either in projects or programs or in their day-to-day work. This type of alignment, or old-fashioned coordination, does not happen often enough and is a major reason for failure. And when alignment does happen, it tends to be ad hoc and entirely dependent on how well the people working on the initiative and beyond get along. However, what's really needed is regular, periodical alignment (see Success Factor 6, Section 2.6.2). In his study, MIT scholar Donald Sull asked 400 CEOs what they think is the No. 1 reason for failure in execution. Thirty percent of them said it was lack of alignment, while 40% blamed insufficient coordination between organizational units. Same difference.

9.3.4 Grossly underestimating "what it takes to tango"

Senior management tend to think that five minutes of explanation, a short email, the manager's charisma and two lines on a flip chart are enough to convey the gist of their decision. They also seem to think their decision will then magically transform into reality because middle and lower management will somehow disperse the initiative to every level of the line organization and throughout all projects. That's wishful thinking. Middle management, who bear the brunt of this attitude, are particularly prone to see this as the main reason for failure. They get scant information from their superiors, but are keenly aware of the high expectations from senior management. If things go wrong at the heart of the primary business processes, middle management is rightfully blamed by lower level employees for not providing sufficient information. At the same time, the board and the administrative departments point the finger at middle managers because of shortcomings in execution. That's an unpleasant position to be sandwiched in, and it points to poor vertical, horizontal and diagonal alignment.[190]

9.3.5 Too much or too little information

Information shortage, information overload and white noise created by overly complicated routing

Communication departments communicate ever more glamorously, socially and cross-medially, but most of all, they communicate more frequently. What is needed, though, is that they communicate thoroughly, systematically, at the right time, in just the right dose, and through the most appropriate channels. What's missing most often is communication at regular intervals, which is vital. All too often, communications grind to a halt just after a New Year's presentation or kickoff, damaging a new initiative's credibility.

Oversimplification in communication

Managers and professionals in strategy execution work hard to set well-defined goals and create clear, simple messages. This is crucial for successful strategy execution. People can only retain a few ideas per communication moment. To avert the risk of oversimplification, however, it's important to compensate for simple messages. This can be done in oral presentations, for example. This doesn't happen nearly often enough, which is why the audience pretty much structurally underestimates the implications of an initiative. In our efforts to convey messages in the simplest possible manner we end up obscuring essential implications that must be communicated sooner or later.

9.3.6 Lack of ownership

Low engagement

One of main reasons strategy execution fails is a lack of ownership everywhere it matters. This problem starts at the level of those who lead the initiative. Even division managers may have a strategy foisted upon them, making it hard to create real advocates among the key actors in the division, business unit or department. This decreases lower-level employees' willingness to embrace the strategy. Ownership is crucial to strategy execution, and no strategy or initiative has legs without it. At the end of the day, what you need to execute a strategy is people, and not just words, processes, systems or control.

9.4 Less Familiar Failure Factors

Some reasons for failure are discussed less often, but are just as crippling to strategy execution as the familiar causes discussed in the previous sections. Unfamiliar failure factors include a lack of differentiation, a crazy portfolio, an unclear execution process, an imprudent allocation of time and money, insufficient attention to the soft change process, an imbalance between top-down and bottom-up change, an imbalance between change leadership and change management, and single-mindedness.

9.4.1 Lack of differentiation, everything lumped together

Lack of differentiation between change and day-to-day executive management

Every organization plots its own course to realize its strategic goals. Those goals can be achieved by daily executive management (the going concern, or Running the Business) and/or by various types of change projects or programs (Changing the Business). The various forms of change are closely interrelated and it can be hard to differentiate between them. However, not making a distinction tween the different types of management is a big reason why strategy execution fails. Many managers feel it's too complicated and time-consuming to make that distinction explicit. They'd rather just focus on the work. But the consequence of neglecting to differentiate is that everything is connected to everything else and strategy execution becomes a catch-all phrase. This is a recipe for failure, because every type of strategy execution requires its own method and management.

Lack of distinction between improvement, renewal and innovation

Everyone would agree that a trip to Antarctica requires a different kind of preparation than a cruise to the Bahamas. When dealing with strategy execution, however, there seems to be this strange idea that one size fits all. Even if the organization differentiates between running the business and changing the business, it seldom differentiates clearly enough between incremental improvement, renewing the existing business model and radical innovation. Each of these three "flavors" requires its own approach. This is one of the main messages in this book.

9.4.2 A crazy portfolio

Too small a project and program portfolio

Too small a portfolio is usually a sign that the line organization is handling too many initiatives that ought to be executed by special project or program teams. Remember that radical change tends to affect several disciplines and therefore requires tackling in a project or program.

A crazily overloaded portfolio

The opposite tends to occur much more often: an overloaded portfolio that grossly overestimates the organization's change or execution capacity. The worst thing is that this happens both on purpose and inadvertently, by adding too many initiatives to the portfolio, but also by adding initiatives with overlapping mandates and scopes. Every senior executive and professional must wonder how it can be that every year more goals are set than can possibly be realized. What a surprise that this comes as a surprise! Everyone can see it coming, even before the annual plans have been presented. Overly ambitious objectives always lead to overloaded annual plans, both for the organization as a whole and for every individual discipline. This is partly due to positive ambition, or stretch, that managers want to build into their organization. Their ambitions are partly based on their faith in what the organization will be able to handle, so it's a leap of faith. But it's also due to increasing pressure from the board in increasingly competitive and declining markets. It's human nature, and especially the nature of the humans who pull the strings. They always overestimate their organization's execution and change capacity. This sets the stage for an organized failure that will almost certainly erode the organization's execution capacity. It's the start of a vicious cycle. What's worse, this process may remain invisible because there is no explicit portfolio management. And surely you agree that self-deception is the lamest form of deception.

Mix-up with line duties

When portfolios are not well thought-out, they also tend to contain activities that on closer inspection are not project or program work, but simply regular line responsibilities. This usually amounts to 25 to 33%. Also, projects might actually be programs and vice versa. This increases the general level of confusion, white noise and coordination efforts, in terms of both the projects and office politics, because of the stakes that people have in the portfolio.

Many interviewees told me execution is hampered by confusion as to whether a particular change should be implemented by the line organization, a project or a program. Dutch management consultant Michiel van der Molen put it aptly in his book *Projectmanagement voor opdrachtgevers* [Project Management for Sponsors]. "Here's a rule of thumb: if your line organization in its current form can do it, don't turn it into a project." [191] Another prominent management consultant from the Netherlands, Freek Hermkens, explains that if changes are not allocated properly, they tend not to last. As soon as the project is over, people revert to their previous behavior because "ownership of the improvements resided with the black belt and the project team instead of the line organization," he writes. [192]

At the same time, some changes are so complex that a project can't hack it and a program is the only appropriate solution. For a clear summary of the differences between a program and a project, I refer you to Paul Roberts' *The Economist Guide to Project Management*.[193]

Burying people in initiatives

If the scope of an initiative is too wide, people are likely to get overburdened. Too wide a scope tends to be the rule rather than the exception and severely reduces chances of success. A working group can identify more improvement issues than the organization can realistically handle. However, too narrow a scope can lead to a restricted view of the issues at hand, a disregard for interdependencies with other processes, and insufficient leverage for the business case.

9.4.3 No clear execution process, but mere "ad hoc" agility

Failure to select a method

Change is the only constant, or so the saying goes. However, most organizations fail to deliberately choose, develop and think through a strategy execution method, framework or tools. They don't use methodologies like agile, Scrum, Six Sigma or Lean, or project management methods such as MSP or Prince. Most don't have enough competent, experienced people to apply these techniques. As a consequence, most strategy execution initiatives lack a good foundation to base decisions on.

Failure to properly "condition" an initiative

Conditioning denotes the extent to which an initiative has been properly prepared for. Underconditioning of initiatives means there is either a bad plan or no plan at all, insufficient resources have been freed up, schedules are not taken seriously, and timely, competent decisions are not made. Problems may also be expected when monitoring, control and management information systems have not been organized properly and there is no professional, regular progress reporting system in place. More problems arise when facilities are not in order, such as meeting rooms, hardware, internet access and secretarial support. Research has shown that professionals rate problems with "small stuff" like this among their top three complaints. "Small stuff," my eye.

Lack of differentiation in size

Initiatives need differentiated conditioning. Research by Turner Consultancy shows that there is often insufficient differentiation between the conditioning of large, medium and small change projects.[194] Too much of a focus on large strategic programs or small operational change projects means medium-size initiatives fall by the wayside. This "banana-shaped" approach shows two extremes: either there is too much emphasis on large top-down initiated programs that are heavily sponsored by the board, or all effort is put into line-based changes. There is a tendency to subsume medium-sized initiatives into regular processes and not award these a separate project status. In practice, this means that 80% of initiatives are neglected. The two extremes are not necessarily perfect, but have relatively high odds of success. It's the middle where things go wrong: initiatives that are too small for conditioning as big strategic programs and too big for conditioning as small line-based change projects. The result is half-baked conditioning, less professional and more monodisciplinary approaches, and hence a much greater chance of failure.

9.4.4 Unwise use of time and money

Burning 80% of resources before the execution phase

"Strategy setting is important. Large corporate boards can take up to eight months to set strategy, and then another eight weeks to discuss it with all division unit managers, who in turn can take eight days to work

Figure 42 — **Why strategy execution fails so often**.

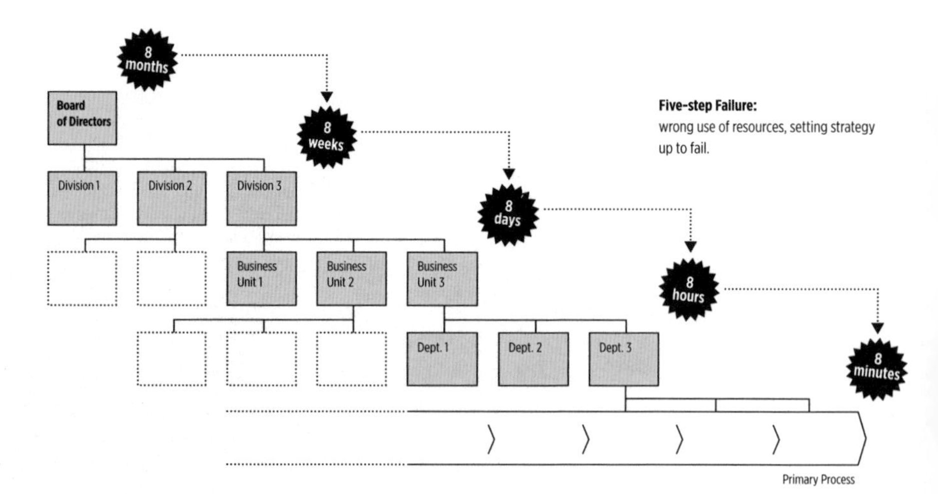

Source: Turner, 2016

out the details with their management teams. I was struck by how top-heavy this is when I overheard an employee saying: 'And then I am told in just eight minutes what I am expected to realize in the coming year!'" This quote from Ben Verwaayen, former CEO of Alcatel-Lucent and British Telecom, perfectly describes one of the main reasons why strategy execution fails in day-to-day business reality (see Figure 42).[195]

Figure 43 — **The three most common archetypal failure-prone approaches: conceptual top-heaviness, speed without effect and evaporating development.**

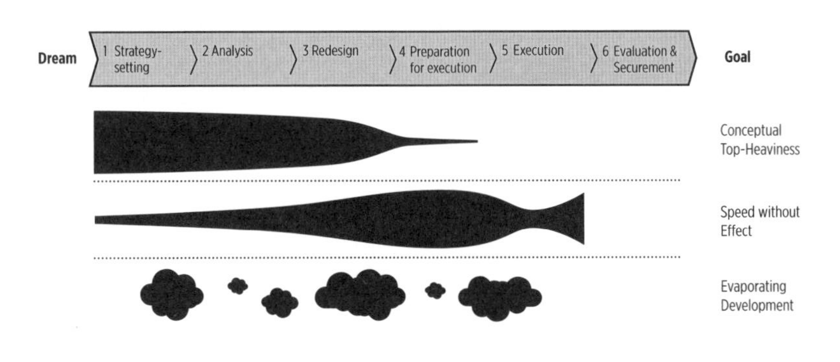

Source: Turner, 2016

This is probably the most important and most frequently occurring reason for failure in any type of organization. It tends to happen most often in large companies where highly educated professionals love to develop sexy strategy and conceptual projects. Yet when it comes to execution, they start rolling their eyes and yawning. Most of them are still up for a new conceptual debate, but their attention span for execution is oddly short. They were selected for their analytical and conceptual competencies rather than action-oriented abilities. This type of failure-prone approach is also known as conceptual top-heaviness (see Figure 43). Failure is caused by a gross underestimation of what it takes to do what strategy is actually all about, namely execution. Often there is an unconscious imbalance in the allocation of energy and resources—time, money, people—over the various phases. Far too much time goes into the conceptual, strategic, analytical and design stages, so that there is nothing left by the time execution is supposed to start.

People find it hard to postpone gratification

An improper allocation of resources points to a poor understanding of the execution effort required. Senior management may have plenty of passion and energy, but lack the stamina to finish the 80% execution. Even if strategy-setting is rounded off and finished on schedule, and even when there are enough resources to finish the job, there may still be a lack of perseverance. Delaying gratification is the hardest thing there is. Remember the Marshmallow Experiment? In a Stanford University lab, kids were left alone in a room with a marshmallow in front of them. They were told that if they refrained from eating it for 15 minutes, they would a get a second one. The children's ability to resist temptation turned out to be a significant predictor of leadership abilities.[196] Clearly, figuring out one of the main reasons for failure does not require profound psychological analysis. We already know the reason: we're bad at deferring pleasure, at disciplining ourselves and persevering.

Want to know more? See Joachim de Posada: Don't eat the marshmallow!

Being too quick off the bat, overly result-oriented
One of the main factors that determines the success of strategy execution is the idea of devoting 80% of your time and resources to execution instead of strategic analysis and course-setting. Doing outstrips thinking. However, doing *without* thinking does not work. Starting execution too soon can be a reason for failure. I call this speed without effect. What is hailed as a pragmatic approach is actually a fruitless, headlong leap into the abyss. Being too quick off the bat and rushing to execution—under the guise of pragmatism and without careful strategic analysis and redesign—is asking for failure (see also Figure 42).

Being too singularly culture-driven
A leading school of thought in change management is one that focuses on corporate culture. Consultants who adhere to this vision always recommend using employees' personal passion and motivation to leverage change. This approach can be professional and down-to-earth, provided there is a connection with hard goals and objectives. Prioritizing corporate culture may be justified when it is the main problem in an organization, but it definitely isn't when the main issue is technology or process-related. In my view, corporate culture is too often characterized as the main or sole issue and cultural change programs as the only remedy. In some cases, corporate culture is misappropriated to create a playground for "fun change management

experiments." Those might indeed be entertaining and inspirational for a while, but if there is no connection to hard goals, none of the changes will last. Three months later everything will be back to the way it was before the cultural change program (see Figure 43, archetype No. 3, Evaporating Development).

As a management consultant, I come across a lot of nonsense and waste in organizations.[197] Passion and inspiration are labels used to convince hundreds of employees that work should be fun, but the sessions used to spread this "gospel" seldom do more than skim the surface. Without a doubt, tapping into passion releases the fuel that drives organizations' success. However, based on the mistaken notion that work should always be loads of fun, passion has become one of the most misused terms in organizations. I call it the tyranny of fun. There are plenty of embarrassing examples from real life: the Chief Fun Officer, the Happiness Engineer, and "fungineering" projects.

Fortunately, the financial crisis has curbed some of the worst excesses. At least, you see fewer tree huggers at conference venues. I completely agree with Oliver Burkeman's article in *The New York Times* titled "Who goes to work to have fun?".[198] In this refreshing piece, Burkeman argues that "fun at work" has become a mantra and that we need to put a stop to it. Research shows that while all this obligatory fun slows down employee turnover, its forced nature also gives many people stress and lowers their productivity. Philosopher John Stuart Mill expressed the problem succinctly when he said: "Ask yourself whether you are happy, and you cease to be so." Far be it from me to say that professionals are not allowed to enjoy their work. On the contrary, it has been proven time and again that happy employees are productive employees. Competent professionals in the right place tend to love their jobs and that's something you want to encourage. What I'm objecting to is a corporate culture in which "fun" has become an objective in its own right, and one that must be experienced and expressed at every turn and without any connection to corporate goals.

9.4.5 Ignoring soft capabilities

Hard capabilities refer to strategy, structure, management, systems and processes, while soft capabilities refer to culture, drive, motivation, representations, expectations, behavior and leadership styles. Hard capabilities are also known as the surface current, and soft capabilities as the undercurrent,[199] as the hard capabilities tend to be explicit and visible, while the soft capabilities, such as motivation and unconscious behavior, are invisible and implicit.

Soft elements are the decisive factor

In the end, it is the soft elements that determine whether change programs succeed. As I discussed earlier, large multinationals like Shell thoroughly prepare their new ventures and acquisitions and evaluate them afterwards. Time and again, it turns out that the success rate of these transactions is lower than expected, and that this is due to lack of attention to these so-called "soft" variables. The problem lies with incompatible corporate cultures, an inability to formulate and pursue a common goal, an inability to bring the synergy outlined on paper to life, and clashes in leadership and management style. Soft capabilities make or break your hard goals.

Soft capabilities are hard-edged

There are several causes for this lack of attention to soft capabilities. First of all, many organizations lack psychological insight and knowledge. We don't know enough about what motivates and drives people. That's strange, because organizations are obviously places where people collaborate. This state of affairs is exacerbated by professionals and leaders' conflicting worldviews and views of humankind. As one researcher put it: "A lot of failures are caused by our wrong assumptions about what people think and feel and how they work."[200] This probably happens without people realizing it. In any case, it's high time we look for ways to change this.

Another cause is that the so-called soft capabilities can have some very hard edges, such as arrogance, complacency, testosterone and ego clashes. Senior management are no stranger to complacency and arrogance. You'd be aghast to know how many acquisitions have been made because of a leader's ego, and how many have failed for the same reason! Or how many execution issues have been badly underestimated, as if they were a walk in the park.

A third cause lies in overestimating people's rationality. There are constraints on all humans' rational capacity, on what they are willing and able to remember and understand.[201] Our rational mind is limited by the available information, our cognitive ability and our capacity and time for decision-making and execution. [202] Our behavior is dictated to a large extent by emotional and irrational motives.

9.4.6 Imbalance between top-down and bottom-up

Many approaches are too bottom-up

A bottom-up approach has little chance of success, because crystal clear frameworks are essential for building up consistent, sensible strategy execution portfolios. Employees want a clear framework, and without one, their energy is unfocused and dependencies are not sufficiently taken into account. Suggesting something new is risky and leads—once again—to waste and planned frustration. This gets in the way of effective strategy execution and leads to countless futile meetings without a clear agenda or a thorough pre-analysis by a core team.

Many approaches are too non-committal
Certain approaches, particularly those called novel or experimental, or those featuring terms like organic, intuitive or incubator, are best met with some skepticism. Such approaches are often intended to mask a lack of analytical thinking. Their attitude says "Let's just get started and we'll see where we'll end up." This tends to lead to a flagrant waste of resources. Of course, sometimes experiments are called for, especially when working on product or services innovations. But generally, changes need a clear framework and a solid plan.

The flip side: excessively top-down
Despite the current zeitgeist, overly top-down strategy execution is still a common occurrence. Initiatives in which senior management have a hand get pole position and are extremely well appointed, even getting their own dedicated Program Management Office (PMO). Senior management's heavy involvement can create a situation in which strategy execution becomes the baby they can't let go of. This has obvious advantages. Sponsorship is well anchored, no question about it. But there are some cons too: a too-rigidly defined plan and execution can be deadly. Sure, clear frameworks are a must, but an unbending framework combined with a regimented approach is sure to nullify any execution capacity at lower levels. Coerced success is never sustainable.

9.4.7 Imbalance between change leadership and change management

It must be one of the most frequently asked questions on business administration, strategy and change management forums: "How do you go from management to leadership?" And "Does your organization have the leaders it needs to navigate through this critical transition?". This time-consuming polarization between change leadership and change management has become a big reason for failure.

In strategy execution, change *leadership* simply refers to vision and leadership development. Leadership is about articulating and promoting your organization's vision, about creating a strong coalition and institutionalizing change, about creating the space, direction and conditions for change to take place. Change *management*, on the other hand, has to do with the instrumental and operational actions that create change. It is focused more on controlling the strategy execution initiatives.[203]

An imbalance between these two poses a risk. Too much focus on change leadership is not smart. It doesn't do justice to change management, which means that, no matter how inspiring your vision is, it will never have legs. On the other hand, too much focus on change management is equally risky, because a strategy executed without vision, without the Big Why, will never reach its full potential. In short, both change leadership and change management are important and must be kept in equilibrium.

9.4.8 Single-mindedness

Our research has also identified reasons for failure that are not caused by an imbalance, but by single-mindedness. In essence, single-minded approaches are types of strategy execution that are overly strategy-based, content-based, change-based or project-based. Failure can also be caused by other shortcomings in the approach taken, for instance if it is too complex, too simplistic or too hyped up.

An excessively expertise-driven or technocratic approach

Strategy execution is sometimes approached as a matter of injecting the right expertise at the right time, preferably in the shape of proven best practices and best-in-class reference models. For strategies pursued in this way, failure lies in wait. Such a technocratic approach does not lead to a widely supported and owned new reality.

A "hostage situation"

One example of what I call a "hostage situation" can be found in execution issues related to the New Way of Working or at startups. Companies all want to be like Google and create noisy, open-plan offices, full of bean bags, slides and dog-sitting facilities. What they should be doing in preparing for the New Way of Working is to ensure that there are enough closed-space work environments so that people can get some work done. Too many organizations fail to think hard enough about both the functional and inspirational requirements that make a good office space. Making sure that there are private offices has nothing to do with curbing people's freedom. On the contrary, most employees are very happy with a work environment that provides a healthy balance between different functions. And I know plenty of organizations that implemented the New Way of Working zealously—the more open-plan, the merrier—and that are now having to undo all of those changes. This runs up bills that could have been avoided if people had more carefully considered the consequences.

Hype-driven or hobby-horse

Another type of approach that is bound to lead to failure is a hype-driven or guru-driven approach. Every consultant, scholar or self-proclaimed guru who swears by a single perspective or method and posits this as the generic recipe for success should be viewed with healthy skepticism. We all know you need to phrase business and change management concepts with an edge and make them sticky, if only to sell them and make sure they stick. But the simple truth is that most strategy execution initiatives are grounded in multiple problems that require a sophisticated, pluralistic analysis and a multifaceted, multidisciplinary solution. People can get really excited about hypes and be blinded to the complexity of real life. Sometimes a hype can even turn into someone's hobby-horse and become a principle that everyone must subscribe to. When concepts such as Blue Ocean, Theory U, Dragons' Den or Big Hairy Audacious Goals have become an end rather than a means, it's a clear sign you've been taken hostage by strategists and experts.

9.5 The New Failure in Radical Innovation

9.5.1 Innovation as a hobby

These days, in the digital age, new digital business models are forcing every organization to get better at innovation. Some innovation gurus have jumped on the bandwagon and shrouded innovation in a veil of mysticism. For example, there's the idea that radical innovation cannot be structured or managed, but that it's a matter of letting a thousand flowers bloom so you can pick only the best. Such gurus suggest that the creativity and brilliance you need for successful innovation are deadened by structure and control, and that metrics are totally reprehensible. But this approach leads to untargeted spraying with buckshot, at enormous costs.

9.5.2 Risky and unnecessary mysticism

The more radical the innovation, the greater the risks and the bigger the odds of failure. Radical innovation cannot take place without failure, because it is trial and error that brings you to the innovation that succeeds. This is the iterative process that is part and parcel of Type 3 innovations (see Chapter 2 on success factors, Section 2.1.2). Because this process is pretty complex and requires a lot of time and money as it is, you shouldn't complicate matters by refusing to structure it. A highly systematic innovation process is key. Too many people overlook this, or think that radical innovation is a mystical force that comes from above. It is not. Radical innovation consists of the systematic and disciplined selection of ideas and then trying and testing them and scaling up what works.[204]

Tech startup spoof

I want to end on a positive note, so the spoof behind this QR-code is meant to make you smile. I hope the success factors, the building blocks and the case studies from this book will help you successfully execute your strategy in the New Normal.

10

EPILOGUE: **IT'S PERSONAL**

A few additional motives for writing this book

10.1 Modern Strategy Execution: Uncharted Waters

Entire bookshelves have been written about strategy. Just as stacks of literature have been published on change leadership, change management, team development, motivation, process management, project management and every other element that has an impact on strategy execution. And yet, precious little is known about how these capabilities must collectively be mobilized to facilitate strategy execution. That is the gap I intended to fill by writing this book. So, my goal has been to connect the various hard and soft approaches and schools of thought. It is an approach that sharply contrasts with existing theories on change management in that it separates the wheat from the chaff. Striving for excellent strategy execution is as inspiring as it is sobering, as I was often told in the interviews I conducted for this study. Board members and senior managers rightly reject the widespread idea that everything should be fun. Which is why many of the success factors we describe can seem arduous or even downright boring. It's high time boring became the new sexy.

Organizations are not learning strategy execution fast enough. The challenges are getting bigger and the demands higher, and organizations are losing ground. They frequently prove themselves incapable of solving hard puzzles, the must-win, wicked assignments. Instead we see *Alice in Wonderland's* Red Queen effect; no matter how hard they run, they can barely keep up, let alone get ahead.[205] So, organizations need to dramatically up their game and get better at strategy execution.

Organizations respond to this challenge in different ways. Some remain passive, either by choice or by default. Others take action. But even organizations that recognize they have to take action often fall headlong into the trap called innovation. They experiment until they're blue in the face. Active responses are either proactive or reactive. The former come from ambitious organizations that want to become or remain a leader in their field. The latter come from organizations that are forced to change by increasing competition, or new rules and regulations—conditions that often apply to the public and semipublic sectors.

10.2 Inspiring and Sobering

Strategy execution is both inspiring and sobering. Half of this book feeds your ambitions and dreams, while the other half brings you back down to earth. What's inspiring is a sense of purpose: the joy of seeing your hard work with your co-workers and clients come to fruition. The payoff in the end is so much more than financial. In a sense, the journey is the destination because our joint efforts to execute a strategy hone our skills and nourish us.

Because the word "inspiration" has been co-opted by the "change Soviets," to loosely quote Nassim Nicholas Taleb, it requires some explanation. To me, inspiration is not something you're entitled to as a fringe benefit of your job. It is, first and foremost, your own responsibility. It takes a lot of your own hard work to become and stay inspired, even though you can't will it, as most of us know.

Obviously, there are moments when your mind starts to hydroplane and ideas just start flowing. I personally experience this while running, speed skating and cycling, and while reading, of course. Well-written articles and books trigger so many thoughts, that I obsessively jot down notes; underline, circle and highlight passages; and fold back the corners of the pages. But inspiration can also come when least expected. You go for long periods longing for it, and then suddenly it pops up.[206] As I said before, I'm a believer in Anders Ericsson's 10,000-hour theory popularized by Malcolm Gladwell. You need to spend at least 10,000 hours of dedicated work and practice on something to get good at it, regardless of how much talent you have or inspiration you feel. In the end, it's all about doing the work, particularly in strategy execution. And this is the sobering side of the equation.

It takes more time to get rid of nonsense than to come up with it. This is a messier part of the reality we face than those other, more elevated motives I've written about. My co-consultants and I have worked for over two decades with executive and supervisory boards, management teams, professionals and blue-collar workers on a single mission: strategy execution. This has given us a unique perspective on exactly what works, and what doesn't. That's why it was so cathartic to write Chapter 9 on failure, the reasons for it and its costs. So much garbage is spouted about failure. It takes far more time and effort to debunk this nonsense than it does to come up with it in the first place. There have been moments when I wanted to pull my hair out in frustration.

I get asked what I think of training sessions and color management consultancy. Training sessions are part of HRM's tool kit to help people develop their skills. I'd like to add that the more specific the training, the better. In my own field—strategy execution—I have grown skeptical about general training courses because the skills they offer are usually too generic to apply to any specific initiative. Methods dominated by training and coaching are too indirect. Such non-committal methods often have poor results. Skills training and coaching only work when the learners are fully committed to put in the hard work to achieve their goals, as David Maister argues in his excellent article "Why (Most) Training Is Useless."[207] While I do teach masterclasses in strategy execution, I always kick these off with a healthy dose of skepticism and kindly ask anyone who's not intrinsically motivated to leave.

Let me say this about color management methods. Concepts such as Insights Discovery, core quadrants and management drives are valuable when applied to the purposes they were designed for. They provide insight into the individual's dominant traits and the consequences these have for their own development and the balance on their team. So don't get me wrong; I use these methods myself, but we don't need a coloring book for everything. These methods are not a suitable replacement for other crucial analyses. Proclaiming yourself a blue organization doesn't absolve you of the need to thoroughly analyze your strategy. Fortunately, the people who came up with these concepts know and stress this, too.

My view of humanity is positive and down to earth. We are all products of our beliefs and experiences. I believe that board members, managers and professionals are like everyone else in that they're primarily out to do good, not just "less bad." That's my view of humanity in a nutshell. Most of us are trying to use our talents to do something good. At the same time, I believe all of us have shortcomings that have to be taken into account if we're going to reach the point where we can execute. I'm not going to put forward a theological treatise on the broken world we live in, but in simple terms, humans are fallible. We want to have a good time, but that's not always possible. Sometimes we need to persevere and do things whose benefits aren't immediately clear, or that are just plain boring and require more persistence, mental capacity and creativity.

In *Thinking, Fast and Slow*, Daniel Kahneman has described our dysfunctionality in terms of System 1 and System 2 thinking.[208] Those systems determine the way we think and act. System 1 is fast, instinctive and emotional. System 2 is slower, more conscious and logical. Kahneman studied several characteristic human traits that are relevant to strategy execution. For example, he observed our tendencies to jump to conclusions and to overvalue human judgement, which is characterized by prejudice. In another interesting section, Kahneman discusses framing. If we say an initiative has a 40% chance of success, we are more likely to give it our all than when we say it has a 60% chance of failure. Both statements are true, but the one you choose and your reasons for doing so have an impact. Another section deals with the sunk cost fallacy and shows that we tend to want to throw good money at things that have already turned bad. We don't want to have any regrets, so we reason that a project is bound to become successful at some point if we just keep investing in it. These tendencies can all lead to big decision-making errors.

Strategy execution requires knowledge from a range of disciplines. Business administration is not mathematics or physics and is only partially a hard science. In hard science, we deal in purely causal relationships. Every question only has one correct answer. But because strategy execution is mainly about people, you can't do without some idea of macroeconomics, philosophy, psychology, theology and social sciences.

It *is* possible to avoid failure in strategy execution. That is the upbeat note I want to end on. Let's recognize that strategy execution is a fantastic profession, and *your* profession. As you've seen, there is a clear distillation of what works and what doesn't, and much of that is universal. You will need this knowledge at your fingertips all of the time, because strategy execution is never done. Everyone knows that change is the only constant, but we also know that it's getting worse. We live in times of permanent beta versions, as management thinker Martijn Aslander put it in *Nooit af* [Never done].[209] Every product and every service is continually revised and upgraded, and every iteration and innovation must be based on down-to-earth feedback about what does and does not meet customer needs. And for this, you need modern, iterative strategy execution. This book can help you get a grip on that.

APPENDIX 1
ACKNOWLEDGEMENTS

For the past three years, my colleagues at Turner Consultancy and myself, as owner and Managing Director, worked on developing a comprehensive overview of the reasons why strategy execution and innovation succeed or fail. We would never have been able to do this without the extremely valuable contributions of numerous high-ranking board members, managers, staff members, program managers, colleagues and partners. Our interviewees represented every possible discipline, from strategy to marketing, sales, operations, IT and financial control. Ours was a qualitative study. First of all, we conducted more than 50 interviews with people from both private businesses and state-run organizations. Secondly, several people made a particularly substantial contribution by sharing their ideas and insights as speakers at the seminars on strategy execution and innovation that Turner regularly organizes.

In particular, I would like to express my appreciation to the following interviewees and speakers:

- Theo van Aalst, Director of Strategy and Development, PostNL
- Annet Aris, Senior Affiliate Professor of Strategy, INSEAD; Member of the Supervisory Board, ASR
- Fred Arp, former CFO, Telegraaf Media Groep
- Karin Bergstein, Member of the Executive Board, ASR
- Lydia Bestebreur, Senior Advisor on Competence, Training & Education, Netherlands Forensic Institute (NFI)
- Arno van Bijnen, Commercial Director and Member of the Executive Committee, PostNL
- Welmer Blom, Senior Vice President Middle East, Gulf & India, Air France KLM
- Lisette van Breugel, COO, Arbo Unie
- Hein Bronk, Co-Founder & Partner, The Review Group; Founder and former CEO, MYbusinessmedia
- Jacques van den Broek, CEO, Randstad

- Harry J.M. Brouwer, CEO, Unilever Food Solutions
- Ton Büchner, former CEO/Executive Committee Chairman, AkzoNobel
- Yvonne Campfens, former Executive Vice President of B2B Netherlands and Managing Director, Springer Media; former Managing Director of the Publication Workflow Group, Springer Nature
- Joke Cuperus, CEO, PWN; former Chief Engineer, Dutch Ministry of Infrastructure and Water Management (Eastern Region)
- Pauline Derkman-Oosterom, Director of Life Insurance, a.s.r.
- Rob Eijkelenkamp, CEO, Studio Piet Boon, former Managing Director of News and Print Media, Telegraaf Media Groep
- Ronald Goedmakers, owner and CEO, Vebego International
- Cees 't Hart, CEO and President, Carlsberg Group; former CEO, FrieslandCampina
- Jan Hattink, former Finance Director, PostNL
- Rienk Hoff, former Director of Enforcement and Surveillance, Municipality of Amsterdam
- Mijke Horneman, former Senior Strategist, CRV Holding BV
- Gert-Jan Huisman, Partner and CEO, Anders Invest; former CEO, Centrotec AG
- Symen Jansma, Co-founder and former CEO, TravelBird
- Patrick Kerssemakers, former CEO, fonQ
- Joop Kessels, Managing Director, Utrecht University
- Agnes Keune, Senior Business Developer, Bol.com
- Hein Knaapen, Chief HR Officer, ING Group
- Antoinette de Kroon, Executive Services Team Manager, Netherlands Forensic Institute
- Jeroen de Munnik, Chief of Institutional Business, PGGM
- Harry Paul, former Inspector-General, Netherlands Food and Consumer Product Safety Authority
- Ton Ridder, former Managing Director, KLM Cygnific
- Audrey van Schaik, former Director of Treatment, Department of Geriatric Psychiatry, GGZ inGeest
- Thijs Stoop, Principal at Roland Berger Strategy Consultants; former Member of the Executive Board, GGZ inGeest
- Kees Stroomer, Managing Director of ISS Facility Services Nederland; former Managing Director, Tempo Team
- Gerard van Tilburg, Deputy Chairman of the Executive Board, Royal Cosun; Member of the Board, Energiegilde
- Tjark Tjin-A-Tsoi, Director-General, Statistics Netherlands (CBS); former Managing Director, Netherlands Forensic Institute
- Herna Verhagen, CEO and Chairperson of the Executive Board, PostNL
- Paul Verheul, Executive Board/COO, Van Oord
- Frank Vrancken Peeters, former Regional Managing Director for Western Europe, Wolters Kluwer

- Menco van der Weerd, former Head of Change at the Life Insurance & Mortgage Division, Aegon NL
- John de Wit, former Program Director, Tata Steel; Director of Global Procurement, Danieli Corus
- Leon van de Zande, former Policy Director for Teaching & Research, University of Utrecht
- Marjoleine van der Zwan, Managing Director, PIV Insurers' Institute on Personal Injury; former COO, MediRisk

I would also like to express my appreciation to the following organizations for providing case studies:

- Aegon
- Alcontrol Laboratories
- Arbo Unie
- a.s.r.
- Royal Cosun
- FrieslandCampina
- FonQ
- An international bank
- A medium-sized Dutch University of Applied Sciences
- Utrecht University of Applied Sciences
- KRO-NCRV
- NautaDutilh
- Nederlandse Voedsel- en Warenautoriteit (NVWA)
- Unilever
- Wolters Kluwer
- Würth

My special thanks to all the board members and scholars who endorsed this book:

- Karin Bergstein, Member of the Executive Board, a.s.r.
- Lisette van Breugel, COO, Arbo Unie
- Jacques van den Broek, CEO, Randstad
- Harry J.M. Brouwer, CEO, Unilever Food Solutions
- Maarten Edixhoven, CEO, Aegon Netherlands
- Prof. Dr. Meindert Flikkema, Academic Director of the Amsterdam Centre for Management Consulting, Vrije Universiteit Amsterdam
- Ronald Goedmakers, owner and CEO, Vebego International
- Henk Hagoort, Chairman of the Executive Board, Windesheim University of Applied Sciences; former Chairman of the Executive Board, NPO
- Cees 't Hart, CEO and President, Carlsberg Group; former CEO, FrieslandCampina
- Kees Hoving, Chief Country Officer for the Netherlands, Deutsche Bank

- Symen Jansma, Co-founder and former CEO, TravelBird
- Patrick Kerssemakers, former CEO, fonQ
- Manfred F.R. Kets de Vries, INSEAD Distinguished Clinical Professor of Leadership Development and Organizational Change
- Agnes Keune, Senior Business Developer, Bol.com
- Hein Knaapen, Chief HR Officer, ING Group
- George Kohlrieser Ph.D., Professor of Leadership and Organizational Behavior, IMD in Lausanne, writer of bestsellers *Hostage at the Table* and *Care to Dare*
- Peter Meyers, CEO, Stand & Deliver Group; Lecturer in Performance and Leadership Skills, Stanford University and IMD in Lausanne
- Heiko Schipper, former Deputy Executive Vice President, Nestlé S.A. and former CEO, Nestlé Nutrition
- Feike Sijbesma, Chairman of the Managing Board and CEO, DSM
- Ben Tiggelaar, Behavioral Scientist, Author, Public Speaker and Consultant
- Tjark Tjin-A-Tsoi, Director-General, Statistics Netherlands (CBS); former Managing Director, Netherlands Forensic Institute
- Herna Verhagen, CEO and Chairperson of the Executive Board, PostNL
- Paul Verheul, Executive Board/COO, Van Oord
- Ben Verwaayen, Supervisory Board of AkzoNobel, Partner at Keen Venture Partners, former CEO of Alcatel-Lucent and British Telecom
- Prof. Henk Volberda, Professor of Strategic Management and Innovation, Director of Knowledge Transfer, Rotterdam School of Management (Erasmus University Rotterdam)

I would also like to express my gratitude to the following colleagues and partners from Turner Consultancy. They are listed in alphabetical order:
Marjolein van Abbe, Joël Aerts, Marjam el Ammari, Martijn Babeliowsky, Mieke Bello, Stefan Bolt, Eugenie Boon, Mariëtte Brouwer, Peter de Bruin, Alexander Bruinsma, Susanne Chamalaun, Mariëlle Companjen, Katinka Cornelése, Alex Crezee, Johannes Crol, Jeroen Dekkers, Eveline Dusseldorp, Bas van 't Eind (oprichter), Jasper Engelbert, Patrick Eppink, Wouter Evers, Wendelina Fieret, Jurgen Frumau, Jop Gerkes, Bas Hafkenscheid, Janwillem Hekman, Evelien Hellenthal, Tjalle Hoekstra, André Holwerda, Joris van Hulzen, Gerrit-Jan Jansen, Relinde de Koeijer, Roel Kok, Coco Korse, Adriaan Krans, Sander Livius, Otto van 't Loo, Dayashri Manohar, Max Meijers, Feike Oosterhof, Ties Rijkers, Bas van Rooij, Joachim Rullmann, Annelieke van Schie, Peter Schreuder, Marga Severs, Dirkjan Takke, Bob Tasche, Dodijn Velema, Lot Verburgh, Jeroen Visscher, Bouke Waltman, Martijn Walvis, Peter Weijland.

My thanks are also due to the following Turner alumni:
Astrid Bakker-Boumans, Erik Bakker, Ben van Berge Henegouwen, Arjan van den Born, Iris Borst, Juliëtte Bos, Jikkelien van Marle, Wido Bosch, Maria van Boxtel, Wouter Bruggers, Ithar da Costa, Martine Daniëls, Patrick Davidson, Juriaan Deumer, Erna Doedens, Andrea Doesburg, Karin van Duuren, Meindert Flikkema, Rutger Gassner, Han Haring, Marcel 't Hart, Jelmer Heida, Gerco Hennipman, Henry Hennipman, Tamara van der Horst, Robbert Jellinek, Salko Kapetanovic, Stefan Karnebeek, Barbara Kaufman, Maaikel Klein Klouwenberg (founder), Wouter Klinkhamer, Regine Kruijsdijk-Oolman, Rosalie Kuyvenhoven, Madiha Leuven-Mouchtak, Steven van de Looij, Alexander Loudon, Pieter Lugtigheid, Erwin Matthijssen, Jan-Willem Meiburg, Rik Meijering, Nicole Messer, Maaike Pol, Ron Müller, Barbara Nederkoorn, Leonique Niessen, Linda Nieuwenhuis, Corrie Nieuwenkamp, Femke van Nieuwkerk, Niels Penninx, Colette Pijl-Leeflang, Carolijn Ploem, Willem Pluym, Suzanne Raafs, Martine Reimerink, Herbert Rijken, Rob Schipper (former commissioner), René Schreurs, Barbara Schrijver, Peter Slikker, Ralph Smeets, Sjors Stoffelsen, Rutger Strengers, Theo den Tex, Esther Timmer, Hugo Timmerman, Marcel van Tol, Joost Tolboom, Ineke Uijtenhaak, Arjan van Valkengoed, Eveline van Veelen, Rose van Velzen, Linda Visser, Enno Wiertsema, Ellen Wijnands, Mark de Wit, Feico de Zwaan.

This book is a richer work thanks to them. In the course of this research, I was once again reminded that a team knows far more than a few individuals.

APPENDIX 2
GLOSSARY OF TERMS

Agility
Agility, or organizational agility, is the ability to continually adapt without changing, according to Lee Dyer and Richard A. Shafer of Cornell University. Agile organizations have an innate "capacity to shift, flex and adjust as circumstances change."[221]

Alignment
Alignment, or strategic alignment, is the process of attuning an organization's actions, divisions and employees to the organization's goals. This strategic alignment ensures that divisions and employees collaborate well and thereby contribute to the organization's results.

Architecture, Open Architecture
The term (Open) Architecture is derived from the field of software programming, where it is used to describe the structure of a product. Open architecture refers to products whose specifications are public, making it easy for other software developers to add components to it. Like other terms (such as agile and Scrum), this notion has found its way into the non-technical arena and is no longer exclusively used in software development. It also refers to the structure of products, prices, processes, organizations and knowledge. In this book, we use the term architecture in the wider sense. In the financial services industry, open architecture has yet another meaning; investment companies with an open architecture give their customers the opportunity to invest in other financial institutions' products as well.

Benefit Realization Management
In strategy execution, Benefit Realization Management refers to the setting up, operationalizing and use of a benefit measurement system. Synonyms for this term are: business case management, performance

management and target monitoring. Benefits are measurable, planned changes that result from a strategic initiative and are regarded by stakeholders as beneficial.

Breakthrough
The sixth building block from the model presented in this book, known as BREAKTHROUGH, is about developing a Minimum Viable Product (MVP) with at least one innovative breakthrough. We see this as an important change that truly influences the existing business model or leads to a new one. The word breakthrough suggests two things: (1) an innovation of a rare caliber that (2) leads to a sharply enhanced performance.

Building Block
The Strategy = Execution Model consists of four accelerators. Each accelerator consists of four Building Blocks, two for the hard capabilities and two for the soft capabilities. Hence, the model consists of 16 building blocks in total. A building block is a brief description of an important issue in strategy execution and of what it takes (which actions in a concerted effort are required) to attain the building block's objective. The first building block of an accelerator is hard and deals with the Why: the goals and benefits. The second building block of an accelerator is also hard and deals with the What: the content of the strategy and the initiatives in the portfolio. The third is one of the two soft building blocks and deals with the How: the execution and change strategy. And the fourth is also soft and describes the Who: ownership of the initiatives and their envisioned benefits.

Business Model
A Business Model describes the way in which an organization creates and appropriates value (i.e. makes money). A business model answers the following main questions: what proposition does the organization offer its customers; how does it serve its customers; what target group does it aim at; how does it create value and how is the value chain set up; what is the cost structure; how does the business position itself and how does it want to compete? A business model's internal organization consists of capabilities: processes, governance and structure, people and culture, technology and resources, data and knowledge.

Business Process Redesign
Business Process Redesign or Business Process Re-engineering (BPR) is a management strategy defined by Michael Hammer and James Champy in the early 1990s. BPR analyzes organizations' internal processes in order to fundamentally redesign them to make radical improvements in cost structure and customer service, for instance.

Capabilities

We define Capabilities as the ability to perform certain actions or achieve results pertaining to an organization's goals. Each component of the business model is a capability. We deliberately distinguish between capabilities and personal competencies, such as knowledge, skills, motivation and ambition, personal qualities and intelligence.

Change Leadership

Change Leadership is a means of spearheading various types of transformation. Change leaders uphold the vision, build a leading coalition, and create the space, direction and preconditions necessary for institutionalizing changes.

Change Management

In the context of strategy execution, we define Change Management as the organization of instrumental and operational actions aimed at implementing and monitoring strategy execution initiatives.

Changing the Business (Execution Excellence)

Changing the Business is the term we use to describe transformation or change management. Changing the business is not the same as Running the Business, which refers to daily executive management of the existing organization. Changing the Business is about fundamentally altering the organization. We subdivide this category into three types of change: 1. Improvement, 2. Renewal, and 3. Innovation. Types 1 and 2 refer to modification within the limits of existing business and revenue models. Type 3 refers to radical innovation of a business or revenue model.

Continuous Development

In this book, Continuous Development is defined as the cyclical redesign and improvement of the Minimum Viable Product (MVP).

Core Competency

A Core Competency is a field or task that a business does best and that gives the business its competitive edge. The term was coined in 1990 by Gary Hamel and C.K. Prahalad in an article in the *Harvard Business Review*.

Cultural Change Program

A Cultural Change Program is a change program aimed solely at changing employee norms, values and conduct. Cultural change programs that are not linked to goals and content never pay off, because corporate culture is the result of the work people do to achieve hard goals and make content-related changes and is therefore not a separate matter.

Customer Intimacy
We use Customer Intimacy to describe a marketing strategy that enables an organization to get close to its customers. Customer intimacy leads to greater problem-solving abilities in customer contact, an improved ability to align products with customers' conscious and unconscious needs, and deeper customer loyalty.

Customer Journey
The Customer Journey describes the phases customers go through while purchasing a product or service, as seen from their perspective. See also Customer Journey Mapping.

Customer Journey Mapping
Customer Journey Mapping is a method used to visualize the phases customers go through while purchasing a product or service, from their own perspective. Organizations often need several visualizations to map out the various scenarios and channels.

Digital Innovation
See Innovation.

Disruption
A Disruption literally interrupts or thwarts a process. Disruptions are almost always the result of innovations, but innovations are not necessarily disruptive.

Employability
Employability is people's ability to carry out their duties in the best possible way. Everyone is responsible for continually developing their employability and enabling others to do the same.

Execution Capacity
We use the term Execution Capacity to describe an organization's maturity and its ability to change. Execution capacity is comprised of both hard and soft change capabilities. This capacity is also known as ability to change.

Execution Coalition
The Execution Coalition is a concept coined in this book. It consists of five key roles that are indispensable to each accelerator: the Chief Execution Sponsor, the Co-Sponsor, the Execution Lead (Program or Project Manager), the Execution Team Member(s) and the Benefit Realization Manager(s). These roles are essential, interdependent and

indispensable to execution and benefit ownership. They encompass every key role in the organization, from management level to work floor, in both primary and secondary processes. An execution coalition does far more to increase the chances of achieving the necessary alignment than separately operating entities (like steering groups, core teams and working and monitoring groups) ever could.

Execution Excellence
In our definition, Execution Excellence describes how well an organization is able to attain its goals using three types of strategy execution: (1) improvement, (2) renewal and (3) (digital) innovation that turns the existing organization into a new one. Excellence is essential to achieve the best possible results.

Execution Resources
Execution Resources are the means necessary to carry out an initiative. Examples include an easy-to-use digital checklist for a new process; a simplified version of processes in the shape of a mini-protocol; a letter of credence in video format; a personal manifesto format; and a Q&A database.

Execution Tool Kit
The Execution Tool Kit is used to transfer the total design and MVP to the various new stakeholders so they can take it from there. The tool kit always contains a crystal clear ten-pager outlining the why, how, what and where of the initiative, the Chief Execution Sponsor's letter of credence and an ingenious selection of design content and the analyses underlying it. In short, it is a mix of hard, content-related, elements and soft, change-related, elements.

Fact Sheet
A Fact Sheet is our name for all sorts of practical planning templates. These are overviews of data that are pertinent to a particular component of the model. The Appendices include several fact sheets about the four accelerators, the portfolio, the MVP and project and program management.

Failure Costs
Failure Costs are the costs incurred because of a failed strategy execution. We distinguish between direct and indirect failure costs. These are often not made explicit, even though it is possible to do so, even in the case of frustration among employees and perceived unused potential.

Failure Factors

Failure Factors are reasons why an initiative ultimately cannot be, or has not been, executed. We differentiate between familiar failure factors and less familiar failure factors. These are discussed in Chapter 9, which outlines the reasons why strategy execution sometimes fails.

Goals

See Objectives.

Habit

Habit, or "automatic pilot," is a term borrowed from sociology and psychology. Behavior, or habit, is influenced by the environment and goals. Behavioral change is most likely to occur when the context and the goals change too. Attempts to change habits without addressing the environment or the objectives are doomed to fail.

Hard Capabilities

Hard Capabilities include business processes, structure and technology (IT). The SECA.NU online research tool, developed to assess an organization's execution capacity, can be used to systematically evaluate an organization's hard and soft capabilities.

Improvement

Improvement is our term for Type 1 changes: a continuous improvement and iteration of the existing revenue and business models, operational excellence, in the existing business processes.

Innovation

Innovation literally means renewal. However, in this book we use it to denote a radical change, usually a digital shift, that necessitates new business and revenue models.

Intervention

A well-directed Intervention is the best way to change people's behavior. An intervention may pertain to means of collaboration, management, ownership, the division of responsibilities, communication and calling each other out on undesirable behavior.

Key Processes

Key Processes are processes that leverage the goals. They are crucial for achieving results. Building Block 6, BREAKTHROUGH, identifies these key processes so they can be leveraged (used) to reach the goals.

KPI
A KPI is a Key Performance Indicator, a metric used to analyze how well a business performs.

Lean
Lean Manufacturing, or simply Lean, is a management philosophy from the field of operations management aimed at realizing maximum value for the customer by eliminating waste and enhancing business process flow. This improves performance (e.g. efficiency) and decreases operational cost. Toyota in Japan contributed greatly to the development of lean manufacturing in the 20th century.

Lean Six Sigma
Lean Six Sigma is a method in the field of operations management for organizing quality and efficiency improvements. It systematically optimizes business processes to improve customer value through a program aimed at continuous improvement of results. The method combines Lean Manufacturing and Six Sigma principles.

Leap-of-Faith Assumptions
In the context of this book, we use the term Leap-of-Faith Assumptions to describe the assumptions that steer innovations. According to Eric Ries, inventor of the Lean Startup Method, such assumptions are the best way to kickstart an innovation.

Managerial Excellence
Managerial Excellence describes executive management and the extent to which an organization is able to use the existing business model to achieve the goals of the current business. We call this Running the Business. Again, excellence is indispensable to achieving the best possible results.

Minimum Viable Product (MVP)
A Minimum Viable Product, or a prototype, is the first marketable version of a product in the early stages of development. Note that "minimum" does not mean sub-par. Instead, it means narrowly defined and manageable. It is meant to bring about the minimum necessary customer experience, goals and functionalities. An MVP enables a business to assess whether the product is economically viable. It is a very basic version of the ultimate product aimed at learning as much as possible from early adopters.

Multidisciplinary
Multidisciplinary refers to activities that involve various disciplines. Most strategy execution initiatives are about complex, multidisciplinary changes, which means that they must involve various disciplines within the organization too.

Must-Haves
MUST-HAVES is the name of the fifth building block. In the Strategy = Execution Model, it stands for the foundations that each initiative needs to be built on: a clear assignment, willingness and a sense of necessity, an answer to the Small Why behind the initiative, a business case and a hypothesis-oriented analysis. This term makes clear that if there is no need for an initiative, it will not succeed.

The New Normal
The New Normal is our name for the times we live in. Digital and other technological and social developments are putting the business and revenue models of many organizations under pressure. These organizations can do one of two things: adapt or eventually fail. The New Normal is also the title of Jacques Pijl's book (*Het Nieuwe Normaal*, 2014), which describes 21 rules for survival in modern times.

Objectives
Objectives are the aims, goals and targets in a business model that stem from an organization's vision, mission and strategy. Objectives are best defined according to SMART criteria: Specific, Measurable, Attainable, Realistic and Time-bound.

Ownership
Ownership is a form of direct employee involvement in an organization or initiative. The term denotes a deep-rooted sense of responsibility and engagement. New initiatives can only succeed if the people in the execution coalition take ownership of them. There are two types of ownership: Execution Ownership and Benefit Ownership. Execution Ownership refers to the responsibility a person feels for completing the execution of an initiative, while Benefit Ownership refers to the felt responsibility to use what has been implemented to generate the envisioned benefits. Employees may assume either or both types of ownership.

Portfolio
In this book, the term portfolio describes all the strategic change initiatives in one organization, of all three types. Building Block 2, SELECTION, is used to create a balanced portfolio. A portfolio needs to be balanced

in terms of the various types of change initiatives, but also in other respects, such as total number of initiatives, types of objective and horizon (see Figure 14). In the corporate and financial world, portfolio also denotes a range of products or services. Originally, a portfolio was a selection of representative work that artists, graphic designers and advertising agencies used to convince potential clients of their qualities.

Product Leadership
Product Leadership is a term coined by Michael Treacy and Fred Wiersema. They argued that product leadership is one of the three disciplines a business needs to master in order to lead the market. The other two are customer intimacy and operational excellence. According to the management thinkers, an organization needs to excel in at least one of these to actually become market leader. In the New Normal, organizations need to score high on all three.

Psychological Check-In
This book distinguishes between psychological ownership and formal ownership. The latter entails formal employee responsibility for an initiative or process. The former refers to the ostensibly soft counterpart of formal responsibility, namely the owner's intention. The main point is whether an employee *wants* to take responsibility rather than *has* to take responsibility. The check-in is the moment the employee takes on responsibility and claims ownership.

Revenue Model
An organization's Revenue Model describes the way in which the business generates money and appropriates value. The difference between value creation and appropriation is important. A business can make money in many different ways, and therefore there are many different revenue models that can be used to do so. A revenue model is part of a business model.

Renewal
Renewal is the term we use to denote Type 2 changes: innovations of the existing revenue and business models aimed at continued healthy operation. Renewal can sometimes be subsumed in the regular business processes, but sometimes its execution needs to be assigned to a separate project or program.

Running the Business (Organizational Excellence)
Running the Business is the term we use for regular executive management in the organization. This refers to activities that are consistent with the existing business model.

Scaling
Building Block 11 is called SCALING and refers to the phase in which the right scaling and rollout methods have to be selected, developed and operationalized. Scaling entails involving more people in the organization in the initiative and making the product available to larger groups of customers.

Scrum
Scrum is a term borrowed from software development. It is an iterative method to develop products. It is a flexible and holistic strategy in which the members of a development team work together to achieve a common goal.

SECA.NU
Turner Consultancy has developed an online Strategy Execution & Change Accelerator (SECA.NU). This research tool provides participants with online and real-time information about their organization's present execution capacity compared to benchmarks. This enhances and accelerates strategy execution. SECA.NU consists of 25 questions that give a very accurate analysis of an organization's maturity in strategy execution.

Secure
To Secure means to embed, integrate and institutionalize: to ensure and protect against dilution.

Six Sigma
Six Sigma is a management strategy aimed at improving the output of business processes by removing the causes of defects and thereby reducing the variability in the processes. Six Sigma consists of a collection of quality management methods, including statistical methods. Typical elements include creating an infrastructure of experts in the organization who continue to build up their capabilities (Green Belts, Black Belts, etc.); a predefined sequence of steps that each Six Sigma project follows; and quantifiable goals (e.g. quality improvement and/ or cost reduction). Six Sigma was developed by Motorola in 1986 and became central to General Electric's strategy from 1995 onwards.

Soft Capabilities
The Soft Capabilities in strategy execution are people-centered capabilities. They include corporate culture, behavior, and leadership and collaboration styles. In contrast to what many people think, soft capabilities are quantifiable too. The SECA.NU online research tool, developed to assess an organization's execution capacity, can be used to systematically evaluate an organization's hard and soft capabilities.

Storytelling
Storytelling is the internal and external communication strategy used to convey the background story to any type of change in the organization to other stakeholders. Storytelling is more than just communication. Effective storytelling creates a desire for change and is a cue for people to claim ownership.

Strategy Execution
Strategy Execution is the full range of activities that an organization deploys to manage, improve and renew its existing business model (Types 1 and 2), and to innovate by creating new business models (Type 3). Management of the current day-to-day business is what we call Running the Business (aka the going concern). Improving, renewing and innovating is known as Changing the Business. Strategy execution enables an organization to simultaneously leverage its existing business model while also innovating with new business models in order to secure future continuity.

Targets
See Objectives.

Time Best Spent
One of the greatest ambitions of the model presented in this book is to radically rebalance the time and resources spent on strategy execution. Rather than spending 80% of the time on formulating strategy, we advocate spending this 80% on the actual execution. We are turning the use of time into a new KPI.

Two-Track Approach
We use the term Two-Track Approach in this book to make clear that radical (Type 3) innovations need to be organized separately and cannot be incorporated into the existing organizational structure. True innovations are developed at a different speed and are so crucial that they need to be managed in a dedicated program or project.

VUCA
VUCA is an acronym of Volatility, Uncertainty, Complexity and Ambiguity. The term is derived from the military and describes the four characteristics that are part and parcel of the New Normal.

Why, the Big Why
Answering the Big Why is the starting point of any strategic analysis and course plotting. Why does this organization exist? What do we want to achieve? Simon Sinek, author of *Start With Why*, has put this question at the top of the agenda again.

Why, the Small Why

The Small Why is derived from the BIG WHY and describes the underlying reason for every strategy execution initiative. Why do we want to execute this strategy? How does this initiative help to answer the Big Why?

APPENDIX 3
INDEX

Index of Terms

Index of Names

W

X

Y

Z